W9-CMJ-231

PN
147
.E46

Write
on
Target

by Connie Emerson

Writer's Digest Books

Cincinnati, Ohio

Salem Academy and College
Gramley Library
Winston-Salem, N.C. 27108

Write on Target. Copyright 1981 by Connie Emerson. Printed and bound in the United States of America. All rights reserved. No part of this book may be reproduced in any form or by any electronic or mechanical means including information storage and retrieval systems without permission in writing from the publisher, except by a reviewer who may quote brief passages in a review. Published by Writer's Digest Books, 9933 Alliance Road, Cincinnati, Ohio 45242. First edition.

Library of Congress Cataloging in Publication Data

Emerson, Connie, 1930-
    Write on target.
    Bibliography: p. 225
    Includes index.
    1. Authorship. II. Title.
PN147.E46   808'.02   81-11668
ISBN 0-89879-062-X   AACR2

Book design by Colophon.

Acknowledgments

After I had signed the contract for this, my first book, the reaction set it. I vacillated for days between elation and sheer terror. Could I really do the kind of job I wanted to do (and the job that the editors in Cincinnati expected me to do)? Then, after considerable research and eraser chewing, I realized that my fear of authorship was ridiculous. I could do it—with a little help from my friends.

Now, more than a hundred interviews later, the information is all together and I've acquired a good many more writing friends along the way. All of them have been a great help, but there are a few of these friends, old and new, who deserve a special thank-you: fellow writers Celia Scully and Judy Davis for their advice and encouragement; Jim Mildon, Caroline J. Hadley, Kathleen Mulroy, Bev Gabelman, Donna Briney, Marian May, and Phil Rose, for the information they so generously provided; Chuck Manley and the staff of the Washoe County Library for their research assistance; Carol Cartaino and Barbara O'Brien for their editorial skill.

Last, but not least, thanks to my husband, Ralph, who through it all remained my best friend.

Permission Acknowledgments

Grateful acknowledgment is made for permission to reprint excerpts from the following:

Allen, Joseph. "Seaside Fantasies," reprinted from *Geo*, April 1981. ℗ 1981 by Gruner + Jahr USA, Inc.

Arden, Harvey. "The Magic World of Hans Christian Andersen," *National Geographic*, December 1979.

"Bette Davis." October 13, 1978. Courtesy of *W*, Fairchild Publications.

Bowring, Dave. "Bluegrass Bucks." Reprinted from *Sports Afield* Magazine, October 1980. Copyright ℗ 1980 The Hearst Corporation. All rights reserved.

Brenton, Myron. "Two-Time Losers," ℗ 1980 *Prime Time* Magazine.

Bruski, Mary Ellen Garvey. "We're Having a Baby," reprinted from *Lady's Circle*, Lopez Publications, July 1980.

Burba, Nora. "Get It All Together at Canyon Ranch," as published in *Phoenix* Magazine. Copyright 1980, Phoenix Magazine Publishing, Inc.

Capote, Truman. *A Christmas Memory*, ℗ 1956 by Truman Capote. Reprinted by permission of Random House, Inc.

Carlsen, Bob, and Masler, Hank. "California's Top 25 Attractions," May/June 1979. Reprinted with permission from *National Motorist*, ℗ The National Automobile Club.

Carlsen, Robert. "Head for the Hills," July/August 1980. Reprinted with permission from *National Motorist*, ℗ The National Automobile Club.

Cassill, Kay. "The Time Clock in Your Genes." Reprinted from *Marathon World*, Marathon Oil Company. Number 1, 1979.

Champlin, Chuck, Jr. "Special Effects: The Devil's Magic." Reprinted courtesy of Halsey Publishing Co. and Braniff Airlines' *Flying Colors* magazine.

Davison, Camille J. "Dressing Up with a King-Size Flat," ℗ *Sun* Magazine, Summer 1980.

Ellis, Marc. "Michelstadt: A Special Joy," *Aloft*, January/February 1979. ℗ Wickstrom Publishers, Inc., Miami, Fla.

Emerson, Connie. "How to Double the Life of Your Car and Save on Repairs." Reprinted from the September 20 issue of *Family Circle* Magazine. ℗ 1977 The Family Circle, Inc.

Emerson, Connie. "Jumpin' Jehoshaphat!" Reprinted by permission, courtesy *Sundancer* magazine carried aboard Hughes Airwest. ℗ 1979 East/West Network, Inc.

Emerson, Connie. "Let Your Freezer Help Fight Inflation." Reprinted by permission of *Ladycom* magazine, ℗ September 1979.

Emerson, Connie. "Nevada Banks Discover a New Handle." Reprinted by permission of *California Business*, ℗ September 1978.

Emerson, Connie. "Reader's Idea Exchange." Reprinted from the September 27 issue of *Family Circle* Magazine. ℗ 1978 The Family Circle, Inc.

Flores, Dan. "Great Plains Gobblers," ℗ *Outdoor Life*, April 1980.

Funke, Phyllis. "Manhattan's Lower East Side." Reprinted from *Mainliner* Magazine, March issue. ℗ 1977.

Gore, Rick. "Journey to China's Far West," *National Geographic*, March 1980.

Gorkin, Michael. "A Warm Family Story Written on Ice," *50 Plus*, November 1978.

"Her Dolls Are a Hit in Hollywood." Reprinted from *Us* Magazine, May 30, 1978.

Kates, Joanne. "Executive Playthings," Air Canada's *enRoute* Magazine, February 1977.

Kosner, Alice. "What to Do When You're Really Depressed," *McCall's*, November 1977.

Kramer, Freda. "Single and Dieting? 7 Ways to Make It Easier." Reprinted from *Weight Watchers Magazine*, February 1980.

Lapinski, Michael. "Trolling for Trophies at Pend Oreille," *Western Outdoors*, October 1980.

Martin, Richard. "Ringtails Don't Come Easy," ℗ *Fur-Fish-Game*, October 1980.

"Mary Martin." *50 Plus*, April 1979.

Mitchell, Ron. "An Angler's Autumn." Reprinted from *Sports Afield* Magazine, September 1980 issue. Copyright ℮ 1980 The Hearst Corporation. All rights reserved.

"Muscle Trikes," ℮ *Easyriders*, July 1980.

"New England's Blend of Sea and Season." Reprinted courtesy *Mainliner* Magazine carried aboard United Airlines. ℮ 1977 East/West Network, Inc.

Olesky, Walter. "It'll Save Energy . . . But Will It Save You Dollars?" Reprinted by permission of *Consumer Life* Magazine, ℮ 1978.

Parker, John. "Legal Clinics—Balancing the Price of the Scales of Justice," reprinted from *Consumer Life* Magazine, ℮ 1978.

Pond, Neil. "Willie's Last Picnic Blast," *Music City News.*

Rudnick, Terry. "Four Records That Won't Be Broken," ℮ *Outdoor Life*, June 1980.

Scully, Celia. "Collecting Postcards." Reprinted from *Travel & Leisure*, December 1978.

Shadoan, Kay. "Nostalgia Lives." Reprint permission *Pace Magazine*, the inflight publication for Piedmont Airlines. February 1976.

Shaw, Nancy B. "Sandstorm." *Alaska* Magazine. October 1980.

Shepherd, William G., Jr. "The Sweet Success of Smell." Reprinted courtesy *Mainliner* Magazine carried aboard United Airlines. ℮ 1980 East/West Network, Inc.

Shuttleworth, John. "Writing (or Rewriting) Articles for *The Mother Earth News*." Reprinted with permission from *The Mother Earth News*, copyright ℮ 1977 by The Mother Earth News, Inc., Hendersonville, NC.

Smith, Robert Paul. *Lost and Found*, ℮ 1973 by Robert Paul Smith. Reprinted by permission of Knox Burger Assoc. Ltd.

Swinnerton, A.R. "Were the Good Old Days Really *That* Good?" *Retirement Living.*

Warburton, Jay. "Best Goose Hunting in the West." Reprinted from *Sports Afield* Magazine, October 1980 issue. Copyright ℮ 1980 The Hearst Corporation. All rights reserved.

Williams, Herb. "The Best Dam Tour in Washington," *Chevron USA*, Fall 1973.

Wiseman, Ed. "Bear Attack," ℮ *Outdoor Life*, January 1980.

Wolf, Frank. "Going Back to College? Here's How to Spot Rip-off Programs," ℮ 1980 *Prime Time* Magazine.

To my parents,
Odne and George Toring

Table of Contents

Introduction

1
Sizing Up
Your Chances

Before you rush off to start analyzing *The Plumber's Helper*, stop. There are ten to fifteen thousand markets out there, without counting trade journals and company magazines. The probability of acceptance at some of them is a mathematical nightmare. Others may be the answer to your writing dreams. This chapter shows you how to evaluate your prospects, take advantage of the odds, and choose magazines that will give you the greatest chance of success. **1**

2
What's Up Front

They say you can't tell a book by its cover, but in magazine analysis, that's not necessarily so. Who reads mastheads? You, if you want to make sales. The table of contents and the editor's page are full of clues that will help you unravel the mysteries of editorial mind reading. This chapter puts you giant steps ahead of the competition by showing you how to extract information from the part of the magazine most readers ignore. **11**

3
Reading the Ads

There's no end to the messages a discerning freelancer can get from a magazine's advertisements—messages that will help you target your material at exactly the audience the editor wants to interest. Since advertising revenues keep magazines in business, it's your business to know what the advertising is all about. **23**

4
Looking at
the Pictures

You can bet your Hasselblad that competition among writers often ends in a photo finish—the writer who can supply good photographs along with his words wins the assignment. You'll need to spend some time studying the magazine's layout in order for your photo submissions to be "picture perfect." This chapter tells you what to look for in all your shots and how to put them in focus. **33**

5
Your Style
Is My Style

Are you singing the successful freelancer's theme song? If not, it's time you change your tune. Although there are editors who claim they'll buy anything as long as it's well written, what they *mean* is, as long as it's well written in their accustomed style. Whether it's a casual article or a factual one, at all times it has to be in sync with a magazine's editorial format in order to sell. Here's how to do it. **43**

6
The Name Game

Titles are among the most important keys to an editor's kingdom. Coming up with just the right name for a piece shows you're on the magazine's wavelength, which is a great confidence builder in writer-editor relations. How do you fashion a custom-made title? Subtitles? Subheads? How do you know when it's your job to write them? This chapter covers all that, and more. **59**

7
Analytical Countdown

Word counts are a tedious business—no argument there. But it *is* business and sure beats spending your time retrieving brown manila SASEs from the mailbox. This chapter reveals what you should count: adjectives, adverbs, and the like. It also goes into anecdotes, similes, metaphors, statistics, and quotes. There are tips on how to come up with just the right phrase, and shortcuts to help you save time.   73

8
Great Beginnings
and Happy Endings

Would you like to write publication-perfect leads in half the time it usually takes? Endings that sparkle rather than fizzle, that make editors say yes? In this chapter, an analysis of the most popular types of leads will help you along the way. In addition, there are time-saving tips on writing leads and an easy-to-use leads and closings file designed especially with an eye to your own editorial conquests. And, to point you in the "write" direction, editors of top publications share their favorites.   81

9
Wrapping It Up
with Analysis

Once upon a time, the story goes, there was an overweight free-lancer who, after spending hours on research and writing the lead, would throw all her notes on the floor. Then she'd pick them up one by one, starting with the paper closest to her, and type the manuscript according to that order. She didn't sell any articles, but she did lose 27 pounds. If you'd like to put your articles in the shape your target editor finds irresistible and lose your weight running to the bank with acceptance checks, this chapter tells you how.   99

10
Hints on How-to's

They're the hottest sellers today—each magazine has its own how-to. To help you separate method from madness, this chapter offers analytical, idea-generating devices, an appraisal of five basic formulas for the personal problem-solving how-to, a list of do's to follow when you're explaining a project, tips on preferred terminology, and suggestions from editors on "How to sell me a how-to."   113

11
Information Please

Informational pieces are often the "biggest" pieces in the books. These cover stories are the articles every freelancer wants to sell. They're articles that tell about the high cost of cattle rustling, the latest fast food craze, medical breakthroughs. No two magazines want the story told in exactly the same way, and there's no reason why you can't slant your story to accommodate the house style. First you have to find a strong story idea. Next, there's the matter of timing it right. Then you must put it all together in your chosen publication's style. Learn from the magazine's past issues. This chapter tells how. **127**

12
The Well-Developed Personality

Profiles, Questions and Answers, A Day in the Life of . . . are all personality types, though Freud might disagree. And since most of us who ply this craft are inveterate busybodies, they're among the most delightful (and most exasperating) articles to write. Each magazine has its own personality, so the one you're writing about must be compatible. Whom would the editor like you to interview? What kinds of questions would he want you to ask? What if the interviewees won't talk? What if your subject takes off for Madrid and you're in Savannah? This chapter tells how to sort through the tangles. **139**

13
Business
(with Pleasure)

Articles about business aren't all work and no play. You don't even have to be dean of a business school to write them. However, being an expert magazine analyst helps. Knowing how many facts you'll need, what kinds, and where to get them; whether to play it straight or with humor will make a difference in your financial future. By analyzing a target magazine, you will zero in on its editorial policy. Can you imagine a Jessica Mitford article in *American Opinion?* **151**

14
Inside on
the Outdoors

Want to exchange library fluorescent research for sunlight and perhaps bring home a creel of trout along with your notes? Before you choose your lures, check this chapter to see what kind of writing bait you'll need to catch the editor you're angling for. Knowing how to recognize basic outdoor formulas, how to analyze such things as the ratio of in-the-field to library research needed, editorial preferences and taboos, will help you reel in a bigger catch. **167**

15
Have Typewriter
Will Travel

If you're a writer who likes to travel, or a traveler who would like to write, this field's a natural. It's one of the fastest growing and easiest for beginners who mind their analysis to break into. Before you put on your traveling shoes, there are some things you ought to think about: point of view, tone, sense of place, reader rapport, human interest, name dropping, emotional enthusiasm, and visual words as they relate to the magazines you'd like to write for. With pretrip analysis, you'll increase your writing mileage. **183**

16
Catching Up
with Your Past

Nostalgia recalls the poignant, the laughable—the "good old days." The idea possibilities, from aprons to fly paper, are inexhaustible, since today's fads and fancies become tomorrow's memories. In order to sell a nostalgia piece, you must analyze the magazine. What one editor considers worth remembering, another doesn't care to recall. To put your reminiscences in the proper perspective, read this chapter. **205**

Appendix A
Going into Analysis—
Two Case Histories

From market research to idea formulation and actual crafting, these two examples show you how successful articles are delivered by the editorial mind reading method.

Appendix B
The Writer/Analyst's Checklist

Bibliography

Index

Introduction

Tailors and writers must mind the fashion.

—**Thomas Fuller,** *Gnomologia,* **1732**

When my first query letter came back with an assignment, I was stunned. Things weren't supposed to happen that way. A writer had to struggle, to write and rewrite until—just when she was about to throw in the carbon paper—an editor bought her manuscript for ten dollars. I got one hundred! dred!

My next piece sold, and the next. Now seven and one-half years later, I've collected checks for more than two hundred and thirty articles by writing an average of three to four hours a day. I won't say there haven't been a few black days at the mailbox, but sales have outnumbered strikeouts by more than twenty to one.

Did I have some slumbering talent that suddenly awakened after forty years? Was I incredibly lucky? No. The truth is that during my years of homemaking, I had become accustomed to learning by using models. I wouldn't dream of making chocolate éclairs without consulting a recipe or sewing a dress without a pattern. So when I decided to write, it was only natural that I automatically studied the magazines I wanted to write for and fashioned my articles as those other writers—whose successes were right in front of me—had crafted theirs.

In so doing, I had stumbled upon the secret of selling nonfiction: Get inside editors' heads. Determine what they will want in the future by studying what they have bought in the past, and you'll make sales.

Although I discovered the formula for successful articles instinctively, I realize that for many writers it's a hit—and often miss—proposition. Scoring editorial touchdowns consistently requires a well-thought-out game plan.

That's where analysis comes in. Before you write a word of your query, before you decide on an article's subject, your first job is to analyze the magazines you hope to write for—from their front covers to back-page ads.

How do you do that? Though every good book on writing advises writers to read the publications they hope to sell to, the mystery of how they should read and what exactly they should look for hasn't heretofore been revealed. This book unravels that mystery. Part I covers basic analysis techniques that you can use to study any magazine effectively. Part II dissects three of the most salable types of articles today. Part III explores four top article subjects in depth, showing how you can obtain information on everything from trends to taboos. In short, you can learn to read a magazine so that you can tailor custom-made articles to fit that publication perfectly—whatever its editorial shape may be.

Time was when an article might fit into any number of magazines. But not anymore. You see, during the past few years magazines have been facing an identity crisis. With dozens of new publications hitting the newsstands each year, editors work overtime to assure that theirs are distinctive, that they won't be lost in the crowd on the racks.

A look through the pages of *Writer's Market* will show you that the day of the general-interest magazine is fading; most magazines now are specialized. There are magazines for potters, record collectors, funeral directors; for tropical fish fanciers, handwriting analysts, and Christmas tree merchandisers. It's a challenge to write for these publications. Most of their readers are already well informed on their pet subjects, so the writer must sharpen his or her research skills. That includes the ability to determine the potential reader's level of expertise. An awareness of the subtle differences in readership of magazines, which to the uninitiated seem all alike, is also imperative.

Enterprising publishers are aware that people's interests are becoming increasingly varied. The magazine-reading public wants to know the latest about its hobbies, favorite sports, interests, and businesses. The publishers also know that magazines make more profit from the advertising space they sell than from sales of copies to readers. Therefore, by putting together magazines that appeal to special-interest segments of the population, publishers can offer unique packages to advertisers, namely, targeted audiences. As a result, the magazine with a limited, well-defined readership is often more profitable than a magazine with a much higher circulation but a general, amorphous readership.

There are thousands of these specialized magazines. And when there is more than one aimed at a very specific audience—say squash players or potato growers—you can be sure that each publication's slant, degree of technicality, tone, and style will be different from the others.

The problem, editors contend, is that the majority of would-be writers don't read the magazines they want to write for thoroughly enough to recognize these differences. Furthermore, they don't become familiar enough with these magazines to know what kinds of material to submit.

Most of the queries and manuscripts editors receive aren't rejected because of bad writing. They are rejected because the subject matter is wrong for that publication.

Editors lament that, all too often, even if the idea is appropriate, the style or approach is wrong. The pieces don't fit their magazines' images. For just as we all have our way of expressing ourselves, every magazine has its own way of presenting its material in a well-defined style that the editors feel is necessary to their publication's very survival.

I've found, in teaching nonfiction writing classes, that it's not always the talented student who makes the sales. Some people who show loads of promise are unable to produce marketable pieces simply because they are unwilling to write articles that conform to what has appeared in a magazine in the past.

Though editors don't like to admit it, in their quest for uniqueness, they're a bit reluctant to stray very far from established editorial paths—unless the magazine is so obviously failing that drastic changes must be made. Good editors have a strong feeling for who their readers are and select what they think those readers will want. Although they may not be averse to finding new directions to go in (if those directions fit the readership they've so carefully cultivated), your chances of acceptance are greatest if you follow established patterns. Clues to the editors' preferences are scattered throughout the magazines they put together. By carefully collecting these tidbits of information, the writer can anticipate the kinds of ideas an editor will like and choose the structure that will be a winner.

Analyzing articles takes time. Studying markets, counting words, and poring over anecdotes, figures of speech, and titles is work. I'm inclined to agree with Olin Miller, who said, "Writing is the hardest way of earning a living, with the possible exception of wrestling alligators." But in my book, hard work is infinitely preferable to rejection. And the best way to avoid those ego-deflating printed forms is to know a publication so well that you can produce articles, time after time, according to its formulas.

Now, don't get me wrong. I'm not suggesting that you become a copycat. If your idea's fresh, the article will be, too, despite the fact that it may have the same ratio of anecdotes, adjectives, and adverbs as the articles printed by the magazine in the past.

What analysis does for you is provide guidelines—parameters within which to craft articles with editor appeal. It's a form of editorial mind reading, enabling you to look at markets, readers, advertisers, and your own writing from an editor's point of view. In short, analysis shows you the way to write on target. And that's what this book is all about.

1
Sizing Up
Your Chances

Luck is what happens when preparation meets opportunity.
—**Jack Valenti,**
Reader's Digest

Every year millions of tourists visit my city of Reno, Nevada, trying to beat the odds. Precious few do. Each year thousands of would-be article writers try to beat the odds, too. Though they've a better chance than the gambler trying to line up all sevens on a four-reel slot machine (1 in 160,000, incidentally), most of them also will be disappointed. The fact is, in the editorial offices of magazines they're most likely to send their hard-written work to, the competition rivals that of trying to find a free parking spot within six blocks of the Super Bowl.

Marian May says that while she was editor of *Chevron USA,* the postman brought her an average of one hundred queries a week. Of these, she asked to see four on speculation, from which one or two were selected. At *Signature,* from the seventy-five manuscripts and queries received each month, only one article is purchased. An estimated one-sixth of the queries are answered with instructions to go ahead on speculation, but only one percent of the articles the editors ask to see on this basis are purchased.

Chevron USA and *Signature* are only medium-size circulation magazines. As circulation size increases, so does the number of competitors. Since there is a high positive correlation between circulation size and payment to writers, one reason for the big books' bulging mailbags is obvious. But there are others. Top pros like the exposure. Having their bylines in front of lots of readers and lots of editors helps ensure that they'll stay in demand. Established writers who haven't yet reached the five-figure income bracket look at the big magazines as the important step up.

But why do unpublished writers try to tackle the publishing world's Goliaths? First of all, these magazines' widespread visibility makes them the ones beginners know about. And secondly, beginners underestimate the difficulty of making those initial sales. Ask any group of beginning writers to list the magazines they plan to submit their articles to. Chances are, the lists will be almost identical—*Woman's Day, Family Circle, Reader's Digest, Sports Illustrated,* with an occasional *McCall's, National Geographic, TV Guide,* and *Good Housekeeping*—all magazines in the top twenty.

Added to the trials that even top-selling writers must face are the editorial boards of the big magazines. A proposal has to make a hit not only with one editor, but with the whole gang. At *National Geographic,* the article selection process goes something like this, according to Associate Editor Joseph Judge: "A planning council made up of nine editors from the technical and picture sides of the magazine meets monthly to consider approximately fifty ideas—survivors out of a batch of several hundred. They may approve one or two."

Sounds hopeless? Not at all. Remember that we've been talking about high-profile big- and medium-size magazines, the publications most writers submit articles to. There are some ten to fifteen thousand others out there, and that's not counting most trade journals and company publications. Many of their editors await mailtime as eagerly as they do their annual vacations.

You won't find most of these magazines on the newsstands. But you may see them in your doctor's or insurance agent's office, or perhaps on a friend's coffee table. Some are distributed only abroad. Others are sent to members of a specific organization, club, church, or profession. When we lived in California, I met a writer who made more than one thousand dollars a month writing for magazines I'd never heard of. Her secret was that most other writers didn't know about them either.

It's encouraging, too, to listen to the reasons one typical editor gives for the majority of his rejections: " 'Does not fit our current editorial needs' from my magazine's point of view can be translated to read everything from impossibly sloppy manuscripts to dull writing to an idea that's been beaten to death. *But most often it means that any idiot should know we don't ever use the kind of material he's sent us."* (Italics mine.)

You can do better than that. There's no excuse for sending your work to a magazine where it hasn't a hope of publication, especially when you realize that successful manuscript submission depends on more than good writing and luck. Analysis allows you to deal with a stacked deck, and in-depth knowledge of the markets becomes your trump card. Since there are so many possible outlets for the writer's wares, every conceivable topic and individual writing style has its place. But in order to find that place, you have to know that it exists.

The writer who decides upon a subject and then tries to find a suitable market can succeed by doggedly searching for a magazine to fit the idea. The proficient market analyst, on the other hand, has a much easier job. By being familiar with a variety of publications at the outset, he can formulate his ideas on the basis of what he knows a particular magazine is buying.

Beginning writers all too often believe that a writer merely writes and doesn't have to spend time on bookwork. They're wrong. Louise Boggess, a successful writer and teacher, freely admits, "First and foremost, I am a business-woman." Other writers estimate that they spend up to 60 percent of their working time studying the markets and marketing their output.

Study of the markets, because of the growing number and increasing diversity of publications, has become more and more complex. I find that my copy of *Writer's Market* becomes dog-eared by the time it's a few months old. Published yearly, the book contains thousands of listings of markets for freelance material. Since the publications are divided into categories such as religious, women's, alternative, and the like, you needn't devour the whole volume to get the information you want.

Freelancers usually think of general circulation magazines when they look for article markets. They don't realize that company publications and trade journals are a larger, often equally lucrative outlet for their writing.

Although the names of several hundred trade journals are included in *Writer's Market,* you can find out more about them and about company publications by looking through *Ayer's*

Directory of Publications, Business Publications Rates & Data, Standard Periodical Directory, Ulrich's International Periodical Directory and *Gebbie House Magazine Directory*. They're available at most library reference desks.

Keeping an eye out for magazines you've not seen before will lead you to still other publications. I never pass a reception room without glancing to see what magazines are on the tables. It's also a good idea to check at a well-stocked newsstand every month or two, as new titles are continually appearing.

Bettering Your Odds

In writing for both general circulation and company publications, you'll give Lady Luck a hand by concentrating your efforts on the most salable types of articles. *How-to's, informational,* and *personality* pieces are examined in Part II of this book, but there are others you will frequently come across in your magazine analysis.

Personal experience/life experience pieces are human interest accounts of how you or some other person has solved a problem, survived an unusual situation, or experienced something out of the ordinary. You see these pieces every month in many magazines—the family that adopted a dozen racially mixed children, the baby who didn't die from a usually fatal birth defect.

Humor is funny—it takes a special talent to put words on paper and make people laugh. When we speak humorously, we rely more upon voice inflection than most of us realize, and we choose our subject matter to fit the occasion as well as the people we're talking to. The written word doesn't transmit humor as readily. There are also wide differences in what people think is funny. Not only is humor highly subjective, the well-written variety is in short supply. So if you can make an editor chuckle, you're almost sure to make a sale.

Inspirational pieces must be crafted subtly in today's sophisticated market. You must uplift the reader's spirits and make your point without preaching. Since writers of inspirational pieces often use material objects to relay a spiritual message— budding trees symbolizing rebirth or new beginnings, a fork in the road representing choices that must be made—the writer who can come up with fresh analogies or new twists on old themes will find a welcome place in this field.

As you analyze markets and article types, don't neglect to analyze your own writing strengths and interests. Those will determine what kinds of articles you will write best.

Just as certain kinds of articles are popular with editors, some subjects sell more readily than others. In Part III we take an analytical look at three of the subjects that are among the most salable today—business, the outdoors, and travel. A good many others, such as sports, politics, technology, religion, and antiques, are also bestsellers. The successful writer is the one who keeps abreast of the types of articles and subject matter currently in demand. He does this by becoming intimately acquainted with as many magazines as he can. Leon Mandel, formerly West Coast editor of *Car and Driver,* now a full-time freelancer, relies exclusively on "reading the book" to learn what he needs to know about potential markets and what they like. At any given time, Mandel subscribes to between twenty and thirty magazines, which he reads cover to cover each month. Other freelancers may read as many as sixty.

Reading writers' magazines is another essential of market analysis. Their marketing news will keep you posted on editorial changes, names of magazines about to begin publication, and current needs of existing publications.

While you're working to tip the odds in your favor, remember that you'll beat a lot of the competition out of the starting blocks simply by preparing a professional-looking submission. That means including a self-addressed envelope with sufficient postage to cover the cost of sending an answer to your query or returning your article. It means, too, that queries should be type-written on plain white regulation-size paper or letterhead—no handwritten letters on memo pads or kitten-decorated note paper. Manuscripts should be neatly and accurately typed on 8½x11-inch white, noncorrasable typing paper (see Chapter 9 for additional instructions on manuscript preparation).

Foolproof Filing
Keeping track of all the freelance markets that use the kinds of material you write would be a much bigger job than following all

the stocks listed on the New York Stock Exchange. So, like the intelligent stock market analyst, study only the markets that hold the most potential for your success. To make the job easier, I compile mini-dossiers on each one.

The system is simple. You begin by making a list of the twenty or thirty magazines you would most like to write for. Your list should include publications you actually read and those with subject matter of interest to you. Whenever you read an article and say to yourself, "I could write as well as (or better than) that," you've found another indicator pointing to market possibilities.

Set up a file for each magazine and begin filling it with a photocopy of the publication's listing in *Writer's Market*. Underline information such as word length, the kinds of material the editors say they need, whether a query is necessary, or if finished articles are preferred. Note whether simultaneous submissions are welcomed or shunned; what size photos (if any) are asked for and if they should be black-and-whites, color transparencies, or a combination of the two. If the magazine isn't listed in *Writer's Market,* get that information, or as much of it as you can, from other sources.

You'll also want to make note of the rate of pay and whether that payment comes on acceptance or publication, as well as if there is a "kill fee" paid if the article is assigned and not used. These factors will be important to you in judging a market's desirability. Since payment on publication means that you'll see your check only after the magazine containing your article has gone to press (and sometimes long after), you've no guarantee that the article will be used and you'll ever be paid. Your editor may be replaced by one who doesn't like the piece. The magazine might go out of business. Your manuscript may lie forgotten in a file. There are all sorts of horrendous things that might, and do, happen between the time a writer is informed that his or her work is accepted and that "on publication" day, so it's wise where possible to pursue markets that pay on acceptance.

Another factor you'll want to take into consideration and make note of when choosing a market is the kind of rights purchased. Most magazines today purchase "First North American Serial Rights," which means that after a work is published, the author can resell it as a reprint. When a publication insists on buying "All Rights" and the writer agrees to the arrangement, he gives up the chance to resell the work to any other market.

Include information about the form in which your target editors want to receive submissions. Some editors prefer triple-spaced manuscripts, while others want them double-spaced. There are still other magazines whose guidelines stipulate a certain number of characters to be typewritten on each line. Include this information in your file.

Editors also have preferences as to the type of query they receive. Occasionally, an editor will prefer telephone queries (often followed by an expansion of the proposed idea in writing). Other editors like what is called the "article outline," "article memo," or "query memo." Though the form may vary, this is essentially a piece of typing paper on which the first two or three paragraphs of the actual lead are double-spaced, followed by a single-spaced paragraph or two in which the writer conveys, in capsule form, essential elements of the entire article. Indicated also are the point of view to be used, some of the writer's sources, conclusion, and occasionally, a complete anecdote or pertinent statistics. In most instances, whatever an editor's pet query form may be, a traditional query letter will do the job if it's well written and your idea is a good one (to sharpen your query-writing skills, read the sections on this subject in one or all of the books on writing listed in the bibliography).

Whenever you see an item about the publication in a writers' magazine or come across anything written by its editor, date, clip, and save it in your file. Bits of trade talk, like editorial changes and which magazines aren't paying their writers promptly, are especially helpful.

I have found that your chances of acceptance are *decreased* if you query a magazine that has been recently written up in a writers' magazine. It's better to clip out the blurb, file it in the dossier, and query six months later. Why? Because just about every freelancer from Fairbanks to Forest Hills reads those items, and they all query at once. The note I received from Dorothy Harvey, editor of *Capper's Weekly,* is typical of responses most writers receive to post-publicity queries: "Sorry to be so slow in replying, but we've been swamped with freelance material the past few weeks following mention in *Writer's Digest*." The note went on to say that while my idea was an interesting one, the magazine was overstocked with material.

Make note of any gossip you might hear about the magazine from other writers. Writers' conferences and club meetings are good sources of information, as long as you're able to sort out fact from disgruntled writers' fantasy.

Send for a sample copy of the publication and its guidelines for writers. Some magazines will send a single mimeographed page; others, several pages of information. One of the most complete writer's guidelines I've seen is put out by *Southern Outdoors Magazine*. It is a sixteen-page brochure that lists the publication's "Ten Commandments" (regarding strong language, liquor, cheesecake photos, and the like) and answers such questions as "Who Can Make the *Southern Outdoors* Team?" ("Anybody. We're what you might call an Equal Opportunity Magazine, discriminating only against 'writers' who should have chosen a less demanding career, such as brain surgery or professional football.") Most guidelines aren't so entertaining, but it's imperative that you have them in your reference file and follow them to the letter.

After you've sold an article to a publication, ask the editor about deadlines. Are they two, four, six months prior to the date of an issue's publication? Put that information in your file. Then, if you have an idea for a seasonal article, you'll know the optimum time to query about it. Knowing deadlines will also let you aim your queries so they won't hit the editor's desk when he or she is busiest and therefore least receptive to your ideas. This is especially important when querying magazines with small staffs, where closing dates could supply material for a five-hour-long Excedrin commercial.

Your files will never be completed unless you decide to write off a magazine as a lost cause or hang up your typing shoes. You will keep adding correspondence from editors of the magazines, pertinent articles that appear in them and, best of all, copies of manuscripts their editors buy from you.

The value of these mini-dossiers is obvious. They eliminate the precious minutes you would otherwise spend pawing through ten years' back copies of a writers' magazine ("I knew there was something about it somewhere") and trying to remember if it was Editor A who advised you to query again in six months. Files will keep your marketing information in an organized form and unmuddle your mind.

Targeting at Dollar Signs

Most writers wrestle with the question of whether to aim first for publications that pay top rates or to begin with those at the bottom. Fran Barnes, a freelancer based in Moab, Utah, is convinced that beginning writers should start near the bottom, trying for markets that pay two or three cents a word. The late Mort Weisinger, whose annual freelance income was estimated at more than $100,000, said to start at the top. Other pros advise writing for magazines you enjoy reading, regardless of what they pay.

Whose advice do you follow? I'd like to suggest that you analyze the subjects you enjoy, your areas of expertise, and your writing ability. Then try for publications that print the sort of material you are capable of producing. There's no harm in starting at the top if you're able to stand up to lots of rejections. Just because you start at the bottom does not mean you will be typecast and have to write for them forever. It is more important than anything to send your queries and manuscripts to magazines whose formats they fit. And although Dr. Samuel Johnson said that no man but a blockhead ever wrote except for money, you may decide it's worth sending your work to magazines that pay only in copies, because having the credit of being published can have value too.

Finding Your Place

Don't be discouraged if it takes some time to find your niche in the writing world. The subjects or magazines you choose now may prove less rewarding than those you concentrate on as your marketing knowledge and writing skills increase. Life circumstances, too, may affect your choices.

Norman Lobsenz, one of the country's top freelancers in the field of personal relationships, started out with general interest articles when he turned from a newspaper career to freelancing. Then, with a divorce, his focus shifted. "In those days," Lobsenz says, "we paid alimony. *McCall's* had a department called

'Speaking Out' and I wrote a piece for it called 'Is It Fair for a Man to Pay Alimony'—a very provocative, deliberately controversial piece." Lobsenz's research brought him in contact with divorce lawyers, divorce counselors, and other experts in this social science area, which led to more article ideas. His knowledge of the markets enabled him to become a specialist. Three decades and hundreds of articles later, Lobsenz still writes of relationships: about everything from how to avoid sexual boredom to new ways of dealing with post-divorce conflicts.

Duane Newcomb, a freelancer with some twenty-five hundred articles to his credit, first chose camping travel as his specialty because of an educational background in forestry. Five years as owner of a retail store and a solid knowledge of business publications led him to change his focus, and he began writing trade articles. During the past few years, his emphasis has shifted to writing books, many of them guides to making money, which came as an outgrowth of his business article days.

Dissatisfaction with the kind of religious education her five children were getting started Celia Scully writing. After selling a few pieces, she studied the markets and found that nonreligious publications which used family life and health-related articles offered wider opportunities and paid more money. Since her husband is a physician, access to ideas and interviews in these fields made them logical choices.

Then, one day, Scully received a phone call from the editor of a magazine for travel agents asking her to cover a regional convention of agents to be held the next week in her town. That assignment led to a contributing editorship with the magazine. It also gave the impetus to investigate other potential markets for the travel writer. She now writes for top travel magazines, including *Travel & Leisure* and *Travel/Holiday*.

The secrets of these writers' success have been their willingness to do the pick-and-shovel, nonglamorous groundwork that lays the foundation for article sales, and a willingness to take advantage of opportunities as they come along.

Those opportunities will come along for you, too. They're waiting in the millions of blank pages editors must fill in their forthcoming issues. All it will take for you to provide the copy they need is a good measure of well-spent time—that preparation some people call "luck."

What's Up Front

The past is but the beginning of a beginning.

—H. G. Wells

We Americans go for products in slick packages. Magazine buyers are no exception. Editors know that a magazine's packaging—its front cover—is what attracts magazine stand browsers. Whether the reader's taste runs to souped-up Chevettes or frosted grapes that look ready to fall off the page, that first visual impression, plus the blurbs advertising what is inside, determines whether he will walk away without buying or turn back to have a second look.

It's no wonder, then, that the writer ought to take a second look (and a third and fourth) at the covers of magazines she hopes to sell articles to. The pictures tell a lot. The words say even more, both in terms of the audience the editor wants to reach and the kinds of articles he or she is eager to buy.

For years, each of the established magazines has gone with the same type of cover, issue after issue, with only minor changes. If you want proof, just look at any issue of *National Geographic* from the 1950s. By comparing it with a current copy, you could tell it was a *Geographic* even if the name weren't there. You recognize the cover drawing without *The New Yorker* logo, and the red-bordered cover of *Time*.

It's not that publishers are in a rut. They want their magazines to be readily recognizable. And editors of new publications realize that one way to become established fast is to come up with an attractive cover format that's identifiable as the magazine's own, setting it apart from the competition.

This competition is perhaps most ferocious in the field of women's publications, where editors are fighting tooth and painted fingernail to keep circulation rates climbing as a chorus

Salem Academy and College
Gramley Library
Salem NC 27108

line of newcomers comes onstage each month. At first glance, these women's magazines seem pretty much the same. After all, most of them feature women on the covers, don't they?

Despite the magazines' proclivities for female faces (though the two big supermarket sellers, *Woman's Day* and *Family Circle,* prove that blueberry pies and cute kids in mom-made clothes sell magazines, too), you'll find that each covergirl's message is more than just a pretty face. *Lady's Circle* cover choices run to wholesome-looking celebrities of the Sally Field, Mary Tyler Moore variety. The models on *Self*'s covers exude the radiant health that comes from jogging five miles a day. *Working Mother*'s cover ladies are usually dressed for the office and accompanied by offspring.

You'll never find a child on *Cosmopolitan*'s cover, though, where the models' necklines plunge ever lower as the sexual frankness of its articles climbs to new heights. *Savvy* features photos of important women in the business and professional worlds; *Good Housekeeping* pictures celebrities or fresh-looking models with a small photo of a fancy dessert or craft tucked among the article blurbs. And so it goes. Each magazine projects a cover image consistent with the kind of material its readers will find inside. When Betty Homemaker picks up a copy of *Family Circle,* with its familiar-looking plate of brownies or granny square afghan on the cover, she expects to find the sort of articles she's come to associate with the magazine. So the editors serve up the same mix of editorial fare time after time and present it in the same kind of package.

It's too often been said that a picture is worth a thousand words. But the words on a magazine's cover can be worth a thousand pictures if you internalize what they're trying to tell you, the writer. Just below the magazine's name, there's occasionally a line of smaller, easily ignored, type. It spells out just who that magazine is for, who sponsors it, or something about the publication's size: *Savvy,* The Magazine for Executive Women (not receptionists, mind you, though receptionists who are would-be executives might read it); *Star*—For the Girl that Wants It All; *Pacific Discovery*—California Academy of Science; *COINage*—World's Largest Circulation Coin Magazine; *Hot Rod*—World's Largest Automotive Magazine.

It's true that many magazines don't have that line of small print, but there is rarely one around today whose cover picture isn't punctuated by blurbs. Since the cover is the magazine's billboard, those blurbs are the lures. To the customer who hasn't read a particular magazine before or buys it only occasionally, these previews of what's inside are there to persuade him or her that the issue is worth its cover price.

The cover lines shout loud and clear which articles are the ones the magazine's editor believes will attract the most readers. Chances are good that article ideas *along the same general lines* on *related or parallel themes* are the ones that the editor will receive most favorably in the future. They will also tell you in no uncertain terms about the publication's slant—the conception a magazine has of its readers' interests and values and the role it wants to fill in their reading. This conception evolves from the editors' knowledge of the probable educational level of its readers, their economic levels, the magazine's own taboos, sacred principles and style, along with a variety of other editorial preconceptions. It's up to you, the writer, to detect a magazine's self-concept. Discerning the differences an editor sees between his or her publication and its competitors will result in sales.

Contrast these blurbs from a cover of *Cosmo*—"*3* Kinds of Men a Nice Girl Had Better Avoid Before She Becomes His Jibbering (and Soon to Be Discarded) Slave," "*Words* to Make a Woman Fall Into the Arms of Her Husband's *Best* Friend," "The (Surprising) *New* Sexual Attitudes of the 80s. Can Less Be More?" "Those Lusty, Legendary Lifeguards"—with those on the cover of *Savvy* for the same month—"FALSE GRIT: You Don't Have to Be Macho to Get Ahead," "A WATS Line and a Company Car: Bargaining for Executive Perks," "Bulimarexia: The Eating Disorder of Perfectionist Women." Now it's entirely possible that the same woman might read both *Cosmo* and *Savvy*. But in regard to the magazines' slants and articles their editors think of as grabbers, an article that would fit like the covergirl's blouse on the one wouldn't cover the prescribed territory for the other.

Editor Helen Gurley Brown says, "There isn't much question that *Cosmopolitan* covers have everything to do with our success—we use *many* blurbs, all written by my husband (for the past fifteen years) and if one of them doesn't grab the reader, another one will. Of course the content of the magazine has to live *up* to the blurbs. . . .we believe that ours does. . .but it is the very personal, frisky, provocative blurbs that lure her in the first place."

In the course of your magazine analysis, you'll ultimately want to put together a reader profile for each of the magazines you would like to submit articles to. The cover is a logical starting point. As you look at its illustration and read the blurbs, ask yourself, "What makes the typical reader who's attracted by this cover tick?" Play amateur psychiatrist and probe his or her needs, dreads, unfulfilled wishes, and fantasies (for more information on reader profiles, see Chapter 3).

Not only will a cover tell you a good deal about your magazine's readership, it will also speak volumes as to the slant you should use. Say that you're irrevocably addicted to gardening and good at it, too. Your roses smell sweeter and bloom earlier than anyone else's. No one will have a chance at winning county fair ribbons until you turn in your trowel. You're also a would-be writer and have decided to write an article revealing your secrets of success.

Since you have a variety of magazines in mind, you can effectively begin your marketing research by studying the covers of back issues. Perhaps one of them almost always features photos of gardening tools. Others consistently display flower arrangements or pictures of unusual gardens. One-half of another magazine's covers are adorned with roses in various guises. You read the latter publication's blurbs—"Rating the Rosebush Pruners," "Ten Ways to Display Your Roses," "Are Your Clematis Dying on the Vine?"—and know that this magazine may well be fertile ground for you to cultivate. It's likely that your analysis will also have produced an abundance of other article ideas.

Casing the Contents

When you have gleaned every possible bit of information from the magazine's cover, turn a page or two until you come to the table of contents. Titles of a magazine's past articles provide one of the most successful mechanisms for generating article ideas to excite its editor. When I study back copies I'm especially conscious of the kinds of pieces that seem to predominate in issue after issue. Are they mostly how-to's, informational, personal experience? Does the editor like a profile or two each month, or are all the articles essentially personality pieces?

If you've the time and a dogged determination to succeed, copy down the titles from three, four, or five years of back issues. Patterns will emerge. The publication may *always* include a piece on bass fishing in its August issue, garage sales in April, or tips on avoiding colds in November. Perhaps there's a traditional Christmas reminiscence, an article on one of our country's founding fathers in July, back to school issues in September, or vacation issues in June—you'll not only get article ideas but information on submission timing as well (at least six to eight months in advance for seasonal articles).

Write down every idea you come up with, no matter how mundane it may seem. You'll find that the subconscious can work wonders with ordinary topics, twisting them this way, turning them that until a new way of looking at the subject—a fresh approach—evolves. Another trick is to take a key word or two out of a title to come up with an entirely different concept. "How to Grow Herbs in Your Kitchen" might trigger your imagination to something like "Growing Mushrooms in Your Broom Closet." With a flick of the pen, "Low-Cost Accommodations You'll Like" becomes "Low-Cost Entertainment Your Family Will Love." A family magazine editor who liked "Goals: How to Set Them, Achieve Them, Enjoy Them" might also be interested in "Helping Your Children to Achieve and Enjoy Their Goals."

This idea-producing technique works with all kinds of magazines and trade journals. It's a much more refined technique than crystal ball gazing or reading tea leaves but, like those pursuits, does require a bit of imagination. Say you're stuck at the shoe repair shop for emergency replacement of your left heel, which fell off (thank the writing gods) *after* you finished interviewing the head of a giant pizza chain. Though your mind is on the interview, the idea-stalking part of your brain spots some shoe-polish-smudged back copies of trade journals published for people in the shoe repair business. You look at the contents page of the nearest magazine and spot an article called "Shoe Lasts

Through the Ages." In another issue of the same magazine there's one on bootjacks in Colonial days. You start brainstorming possibilities. Baby shoes? No, too ordinary. It had to have been done in the past. A history of cowboy boots? Maybe. Chances are the editor would go for a piece on Mrs. McGillacutty's shoelace collection, or what about a piece on shoebuttons? When the shoe is repaired, you ask if you could possibly borrow the magazines and return them when the other heel falls off. Most likely, the repair person will tell you to keep them, since most of his customers seem to prefer *Sports Illustrated*. You go home happily, left heel intact, interview notes in your notebook *and* a couple of article possibilities literally in your pocket.

Editors bemoan the fact that the contents pages of their magazines aren't read thoroughly. According to Caroline J. Hadley, editor of *Nevada Magazine,* about 80 percent of the freelancers who query her or send manuscripts miss the mark completely as far as subject matter is concerned. They wouldn't be off target if they would only look at the cover and read the page listing her magazine's articles, she says.

"It says right here that *Nevada Magazine* is published monthly by the state of Nevada," she says, pointing to the cover. "Obviously, that's going to mean propaganda. Otherwise, why would they do it? Look at the titles: '1980 Goldigger's Guide: where to look for gold, how to pan and other rules of the prospector's art.' That should tell the writer that we do how-to's; we want people to get into the state of Nevada, to become a part of it. So anybody who has an idea on a feature how-to that suits our slogan—The Magazine of the Real West—has a good chance of a sale. Here's a historical piece and two on people—'The Man Who Created Las Vegas' and 'How Ohio's Yeast King Became Nevada's Biggest Sugar Daddy.' Anybody who has done something important here is good material, but if the writer checks our contents page he knows that person doesn't have to be the head of a casino or the governor of the state. It can be a little old lady who comes to Nevada every week to play the slots." Hadley, in pointing to her magazine's Events department (a department that uses short pieces) says that freelancers should be on the lookout for mini-features in any magazine. They're the easiest way to break in, to show the editors that a writer is reliable, reasonable, and competent.

When you can't come up with ideas easily, the reference section of the library will come to your rescue. If you're zeroing in on a magazine that goes heavily for how-to's, take the drawer out of the card catalog, and start reading. There are hundreds of how-to books even in a small library. Perhaps the general interest magazine you'd love to write for likes articles on technical breakthroughs written in layman's language. Check through recent issues of scientific magazines for ideas. Some magazines lean toward the occult or unusual happenings. You'll get ideas for them from reference books that deal with the bizarre.

Nostalgia themes abide in abundance in copies of magazines from the early 1900s like *Vanity Fair*. Your public library may not have them, but college and university libraries often do, and they can be obtained through interlibrary loan. There are also a great many books written lately about the good old days that are full of potential article ideas. *Statistical Abstract of the United States, World Almanac, Who's Who, Standard & Poor's*, encyclopedias, phone books, and reader's guides will provide other topics for salable articles. And don't forget to read the newspapers for still more ideas.

Getting in Focus

If you study the titles of articles, you'll be able to determine their scope, to tell whether they deal with broad subjects, several aspects of a subject, or a very narrow, sharply defined segment. You'll want to sharpen your focus when you analyze the articles themselves, but the titles alone can often tell you a great deal. By way of illustration, look at this one: "The Amazing World of Plant Genetics." That subject is very broad. Now consider "Crossbreeding—The Way to Increasing the World's Food Supply." We're still talking about plant genetics but limiting the scope of the subject to a marked extent. "Hybrids in Your Garden" narrows it more, and "The Newest Field Corn Hybrid" cuts it still further.

It's rare that a magazine's breadth of focus is consistent in all the articles it prints, but as a rule of thumb you'll find more broadly focused articles in general interest magazines, more sharply focused pieces as the degree of specialization of the magazine increases. "The Amazing World of Plant Genetics," for example, might appear in a general interest magazine, an airline inflight, a fraternal publication, or any number of categories of magazines. The piece on crossbreeding would fit into almost as large a variety of publications. "Hybrids in Your Garden" would appeal to yet a smaller audience, and it's doubtful whether "The Newest Field Corn Hybrid" would sell to any magazine other than one aimed at people in agribusiness.

Take any subject—diets, the energy crunch, inflation—and think of it as a pie. As you study titles, ask yourself if you're looking at that whole pie, a large piece, a medium-size portion, or a sliver.

There are clues on the contents page to the depth of treatment an editor prefers, too. By determining the number of pages in a piece and coordinating that information with the breadth of focus, you'll be able to get some idea of how deeply the magazine's writers delve into a particular topic. Since the amount of art accompanying articles varies so greatly, and many pieces are continued in columns at the back of the book, you'll want to get a rough word count by looking at the articles themselves.

Masthead Messages

At some point in your analysis, locate the magazine's masthead (the listing of members of the editorial staff, editorial and advertising office locations). If it's feasible, tear the masthead page out and place it alongside the contents; if not, make a photocopy so you won't have to keep flipping pages. The masthead and contents pages together serve as your chances-of-success calculator.

The masthead gives the name of the current editor and in many cases tells you which department editor to submit your material to. A friend of mine, formerly assistant editor of a medium-size magazine, once characterized her office as "a perpetually revolving door." The magazine had five different editors in a period of three years, and the assistants were either shifted or replaced with mind-boggling regularity. This isn't an isolated example. Although a few editors have been at the same desk for decades, by and large editing is an extremely mobile profession.

Publications like *Writer's Market* and other market listings often have gone to press just as an editor resigns, so you should always check current issues of the publications to see who is editor. Address your correspondence to that person. Never, ever, begin a query or a cover letter with "Dear Sir."

Compare the article bylines with names of staff members to find out how many of an issue's pieces were written by freelancers. In a magazine of from seventy-five to one hundred pages it's an easy task to tell which of the articles were staff-written or written by contributing editors. A bigger magazine with a large staff takes more time. But this step of the process is essential, as the following notes I took from one issue each of *Family Circle, Woman's Day,* and *Lady's Circle* will show.

Family Circle:

19 articles with bylines
—8 by staff members (or authority with staff member)
—1 by celebrity
—10 apparently by freelancers

Woman's Day:

11 articles with bylines
—5 by contributing editors
—1 by celebrity
—2 by staff members
—3 apparently by freelancers

Lady's Circle:

19 articles with bylines
—2 by department editors
—1 by a contributing editor
—16 apparently by freelancers

I qualify the number of articles by freelancers with the word "apparently" for good reason. Many of the smaller publications have editorial staffs of two or three people. Some are even one-person operations. Editors often want to, or have to, write several articles that appear in a single issue. They're reluctant to let the world know how short-staffed they are, what a skimpy budget they're forced to work with, or how much they love to see their own words in print, so they write under other names. One editor writes under five different pseudonyms (both male and female) that I'm aware of. Several others I know use one or two pen names. This practice isn't so common in the big publications' editorial offices, but it does happen, so be aware that the articles may be more heavily staff-written than your statistics indicate.

I don't ever let the "apparently" qualification stop me from submitting, even though I suspect some of the bylines are fictitious. Who knows? The staff may have been forced to write pieces simply because they couldn't find the kinds of material they wanted in their submission piles.

While I'm studying the names of the freelancers, I put a check mark opposite those whose work I've seen before in the magazine or remember from other publications. Writers whose names appear frequently in a magazine I assume to be in the editor's "stable," writers relied upon through the years who are thought of first when the editor makes assignments. They have the inside track, since they're known quantities, and they write the bulk of the articles for a great many publications. One magazine I write for publishes about forty articles each year (it appears quarterly). Of those, I have written as many as six during a twelve-month period and I know, by reading the bylines, that there are a couple of freelancers who contribute as many or more.

Don't let the appearance of these regulars keep you from submitting to a magazine, for a successful sale or two might find you a stall in that stable, too. But if you find, upon studying six or more back issues of a magazine, that almost every byline belongs to a staffer, contributing editor, regular contributor, or big name, you'll probably want to write that particular publication off your list of prospects. The competition is just too tough to waste your energies on. The exception here is if you have an article idea that's perfect for that particular magazine and that only you can write. In general, however, concentrate on those magazines that buy most of their articles from freelancers.

The masthead often includes the names of contributing editors who are authorities in their particular fields. This information is valuable in weighing a certain article idea's chances. If you have a great slant for an astrological article, for instance, but one of the contributing editors has written several books on astrology, you'll have more success contacting an editor who doesn't have an astrologer on standby. Since many magazines are strong on articles authored or coauthored by experts, check the contents page to see if you'll need the collaboration of one on your proposed piece. If all personal relationship or mental health pieces, for example, have an authority's name as part of the byline, it's likely that the editor won't even consider an article without one.

A contents/masthead bonus is finding articles written by the editor. You will definitely want to read, and perhaps reread, those in order to familiarize yourself with the phrases she likes, words he seems fond of; her slant, his structure. And if the article's subject can be treated in somewhat the same way as the subject you plan to write about, you'll want to include it in the group of pieces you plan to analyze (see Chapter 7). Some writers also suggest that if you know an editor occasionally freelances, it's worth your while to check *Reader's Guide to Periodical Literature, Access,* and *Popular Periodicals* to see if any of her articles are listed. Analyzing them will give you added insights as to the format and style she likes.

Editors often confess that they're frustrated writers. One of them says she looks forward all year to the annual article she allows herself to write for the magazine she edits. Another admits that what he would rather be doing is freelancing. The only place most of them get to flex their pens instead of their blue pencils is on the editor's page. And then, alas, most of the readers skip over it. Don't you dare.

On these pages you'll see mention of authors who are new to a publication, as well as old-timers. This information will help you size up your chances, but the most important discoveries you'll make will be about the editors themselves. Of course, there's nothing quite like getting to know an editor face to face. But when that's impossible, getting to know one via the editor's page can provide an adequate substitute, for personality clues are sprinkled all about. When an editor writes about the articles that appear in the magazine, enthusiasm for particular pieces and photographs shows through. Some pages, such as those written by Diane M. Dudley, editor of *Sunshine Magazine,* give insights into the editor's philosophy of life. Helen Gurley Brown often takes part of her column to talk about her personal life. Editors sometimes write about their favorite things, or their pet peeves. As one editor says, "No freelancer can possibly know all of my magazine's taboos without knowing me. Some of those taboos have nothing at all to do with the magazine per se, but have everything to do with how I feel personally about certain subjects."

Reading editor's pages won't clue you in on the editorial decision-makers' every enthusiasm, attitude, or prejudice, but the information you garner will give you a definite advantage over your competitors. If you have an idea that dovetails with an editor's cherished cause or deepest concern, one promoting a favorite avocation or condemning a practice he deplores, you'll be well on your way to a sale.

You'll want to take note not only of what an editor says, but of the way in which it is said. Then, when you're ready to write your query, you can fashion it in both the magazine's and the editor's image. Use some phrases he likes. If he's exhibited a penchant for short, punchy sentences, let your query sentences be short and punchy, too. Though you'll want to study the magazine's articles for style before you polish your proposal, analysis of the front pages will set the tone for what you write.

To give yourself an extra boost, read the letters to the editor. Pay attention to the kinds of articles that evoke the most response, for they're the kinds the editor will be looking for to keep interest up in forthcoming issues.

3

Reading the Ads

You can tell the ideals of a nation by its advertisements.

—Norman Douglas

Have you noticed how often articles on summertime skin care are flanked by ads for sun creams; pieces on do-it-yourself car repairs adjoin full-page advertisements for automotive parts; a baking chocolate ad just happens to be next to editorial columns featuring chocolate desserts? Have you ever wondered why different ads for the same product appear in various magazines? Coincidence? Not on your editorial life.

Advertising revenues are what keep most magazines published.

And there's almost always a direct relationship between the kinds of articles in a publication and the kinds of products that are touted in it. Therefore, it behooves every determined free-lancer to become an expert in ad analysis. For the pictures with their persuasive pitches—sometimes comprising more than half of a magazine's pages—are worth more than a thousand words in directing the writer toward the kinds of articles that will make him a super-salesman.

Since Hammurabi ruled Babylon, 2,000 years before Christ, advertising has been a part of business. The Babylonian barkers who shouted the virtues of their employers' wares have been replaced by more sophisticated methods of sales seduction. But the message remains the same—"Buy Me."

Magazines, along with newspapers, TV, and radio, are the manufacturers' and businessmen's media for proclaiming their products' tantalizing qualities. That's why it's so important for writers to find out about advertising's impact on editorial content in general, and on their targeted magazines in particular.

In order to understand how a magazine's ads affect—and are affected by—the articles it publishes, you must know how the ad-placing process works. It goes like this: manufacturers and businesses know what kinds of people buy their products, through customer surveys and feedback from their salespeople and dealers. Because advertising a product nationwide, regionally, or even locally, is a bigger job than the majority of companies care to handle within their organizations, most of them rely on advertising agencies.

The ad agency, with knowledge of what a product's users are like, determines which of the media, or combination thereof, will be most effective in reaching potential customers, then produces ads that will do the job of persuading. To do that job, the creators of the ads must know exactly whom they are speaking to. Top ad agency people, like successful freelance writers, have an extensive knowledge of individual magazine's readerships. They get this information from readership profiles provided by the magazines themselves.

These profiles are as different from one another as the magazines whose readers they describe. The profile that *Sunset Magazine*'s research people put out, for example, compares its readers' socioeconomic characteristics with those of the general population in the United States and in the western states (Arizona, California, Colorado, Idaho, Montana, Nevada, New Mexico, Oregon, Utah, Washington, and Wyoming). Median household income figures are augmented by information on size of household; age, educational level, and occupation of head of household; length of residence in present home; estimated value of that home; and the number of readers who live in cities, suburban or rural areas.

Sierra, published by the Sierra Club, distributes a profile that, in addition to demographics, tells potential advertisers that 88 percent of its readers drink wine (64 percent drink beer); 80 percent use national credit cards; 48 percent hold valid passports. By reading the profile you know what sports these people enjoy, how much they spend on film and developing, what kinds of consumer goods they own, and what other publications they read. Other magazines' media packets tell such things as the percentage of readers who travel long distances more than three times a year, how many have savings accounts and own common stocks, and how they entertain.

Magazines don't use these profiles only as advertising tools. Through them, the editors get to know their readers and learn to cater to these readers' interests when choosing articles for publication. Since advertising is slanted toward a magazine's audience, by analyzing the ads you can see that readership through the editor's eyes.

You, as a freelancer, can use the advertising agencies' techniques in targeting your articles. It is possible, in many cases, to obtain a magazine's media packet by requesting it from the sales department. But with or without this packet, you'll want to study the actual ads displayed in several issues of your chosen publication to find out more.

Who Gets the Message?

Ad analysis will do two things for you: 1) help you form an accurate idea of what the "typical" reader of a magazine is like (his interests, economics, hopes, and priorities), and 2) allow you to zero in on subjects the editors think will interest both readers and advertisers.

The first question to ask yourself as you analyze is what kinds of products are advertised—luxury items, necessities, gimmicks. Then look at the people in the pictures. Are they young, old, men of the world, sexy ladies? Do you get a mental image of readers who are matter-of-fact, intellectual, gullible? And what messages—both explicit and implicit—are the advertisers trying to communicate?

There's a world of lifestyle difference between the readership of a magazine whose ads show distraught mothers with mud-tracked floors, stained baseball jerseys, and coffee that isn't pleasing their husbands and the magazine whose advertisements feature a succession of well-dressed men drinking Perrier water. You won't find much audience overlap from magazines whose ads include taxidermy services to those advertising T-shirts saying "Save the Whales." Ads for home permanents and couturier fashions, calfskin briefcases and mail-order bartending courses, luxury hotels and beer-brewing kits won't appear in the same magazines unless their circulations are large.

You won't have much chance of selling a scholarly article to a magazine that goes in heavily for muscle-building and bust-development ads; or do-it-yourself pieces to publications whose advertisers sell Cartier bracelets, sterling silver adjustable collar stays, and Lladró porcelain. The editor of the first magazine, however, will most likely go for self-help articles that can make readers feel more desirable; the editor of the latter will be interested in pieces slanted toward affluent readers.

Let's get more specific and compare the ads in three of the women's publications we talked about in Chapter 2, *Cosmopolitan, Savvy* and *Lady's Circle*. *Cosmo*'s ads are, for the most part, sexually oriented. You'll see advertisements for at-home pregnancy tests, sun care products, cosmetics and perfumes, contraceptives, underwear, liquor, and cigarettes. Almost all the models in the ads' pictures seem to be between the ages of twenty and thirty-five (the magazine's blurb in *Writer's Market* says "For career women, 18 to 34"). Children and people with gray hair are rarely pictured, and when they are, only in supporting roles. Advertising messages are loud and clear: Use these products and you'll be popular, desirable, with it, happy, and/or entertained.

Savvy's advertisements, by contrast, though heavy on cosmetics, primarily feature luxury items: cars with five-digit price tags, furs, expensive jewelry. They also include ads for business publications. The age range of the models is wider; they tend toward the sophisticated rather than the glamorous, and are rarely shown in any state of undress. The message here is: You're a success. Buy me and you'll be even more successful and look the part as well.

Many of *Lady's Circle* advertisements are aimed at people who want to lose weight or cure ailments by taking pills. Several pages of advertising space are also taken up by promotions of other *Lady's Circle* publications and patterns—needlework, knitting, crochet, and patchwork quilts. The models in the weight-reducing ads are suggestively clothed; those in the needlework ads look like housewives you would see in the supermarket. The message to the ad dissector at first glance seems a schizoid one, but on closer inspection it makes sense. Advertisers see the typical *Lady's Circle* reader as a homemaker looking for formulas to solve her problems, whether they involve making clothes or shedding pounds.

Your analysis job will be easier if you make a checklist and enter your findings on it. You may have nothing to submit to a particular magazine until sometime in the future. If you have the ad information in your file, it will come in handy at that later date. The checklist might look something like this:

1. What kinds of products are advertised?
    a. necessities
    b. luxuries
    c. get-rich schemes
    d. do-it-yourself aids
    e. gimmicks
    f. food
    g. clothing
    h. home furnishings
    i. business-related products
    j. beauty and health products
    k. books, tapes and records
    l. sporting goods
    m. recreational equipment
    n. trip destinations and tours
    o. other
2. What age people are pictured?
    a. children and infants
    b. teenagers
    c. young adults
    d. middle aged people
    e. senior citizens
3. What sort of people are they (professionals, blue-collar workers, athletes)?
4. What messages are the advertisers communicating?
    a. pleasure, happiness
    b. popularity, desirability
    c. efficiency
    d. style, beauty, handsomeness
    e. prosperity, success
    f. health

g. advancement of goals

h. helping others

i. problem solving

j. entertainment

k. security

l. other

There's a second type of advertising you will come across in many magazines—the mail order ads. They are usually placed toward the back of the publication, generally printed in black and white, and include an order blank or mailing address. Aircraft preheater systems, leather moccasins, Christmas cards, and mosquito repellent are only a few of the thousands of items marketed by this method, so don't overlook the clues they provide.

As you scrutinize the ads and note your findings, you'll see a readership profile emerging. The larger the publication's circulation and the more general its editorial content, the more facets that profile will contain. Study of specialized magazines with relatively small readerships will result in more sharply defined "typical" readers.

The Ad/Editorial Connection

The degree to which advertising influences the copy in a magazine depends both on the advertising agencies involved and the magazine's decision makers. Since advertising is often a magazine's lifeblood, editors use editorial copy as bait to entice potential accounts. They solicit these customers on the basis of articles they plan to run in upcoming issues. Their advertising salespeople approach a prospective client armed with a printed sheet that lists future articles, one or several of which are on subjects of interest to the people that client wants to present his message to.

Many agencies place their business with no strings attached. They agree to have a certain number of ads run at specified rates. Others stipulate in their negotiations that they will place the ads only if an article relating to the business or product appears in an issue of the magazine. Most, but by no means all, people with editorial power will reject such proposals.

On the other hand, in cases where there has been no attempt at coercion, editors will frequently place ads in the layout where they will give their advertisers the most mileage. This is not as contradictory as it may sound. These editors' code of journalistic ethics says that they will not be forced into having advertisers dictate editorial copy, but it allows them voluntarily to position ads next to articles that will complement them.

To take advantage of any advertising/editorial content tie-ins, whichever way they have come about, it's a good idea every now and then to skim the pages of *Advertising Age, AdWeek/ West,* or any other major advertising agency publications. These are the Bibles of the agency trade. They tell who has landed what account and often give particulars on upcoming advertising campaigns, including (and this is what you want to know) the magazines in which the ads are scheduled to appear. Magazines switch roles and become the advertisers in these publications, with their ads often including readership profiles—another incentive for the freelancer to study them.

Whether there's an advertising/editorial content tie-in or not, one cardinal rule exists at all magazines: *Never antagonize an advertiser.* A leading car magazine in the early 1970s was asked to testdrive and report on a new model automobile. Their finds were negative, to say the least, and the car, surrounded by a pigpen, graced the magazine's cover. As a result, a former member of the staff says, the magazine lost $100,000 in advertising from the car's manufacturer. This incident was the Halley's Comet of the editorial world. It won't happen again for a very long time.

As a freelancer, you won't score points or sell articles by writing pieces that will deeply offend one of a magazine's big accounts. Editors are sensitive about advertiser alienation to the point that they will have their advertising people check out an even slightly questionable article with the advertiser before they will run it.

Sponsoring organizations have a very large say and tremendous veto power over the magazines put out under their auspices. Although the editor may be hired by a publishing company that is not a part of that organization, he and the publisher know that their existence depends on keeping their sponsors happy. If that sponsor is an automobile club, for example, they know that the magazine won't survive long on a diet of mass transit and anti-driving articles; in fact, one issue with one such offending article will most likely result in someone else taking over at the wheel. By the same token, a publication sponsored by a travel credit card company won't be receptive to articles on cutting vacation costs by picnicking or camping.

In all cases, the sponsor's purpose must be advanced by the material that appears in its magazine. Usually, you can tell if a magazine is sponsored by looking at its cover or masthead, where the words "The Gulf Auto Club," "Official Journal of the National Geographic Society," or "Official Magazine of the Aircraft Owners and Pilots Association" are printed. The connection is not always so obvious. That's where examining the ads comes in. If you notice that many of the ads tout the same products (or causes) there's a good chance that the publication is linked, if not by outright monetary sponsorship, at least philosophically, with a sponsoring group.

If you have a year's back copies of a publication available for analysis, chances are you'll realize that like those of us who go on our annual bathing suit diets, most magazines become skinnier during the summer months than any other time of the year. Why? Because advertisers know that people spend more time outdoors and less of it reading than during the colder months. Thoughts of buying other than summer-use items are more appealing when there aren't so many options for other entertainment.

The decrease in advertising means that there won't be as many pages of editorial copy either, since the amount of advertising determines how much space will be allotted for articles in most magazines. As a freelancer, you'll want to take advantage of this slimming and fattening cycle by submitting queries for nonseasonal material during summer and autumn when editors are thinking about production of the larger issues in the months ahead.

To illustrate the practical application of ad analysis, let's look at how an experienced freelancer puts her findings to work. This writer specializes in travel pieces and is planning a trip to the Far East with visits to China, Japan, and Hong Kong. She has collected back issues of several magazines that she knows from past study use material on foreign destinations. Since the Orient has been a popular topic for recent travel articles, our writer must have fresh angles in order to make sales. To get ideas and choose the most likely markets, she begins studying the ads.

The first thing she notices is that all the magazines are appreciably thinner during summertime. This fits in nicely with late autumn queries, since spring is a much more pleasant time than summer in which to visit the area. And the spring issues bulge with ads, so the editors will be looking for a proportional amount of editorial copy.

One magazine's advertisements are heavily slanted toward luxury—five-star hotels, expensive luggage, elegant silver. It also consistently carries advertising for art/antiques auction firms such as Sotheby's. People pictured in the ads look affluent and tend to be in their forties and fifties. The reader profile is clearly focused—mature readers who like and can afford high quality merchandise and first class travel.

The second magazine's ads are directed toward people who like to spend their leisure time out of doors. Backpacks, dehydrated foods, books on flora and fauna, and build-your-own-sailboat kits are among the products advertised. The ads' models are young, robust-looking, and casually dressed.

According to the third magazine's ads, its readership consists largely of people with families, as many of them picture a parent or parents with their children. The kinds of goods and services offered for sale are in the mid-price range, with some do-it-yourself items.

When the writer has finished analyzing these three magazines, she has a list of more ideas than she will have time to use. The ideas for the first magazine include how to tell fakes from the genuine article when buying antiques in Hong Kong, Japan's Living Treasures (a select group of skilled artisans who are looked upon as treasures by their government), and tours of China that focus on art and antiquities. Among her query possibilities for the second publication are pieces on Oriental foods that can be adapted to backpacking, and camping in Japan's national parks. The third magazine seems to be a natural for articles on what to do with the kids in Hong Kong, the advisability of taking children on a China tour, and Japanese toys. Each of the magazines, the writer concludes, might also want pieces on shopping, restaurants/food, or accommodations, slanted in their individual readerships' directions.

By following the same analytical procedure with any magazine you'll be able to pinpoint the audience that you, and that important editor, want to reach. Advertising pays, say advertisers. Advertising analysis, I'm convinced, will pay off for you.

4

Looking at the Pictures

The concept of the photograph precedes the operation of the camera.

—Ansel Adams, The Print, 1950

One of an editor's jobs—a job that readers and many writers don't give a second thought to—is deciding how the magazine should look. There are considerations that go beyond making it attractive, like suiting the purpose of the magazine. A publication promoting tourism, for example, won't have pictures of city street muggings illustrating its articles. Compatibility of stories on the same spread (two pages facing each other) and placement of continuations of articles to other pages must also be considered. Editors also strive to avoid conflict—an article on oil spills on the same page as the ad for an oil company just isn't politic.

Then there's the matter of consistency. The editor wants readers to feel familiar with his publication and that means laying out the material so that each article has commonalities with the others, not to the point of being boringly repetitious, but involving enough sameness to identify each page as being part of the magazine. Perhaps the editor almost always uses "kickers," those large boldface quotes from an article that punctuate the text. He or she may rely heavily on blurbs to hook readers into reading on. Picture captions may always be complete sentences, or may merely be labels. Then there are the pictures themselves.

Editors display their consistency most graphically in the kinds of pictures they choose. Therefore, the right photographs, as well as the right words, are what sell articles. I'm convinced many of my sales would never have been made if I hadn't supplied the pictures. Most freelancers proficient with both pen and camera agree. To quote one, "It's hard to say sometimes whether editors bought a piece because the pictures were there or the words were there; but most often it's because *everything* was there and they didn't have to do much more to get the piece ready to run."

It's easy to understand why most editors prefer to get text and photos in one simple-to-slip-into-an-issue package. Hiring a photographer to illustrate a story is expensive—not only the hourly rate, but also travel expenses. Getting just the right pictures from a stock photo agency costs a lot, too, both in money and time the editorial staff has to spend on the project. Even rummaging through their own photo files takes valuable time. So the writer who is able to provide good photos gets the nod over another who has produced an equally appealing article sans illustrations.

Not only do most editors prefer that the writer supplies photos, some of them require pictures since that's the only way they can obtain them. Outdoor and travel writers, especially, find that if they're doing pieces on fishing for arctic char or coon dog water races in a remote corner of Kentucky, the availability of photos is what makes the difference between an acceptance and an "I wish I could buy it but. . ."

Ideally, you have enough technical competence to take salable shots or are willing to learn (for some good, straightforward books on photography, see the Bibliography). If for some reason you can't or don't want to combine photography and writing, you can team up with a freelance photographer on assignments. Or you may find that you are able to get the pictures you need from government agencies, travel bureaus, businesses, and other sources. You can ascertain whether the latter type of photos will do the job by reading the photo credits in back issues of your target magazine.

Before you load your camera or send those requests off to photo sources, investigate the magazine's basic photo requirements. Does it print only color, black-and-whites, or a combination of the two? It's futile to send black-and-whites to a publication that uses only color, and expensive (and therefore often not worth the expense) for a magazine to convert color to black-and-white. Does the editor want to see transparencies or 8x10 inch glossies or contact sheets? Many amateurs make the mistake of sending color, polaroid, or instamatic prints along with their manuscripts. Few magazines will consider using them.

Most editors will require that your shots be captioned. The preferred way is typed on paper and attached with tape to the back of black-and-whites, listed on a separate sheet correspondingly numbered for transparencies. To get the specifics, write for the magazine's photo guidelines if they are available and check the requirements listed in *Writer's Market* and *Photographer's Market*.

However you obtain your photos, it's vital that you send your editor in-focus shots that click with the magazine's image. And that means more analysis. The most salable kinds of pictures you'll encounter fall into half a dozen groups: scenics (landscapes, seascapes); buildings, skylines, and street scenes; people; animals; inanimate objects (motors, automobiles, and objects of art); and processes.

According to freelance photographer Jim Mildon, these groups can be categorized further, into shots that are posed and unposed. Mildon, whose photos have appeared in dozens of magazines, including *Travel/Holiday, Elks Magazine,* and the *New York Times,* likes to have at least twelve back copies of a magazine at hand when he begins his study of photographic style.

First, he looks them over to get a general impression, taking note of the ratio of horizontal to vertical shots that are used. "Most magazines deal with horizontals," Mildon says. "That's just because when you open the magazine up it's usually a horizontal layout to begin with—wider than it is high."

Next, Mildon studies the size of the pictures, since size has an effect on the kinds of pictures you should submit. "If a magazine plays pictures very small, you should not send pictures of intricate things; things which cannot be seen in a small space. Many pictures cannot be reduced and still be read," he says.

Christopher Springman, who has photographed such diverse subjects as Willie Stargell for *Friends* and petri dishes for *Smithsonian,* sees adapting his style to suit the magazine as a challenge. He says he "literally unstaples" six back issues of the publication he's shooting for in order to zero in on its photographic personality. Before he goes out to take the pictures, he has a list—either in his mind or on paper—of the shots he wants to get. "Ninety-five percent of your good shots," he maintains, "don't just happen. They're the result of careful planning."

In addition to giving editors the kinds of shots they've indicated past preferences for, Springman includes photos that incorporate fresh angles (pictures of business executives in the factory with the workers or standing by the company logo in addition to traditional behind-the-desk shots; a check being handed over at the site where the money is to be spent as well as the usual check-presentation shot taken against a plain wall).

Dave Bartruff, award-winning photographer whose work has appeared in *Travel & Leisure, Realites, Odyssey,* and *New West,* also relies on "reading the book" to determine what photographs he should shoot or take from his 100,000-picture stock photo file when he has an assignment. Since his field is travel photography, he is especially conscious of the techniques travel editors like to see in photos—scenes in overviews, then shown tighter, and finally telephoto shots for a magnified slice of the first general shot; details such as the arts and crafts of an area, the closeup of the face of an ethnic doll, textures of old buildings, cobblestone streets, signs in the local language.

Mildon, Springman, Bartruff, and other successful freelance photographers have evolved formulas containing many other elements for reading pictures. They look to see whether or not an editor uses captions to carry content that's not in the article. Most magazines use pictures as art in the layout to break up a page or make it graphically attractive. But when the writer/photographer finds that pictures are supposed to carry their own communication, he can adjust his text accordingly. Five paragraphs describing what a rotary engine looks like may not convey the information that a little picture of that engine will, so the writer can briefly describe the engine and let the picture do the rest.

When examining pictures of people, the professional asks himself if the editor goes for posed or unposed shots. He notes whether pictures are taken indoors or out; if they're taken at nighttime or during the day; at dawn or at dusk.

Focusing on Details

You can adapt these techniques of the pros and add some more when planning your pictures. I always pay close attention to the ages of the people in a magazine's pictures, whether they're children, teenagers, adults, senior citizens, or a variety of ages. Then I look to see how they are dressed, casually or in their best clothes. You'll also want to notice if the pictures are head shots, if the subjects are staring at the camera or involved in some activity.

Getting the right kinds of people in your photos is vital. I once took an entire roll of film before I realized that every person in every shot was over the age of sixty-five—not exactly appropriate for the family-oriented magazine I had planned to submit them to. And you'll have better success if you avoid nonphotogenic types. Scruffy-looking, obese, or angry-looking people don't have editor appeal when it comes to articles that don't pertain to sloth, overweight, or hostility. Look out for litter, telephone wires, and the like, too, unless you're writing about those subjects.

In your picture perusal, determine the amount of action an editor demands. We've all seen publications that feature at least one blurry shot in every issue, connoting speed. Some editors thrive on peak action shots, such as the basketball star jumping with the ball suspended in midair and the cowboy flying off the bronco's back. Other editors go for less vigorous action, such as people walking or knitting or looking through telescopes. There are also those who prefer no action at all—joshua trees under a desert sun, the reflection of a lake on the mirrored wall of a skyscraper, a castle next to a thatch-roofed cottage. While few editors always use peak action or consistently choose static shots, some of them do. What you'll find most often is a mix, but within that mix a consistent pattern.

A magazine's subject matter dictates in large measure the degree of activity or inactivity its illustrations portray. However (and in analysis, there seem always to be howevers), individual editors see the visual presentation of subject matter through as many different eyes as they do its printed treatment.

To prove this to yourself, examine two magazines that revolve around food and wine, *Gourmet* and *Bon Appetit*. While both magazines use color almost exclusively, most of *Gourmet*'s photos are static shots of various dishes or table settings, whereas those in *Bon Appetit* augment food photos with those of people preparing and eating the featured dishes. There are also more people in the photos accompanying *Bon Appetit*'s food-focused travel pieces than in *Gourmet*'s.

Most editors, whatever their other preferences, like people in their pictures, whether they be incidental or the featured subject. But there are editors who do not. They prefer their pastures left to the cows, their mountains free of climbers. In almost every picture of a landscape, seascape, or building, though, you'll find some object of recognizable size. Perhaps it's a wildflower or a fire hydrant in the foreground. Editors realize that without this recognizable object there's the problem of scale. It's impossible to gauge the bluff's height or if a valley is ten or one hundred miles wide.

I also try to determine the angles from which an editor likes pictures taken, whether he goes for framing (the ruins seen through an arch or the park bench framed by tree branches), if he seems to like reflections, or any other techniques that give his preferred pictures an unusual quality, a certain something that says, "That picture looks like one from 'blank' Magazine."

In studying sponsored magazines, I pay special attention to the frequency with which the sponsor's product pops up in pictures illustrating the articles. Burton Unger, editor of Volkswagen's *Small World,* says that excellent photographs will frequently sell him on a mediocre story as "it's much easier for an editor to improve words than pictures." But you can be sure that one of those photos, at least, includes a recognizable portion of a VW, for almost every article is accompanied by a picture of the same.

You'll find that magazines catering to a specific activity look for photos reinforcing their reason for being. *Trailer Life* has a travel trailer pictured at least once with each article, whereas *Family Motorcoaching* pictures motor homes. And rejection awaits the writer/photographer who confuses the two. Articles in *Tennis Magazine,* to no one's amazement, are abundantly illustrated with photographs of people playing the game.

When products are present in pictures, it's also important to note whether the brand of that product is obvious or in some way obscured. By reading what's in the pictures (and what is not), you'll be able to establish whether the publication has taboos. You'll see, for example, that *Teens Today* photos feature senior-high-age boys and girls interacting with people of all ages. But they're pictured differently from the young people in such magazines as *Seventeen* and *Teen*. Since the magazine is published by the Church of the Nazarene, you won't be surprised to find the photography rather conservative, but without studying the pictures closely there's little chance of discovering the less obvious taboos. By examining the photos carefully, you'll see that none of the subjects is dressed in sleeveless clothing, tank tops, body shirts, or shorts. They rarely have jewelry on and the girls never wear earrings. Small details? Unimportant? Not if you want to sell to that market. For the first rule of publishing is "give 'em what they want."

Who's to Choose

Though we've referred to pictures an editor likes, he or she is not the only person involved in picture decision making. Most magazines have art directors or photo editors, either in-house or free-lance. At the majority of these publications, the editor and art director/photo editor together determine which photos and art will decorate the magazine. Each has his or her own ideas about what makes a terrific picture, but there are certain criteria, expressed by *Desert Magazine*'s art director/photo editor Tom Threinen, which should please them all: "I look for good quality (sharp focus, exposure perfect or slightly on the light side since the image tends to get darker when printed, clean, undamaged transparency). I expect the technical requirements to be met, first of all, before the artistic merits are considered. When I look at the image, I look for a strong composition (dramatic or classic or minimal or busy—something to take it beyond just a snap-shot). The photographer should have attempted to portray something specific—anything from a mood to the lighting to the location to an explicit subject matter (person, plant, etc.). And, of course, the photos should relate to the text, usually directly. But I like to choose photos that also add something to the story, such as a mood or a visual detail."

Threinen's and other photo editors' insistence on good quality is not based on whimsy. The process of reproducing a print on paper will cause a marginal print to go to pieces and be unusable. It's all too easy to look at a magazine that's printed on poor quality paper and say, "They'll take any kind of picture. The ones in here are so bad." The photos you scoff at probably were fairly good to begin with; they merely lost a lot in the reproduction. Your best chance of shooting pictures that will reproduce decently on low-grade paper is to take them between ten in the morning and two in the afternoon, at eye level with the sun at your back. It's the standard formula and almost guaranteed to produce usable pictures, though perhaps not the most interesting ones. If the magazine you're shooting for is printed on top-quality paper you'll be able to go after those pictures that readers want to look at twice—those shot at other times of day and from more exciting angles—without fear that the quality upon reproduction will be compromised.

When You Can't Snap

Even if you do your own photography, there are times when you won't be able to get the pictures you need because of camera catastrophes, rain, and simply not being there. That's when you explore other sources.

Most businesses, chambers of commerce, and other organizations are anxious to have their names before the public. The chance you're offering them, photo credit and having their product on visual display, spells the kind of publicity that money can't buy, so if they can oblige you, they will. Reading photo credits will give you ideas about people to contact that you hadn't thought of. Going through lists of public agencies, organizations, and industries at the library will provide even more. I have one little gem in my reference library called "1001 Sources for Free Travel Information," which lists tourism offices in all fifty states and two hundred countries as well.

Another possibility you'll come upon as you're reading photo credits is other magazines. If they aren't in competition, editors of regional publications especially are willing to have photos from their files printed in other magazines. I was stuck for photos to go with an article I did on the Elko, Nevada, Basque

Festival. My logical source was the Basque Studies Institute at the University of Nevada/Reno. The only suitable pictures they had were a group that had been taken by *Sunset Magazine*. I was given the shots with the stipulation that the editor of the magazine in which my piece was to appear must get *Sunset*'s permission before using any of them. Next, since my intended publication also uses color and the *Sunset* photos were black and white, I approached *Nevada Magazine*, a publication sponsored by the state department of economic development. They turned me loose on their photo file and I was able to choose the other pictures I needed.

When several photographers receive credits in one article, there is no sure way to tell whether those photos were supplied by freebie sources or obtained from stock photo agencies, or who did the scrambling to get them together, the editorial staff or the freelancer. I've found that when I can't get free photos, it's better to let an editor know that pictures are available from big stock photo agencies than procure them myself. The first reason is economic. Fees at most agencies start at around twenty-five dollars for one-time use of a black-and-white picture and can run as high as hundreds of dollars for some color transparencies. Unless the writer's payment for photos from the magazine will amount to more than these charges, obtaining them is unprofitable and time-consuming. Some agencies set their rates in accordance with the publication in which the pictures will appear, so the writer can't be sure there will be a margin of profit.

There can also be additional costs in the form of research fees. These are refundable or deducted from the total bill after a magazine makes its selection. But if none of the photos is chosen, there is a possibility that whoever contracted for them will be stuck with paying the research fee. A penalty charge for keeping the pictures longer than a specified period makes the use of these pictures impractical, too, when you're submitting an article on spec or one for which a publication date has not been set.

And there's still another pitfall. I desperately needed transparencies for an article and telephoned the company to inquire about available photos and charges, then asked them to send a selection of forty slides. When they arrived, I read the fine print on the use agreement and found to my horror that in case they were lost or damaged I would have to pay fifteen hundred dollars for each of the originals and a smaller sum for each duplicate. Since almost all of the transparencies were originals, my total liability could have amounted to about sixty-five thousand dollars. Needless to say, I immediately rebundled the package and drove very carefully to the post office to send it back registered and insured. I had to pay the research fee, but twenty dollars was a small price for the lesson I learned.

Studying all the pictures in the book isn't only profitable, it's fun. And when you're submitting photos on the basis of what you have learned, remember to include some with light space at the top for the magazine's logo. After all, if you've done your homework well, one of your pictures could wind up on the cover.

5

Your Style
Is My Style

Every style that is not boring is a good one.
—Voltaire

"All the fun's in how you say a thing," Robert Frost once wrote. And saying a thing in the way an editor likes it said makes it even more fun as far as I'm concerned, because I love to fill out those deposit slips at the bank.

How you say a thing is actually a good definition of style—the ingredient that goes a long way in tempting editorial palates. It's the quality that gives distinction to writing, one of the means whereby a magazine develops that flavor its editor is eager to perpetuate. But since editors' tastes are so diverse, it is essential that you analyze what they've bought in the past to determine how you should serve it up in the future. You'll find that some editors like large helpings of folksy chatter. Others prefer their copy sprinkled with sophistication. Still others want theirs straight, with no garnishes.

You may have your subject matter down cold. Your grammar and spelling may be above reproach; your title, terrific; your manuscript, unsmudged. The idea may fit its intended publication like a wetsuit. But if you haven't written that article to the editor's stylistic appetites, be doubly sure there's enough postage on that SASE.

The successful freelancer is a writing chameleon. He blends at will with the surrounding editorial pages of whatever magazine he's writing for at the moment, changing the coloration of his prose as he moves from piece to piece. There are a few writers who are able to live handsomely by specializing in one field and writing for only a handful of top-paying slicks. The operative word here is *few*. Most of us, in order to subsist at above-poverty level, must be able not only to write about a variety of subjects, but also to pull, push, and pummel our writing styles about like chunks of Play-Doh. It stands to reason that the greater the number of publications we're able to write for, the more chances we have of seeing those five fascinating words, "Pay to the order of."

This verbal blending allows you to write in a breezy, free-wheeling way one day, with authoritative, no-nonsense sentences the next. It's not difficult to emulate a certain style if you've done your analysis homework. After all, you don't talk about the same things or in the same manner to your best friend as you do to your father-in-law, your children, or the newsboy on the corner. When you have a clear picture of a magazine's readership, of the working of its editor's mind (at least during business hours), and the kinds of articles she has gone for in the past, style transformations become automatic. Look at these excerpts from articles in three publications and you'll see what I mean.

> Professor William Steed, DFP, is an original—a combination educator, favorite uncle and flimflam man. Although he has been likened to both Will Rogers and Harpo Marx, there's a sprinkling of Professor Harold Hill, Captain Kangaroo and the Wizard of Oz thrown in just for good measure. For when the professor puts on his top hat and frock coat to talk about Croaker College, you can't help wondering if what he says is on the level or if he's spinning you the greatest yarn ever told.
>
> Professor Steed, DFP, is dean of the world's only institution of higher learning for frogs. And if you haven't already heard, Steed's school has gained a worldwide reputation for producing champion calibre jumping frogs. To clarify the importance of his stature, the letters after Professor Steed's name stand for Doctor of Frog Psychology.

That article, called "Jumpin' Jehoshaphat!" appeared in an airline flight magazine. The next one was printed in a business publication.

> Nevada banks are betting a change in that state's laws will enable them to get a piece of the biggest gambling pie: slot machines.
>
> Assembly Bill 211, passed by the Nevada State Legislature in its 1977 session, allows banks or bank subsidiaries based in the state to lease gaming equipment without obtaining a gaming license. Before the law's passage, banks were allowed to make loans on all kinds of gaming equipment and lease such gambling devices as 21 tables and Keno equipment, but were prohibited

from leasing slot machines, backbone of the state's multimillion dollar gaming industry.

The third example is part of an article that appeared in a women's magazine.

We're all battling to make our food budgets stretch as far as possible these days. But many homemakers don't realize that their freezers (and refrigerator freezing compartments) can be their staunchest allies in the struggle against rising prices. A well-managed freezer means food economy as well as better meals. Bargain strawberries tucked away in June taste twice as tempting in December; Chicken Parmesan prepared on a day when you're not busy can be a money-saving meal-saver on a day when you are. All it takes to enlist the aid of your freezer is a bit of planning on your part.

As you can see, the first example is written in a carefree, relaxed style. The second is reportorial and the third is written in an instructional manner that sounds like a home economist talking to a group of homemakers. I wrote all three articles within a few weeks' time. But they were written about different subjects, for different audiences—and most important, for different editors. By studying the magazines, I found it was easy to adapt my style to their individual tastes. Without that analysis, the job would have been far more difficult.

Though it's possible to adapt your style to hundreds of publications, don't be dismayed if you can't become a man for all magazines. Few writers can. You will find that there are some you simply cannot write for—but often, not for the reasons you would imagine.

Once upon a time, I queried a magazine without ever having seen it. When the editor replied with a go-ahead on speculation, I started gathering back issues, something I should have done in the beginning. Each time I'd try to read the articles that the editor presumably had thought interesting, I would find it impossible to concentrate. Though many of the subjects were compelling, the writing was extremely stiff and inordinately dull. I wouldn't do that to *my* exciting topic. So I wrote the piece in a style I liked. Needless to say, my brown manila came back to me with a stiff, dull note saying that unfortunately it wouldn't fit the publication.

It's also difficult to write for a magazine whose subject

matter doesn't interest you or is well beyond your experience level. You're not going to be able to do a satisfactory piece of contemporary political satire if, like me, you have trouble understanding Doonesbury. If searching out the sidewalk cafe where it's ultimate status to sip an aperitif isn't your scene, you'll probably have difficulty coping with the style of articles appealing to would-be jet setters.

An occasional editor has a penchant for complicated words. Whether or not you're a wizard with complex language will determine your ability to produce copy for the ultra-literates. But even if your everyday conversation isn't peppered with polysyllables, you'll find that you and your trusty thesaurus are better able than you think to write for magazines whose editors prefer a Bill Buckley vocabulary.

Often when you find yourself incapable of imitating a magazine's style, the reason isn't your inability to write. It's because you don't have enough material that lends itself to that particular way of telling the story. Perhaps you are short on anecdotes or don't have enough facts. You may have neglected to obtain the kind of information the editor likes writers to use in their leads; it might be that you need more authoritative-sounding quotes. I've found that impossible-to-write pieces almost fell out of the typewriter once I'd collected the missing parts.

Elementary Elements of Style

Read a variety of articles to find styles compatible with *your* writing. Which do you find most interesting and enjoyable to read? Chances are, it will be easier for you to write in those styles, too.

But before you begin analyzing the styles of individual articles, it's a good idea to analyze the components of style itself. They are tone, point of view, sentence lengths and types, descriptive words, reading level, kinds of verbs, and personality devices.

Setting the tone. *Tone* determines whether a piece will be academic, formal, straightforward, instructional, reportorial, conversational, chatty, or breezy; whether it will be serious, lighthearted, or humorous. To say that subject matter dictates tone in many cases is true, but it can also be an oversimplification. Take houseplants, for example. Scholarly botanical journals require formally written, technically complex articles about them. General interest magazines will usually go for a conversational, less technical approach, while houseplant articles in magazines devoted to house and garden generally fall somewhere in between. While most pieces on the subject are of the serious, informational variety, it's possible to treat the topic with a light touch, even with humor; or a negative rather than a positive slant—"To Hell with Houseplants" or "I'm Splitting with My Philodendron."

Tone is established primarily by the kind of language used—formal, informal, or colloquial. Formal language is textbook English, the kind you were supposed to use in high school compositions. Pronouns and auxiliary verbs are always written in full. Slang or trendy phrases are never used, except as a point of discussion, and then they're enclosed by quotation marks. Punctuation, complete with colons and semicolons, is written according to standard rules.

Informal writing is far more relaxed, and most editors today prefer it for conversational rapport between writer and readers. Strangely enough (since we've all been talking in a casual manner for years), writing informally is a problem with most beginning writers. Even those of us with more experience have trouble occasionally with stilted writing. Whenever I feel my style needs relaxing, I tell the story I'm trying to write to my tape recorder. By pretending it's a conversation with a friend, I can make the ghosts from my English-theme-writing days disappear, and the narrative flows.

There are other tricks you will learn from the magazines you're studying. Use contractions. *He's* reads more informally than *he is, they're* rolls off the eye less stiffly than *they are*. The first person and second person techniques have been adopted by many editors not only for purposes of reader identification, but also for their more informal style. You'll find, too, that some editors don't object to a sentence fragment now and then, if the meaning is clear to the reader. Stream-of-consciousness writing generally doesn't work, though, because associations have to be clear to everyone reading a piece, not just to the few whose consciousness streams in the same channels as the writer's.

Another technique involves throwing in an aside now and then or using parenthetical material. Punctuation, which dictates the way material is read, also goes a long way toward informalizing style. Somehow, a parenthetical expression set off by dashes becomes less formal than if commas are used. Colons and semicolons stiffen the tone. In colloquial writing, quotation marks or italics are seldom used to set the down-home phrases apart; words are allowed to flow visually unimpeded.

Colloquial writing incorporates words and phrases that have become a part of language because of their use in everyday speech. These words and phrases may defy all the rules of grammar—ain't, have gotten—but some editors see them as part of their magazines' images. We tend to think of colloquial writing in terms and phrases from bygone eras or such regions of the country as the South or the Ozarks. Colloquial to us means younguns, y'all come, folk. But there are contemporary colloquialisms as well. Hip words are the stock and trade of magazines like *High Times*. Country western magazines have their own vernacular. And the bikers. . .well, take a look at this excerpt from *Easyriders* called "Muscle Trikes":

> Bout three in the mornin' a few bros were swayin' around the last vestiges of the run fire an' slurrin' a few sloppy syllables about speed. You know how that number turns—first they mumbled misinterpreted memories of goin' fast, then the teeth grindin' turned to the means by which to go fast. Shortly, one bro turned to another and made an offer: "Say, b-b-bro, how'd ya like to ride my 92-incher?"
>
> "Far out," the ol' scooter tramp replied.
>
> "And when the sun makes a showin', ya can ride my 289."

When you use colloquialisms, pay special attention to how they have been treated in past issues. Although most editors look upon the enclosure of colloquial phrases in quotation marks as affectation, some of them do use quotation marks, while others italicize the words.

It is difficult to capture colloquial speech, so difficult in fact that many authorities on writing argue against trying. But since there are editors who like their articles flavored with the vernacular of an area or group of people, the writer who wants to sell must go counter to the experts' advice, proceeding with care and caution so as not to sound patronizing.

There's also a nonmechanical component that enters into the tone-altering process, one by which the writer gains a feel for the mood and tone he or she wants to produce. I've found that writers have a variety of gimmicks for changing their inner voices, many of which involve role-playing. When I'm writing a straight news story, for example, I picture myself as a sort of nonabrasive Barbara Walters. From first interview to final paragraph I'm all business, and while writing I sit at my typewriter, notes in organized piles on the desk.

By contrast, when I'm writing a "you are there" travel piece, I flop on the sofa, listen to music of the country I'm writing about, and look at pictures of the places I want to recreate for my readers. Not long ago I met a writer who, whenever he wants to do a free-wheeling, relaxed piece, takes to his bathtub (with notepad, pencil, *and* boats). Whatever props and fantasies work for you, use them.

How do you judge what tone to use? By analyzing previously published pieces on parallel themes, by developing a feeling for what is appropriate to the particular magazine, by becoming sensitive to the publication's readership. Words and phrases like "of course," "obviously," and "as you know" may work in an article for one magazine and sound condescending in another. A flip approach to a serious subject can be the answer to an editor's prayers, or anathema. What's considered good taste varies tremendously among publications.

I, you, or they.   Another element that determines style is *point of view.* You'll notice that most articles are written in the third person, but there is a growing trend toward first-person accounts. The former is standard in informational articles, especially those about technical or semitechnical subjects, and in personality pieces. First person, though very much in vogue during the nineteenth century and first few decades of the twentieth, was out of favor until recent years. Now, first-person accounts are back in editorial fashion, but are unlike those of times past, which sounded like pages from diaries.

Careful study of published articles will show you how to craft your first-person accounts. They usually begin with first person, then after a paragraph or two slip into third, catching up the first-person thread at intervals throughout the piece. How often that thread is caught up will come to light as you read first-person articles in varied publications. Another secret of successful first-person writing is to avoid straight chronology, except in a few publications which go for personalized blow-by-blow recapitulations of experiences. Even then, you will notice that the articles don't recount every detail of the experience—in travel articles, for example, brushing your teeth and parking the car aren't mentioned unless they're relevant. (*How To Write and Sell Your Personal Experiences* by Lois Duncan will give you lots of good information on this type of piece.)

Second person is the predominant form of address in how-to articles, especially those which explain projects. There, the imperative form of the verb (Measure three inches; Glue the corners; Solder wire A to terminal B) is used. Second person is also combined with first and third in pieces whose purpose is to rouse the reader to action (Write your congressman; You can help by . . .) or to acquaint him with a place, event or pastime (You'll find that . . .; Across the river you'll see . . .; And don't miss the . . .).

The point of view you choose can have a direct impact on your sales success. Editors who always buy third-person articles almost never consider others, and editors who print only first-person pieces won't look twice at those done in second or third, no matter how well they're written.

Give 'em the (right) word. The nouns you use are important, but you'll realize as you read articles analytically that it's the adjectives that set the outstanding pieces apart. The quantity of *descriptive words* used in an article does much to establish its style, and the number of them that different editors like varies widely. Be on the alert for adverbs, too, and notice the changes they make in how an article sounds.

You will find in your reading that most editors prefer *active verbs*. They give an article zing, while the passive voice makes it drag. But there's a great deal of difference among active verbs. In some magazines they are definitely punchy; in others they seem to be there only as a necessary part of each sentence. If an editor has shown a preference for such powerful verbs as *ricocheted, sizzled,* and *careened,* he's sure to want equally colorful ones in the future. And speaking of future, note what tense the editor prefers. Usually you'll see that it's a combination, but you will find magazines in which almost all verbs are in present tense. This gives an immediacy to style that other tenses do not. (There's a wonderfully helpful discussion of active and passive voice in *The Careful Writer* by Theodore Bernstein.)

Beware the fog. Since editors are aware of the average educational level of their readerships, they are careful not to print material those readers might have difficulty comprehending. In fact, they work to make reading both easy and enjoyable. Zeroing in on the readability of a particular publication is one of the easiest jobs in analysis.

For some thirty-five years, the late Robert Gunning overhauled the prose of more than two hundred publications, including the *Wall Street Journal*. In the process he invented the "fog index," a way to compute the years of schooling needed to understand a piece of writing. By using this "fog index" you can analyze various pieces in your target publication and see whether your article's readability corresponds. Here's how you use this handy formula:

1. Find the average number of words per sentence in a sample of one or two hundred words. Treat clearly independent clauses as separate sentences.

2. Figure the percentage of words having three or more syllables. Don't count capitalized words, easy combinations like "lawnmower," or verbs that have three syllables because of the addition of *-es* or *-ed*.

3. Add the average sentence length to the percentage of big words. Multiply the total by 0.4. The number that results indicates the years of schooling needed to understand the piece.

4. Repeat the process for several samples in various parts of the article and average the results.

As a rule, as the circulation size of a magazine increases, the fog index goes down. *TV Guide* has a fog index of six. *The Wall Street Journal, Time,* and *Newsweek* average about eleven.

Superstructure your sentences. We've all read that the writer should vary *sentence lengths* and *types*. Generally, that holds true. But while some editors have a passion for forty-word sentences, others prefer an almost staccato style. There's variation in length, all right, but that variation may be between thirty-five and sixty words, or between four and eight. As a rule, the average sentence is shorter in large-circulation magazines than in those with smaller circulations, since widely-read publications are aiming for reading ease.

You'll find definite editorial preferences as far as sentence types are concerned, too. In your analysis you will encounter not only the three basic structures—simple, compound, and complex—but a host of different sentence patterns as well. The twenty-five most common ways to begin a sentence follow as an example of construction diversity:

1. **Noun-verb:**
   Winter arrives early in Finland.
2. **Personal pronoun-verb:**
   He ran from the burning vehicle.
3. **Inverted verb:**
   Perched atop the archway were two bronze cherubs.
4. **Prepositional phrase:**
   At the top of the pile was a sealed document.
5. **Adjective:**
   Large profits can be expected in the next two years.
6. **Adverb:**
   Steadily the waters advanced toward the campsite.
7. **Adverbial phrase:**
   Ahead of time, make arrangements to ship the merchandise.
8. **Adverbial clause:**
   When the water has begun to boil, add the noodles.
9. **Coordinating conjunction:**
   Nor does the broom do as thorough a job as the vacuum cleaner.
10. **Direct object:**
    Tacks you can store in a small container.
11. **Indefinite pronoun:**
    Such is the case when a new travel destination becomes popular.
12. **Series:**
    Date, hour, and meeting place were decided upon.

13. **Participial phrase:**
    Reaching your goal, you may want to celebrate.
14. **Participle:**
    Baked, the cake looks very much like brownies.
15. **Gerund:**
    Jogging can become addictive.
16. **Gerund phrase:**
    Running long distances should be done during the cool part of the day.
17. **Infinitive:**
    To win, a player must score the most points.
18. **Infinitive phrase:**
    To pay by credit card has become the accepted form of business.
19. **Noun clause:**
    That you may learn Spanish in ten days is not as impossible as you think.
20. **Imperative:**
    Take as much time as you need.
21. **Connective:**
    However, the decreasing availability of fuel may cause rising prices.
22. **Transitional phrase:**
    By the same token, they are generous with their possessions.
23. **Appositive:**
    An acknowledged expert in his field, the curator is on hand to answer visitors' questions.
24. **Adverb of question:**
    Where can you find the proper instruction?
25. **Absolute phrase:**
    The forms placed in their positions, you can begin mixing the cement.

These types of beginnings are only starters in the sentence-patterning game. If you really want to delve into the subject, consult *American English Rhetoric* by E.G. Bander, which you can find at most libraries. Another classic, the favorite of many freelancers, is Strunk and White's *Elements of Style.* Whether you read these books or not, you should learn to recognize the different types of sentences. Most often, you will find a variety of types in an article. You'll rarely see a series of sentences that involves mechanical symmetry, for several compound sentences in a row, all with the same conjunction, become boring. For the same reason, sentences beginning with phrases don't often follow one after the other.

House rules.   There's a second meaning of style that writers should know about. It's what is referred to by publishers as *house style* or *press style,* and involves the rules regarding the mechanics of written communication—spelling, punctuation, capitalization, and the like (we'll talk more about punctuation in Chapter 9). Editors commonly use *style* as a verb in the context that styling a manuscript means to fix the capitalization, hyphenation, and spelling in conformity with house rules.

Most editors don't expect writers to be completely aware of their publications' mechanical styles, but it *is* important to prepare your manuscripts in conformity to some sort of style (The University of Chicago Press *A Manual of Style* and the *Associated Press Stylebook* are two excellent references). If you *can* zero in on a particular editor's mechanical style preferences, however, you'll have tallied up another plus

Personality producers.   The preceding elements of style are largely mechanical. The final element, *personality devices,* gives an article soul. Some kinds of pieces, granted, don't lend themselves to artistic expression. But if zestful writing is a feature of the magazine you wish to sell to, yours had better be just as lively.

Personality devices include quotes, anecdotes, figures of speech, and sometimes the descriptive words mentioned earlier in the chapter. When you're analyzing a magazine, notice not only the sort of quotes that are used, but also their length, their source, and their tone (humorous, instructional, startling). Note also the function of these quotes. Are they used to lighten the piece, to add credibility, to increase the human interest quality?

An anecdote, according to Webster, is "a narrative, usually brief, of a separable incident or event of curious interest, often biographical." In simpler language, it is a short story that serves to amplify, a device many editors like used in liberal doses but others ignore. While you're on the lookout for quotes in an article, notice anecdotes, using the same guidelines to determine what kind an editor likes. You'll find that some of them are everyday "slices of life"; others recapitulate important events. They range from a few sentences to several paragraphs in length.

When you're reading, be conscious of any *figures of speech* the writers have used. In case you've repressed memories of high-school English classes when you had to write ten examples each of metaphor, simile, and personification, here's a quickie refresher course. A *simile* is a figure of speech by which one thing, action, or relation is likened or explicitly compared, often with *as* or *like,* to something of different kind or quality. (I remember what similes are by recalling the line from "Oh, What a Beautiful Mornin' " about the corn being as high as an elephant's eye.)

Metaphor is the use of a word or phrase literally denoting one kind of object or idea in place of another by way of suggesting a likeness or analogy between them—the ship plows the sea; a volley of oaths.

Personification is attribution of personal form, character, and the like to an inanimate object or abstract idea as endowed with personal attributes—the city opens its arms; the countryside, dressed for spring.

Some words of warning: Though figures of speech can be exceedingly effective, they won't bring any editorial plaudits when they're not done well. Be sure that your similes are apt *and* fresh, that your personifications are within the realm of your readers' imaginations. Beware of clumsy or mixed metaphors.

Concocting the formula. After you have studied several articles in a publication, you will be able to mix together the proper proportions of stylistic ingredients for your own piece. If the content of your article lends itself to two or three different styles the editor seems to like, go with the one that will result in the greatest reader arousal. A recent study by the University of Kentucky Department of Communications showed that readers react more positively to the narrative story with strong descriptive adjectives and verbs than to any other. Readers also express preference for pieces containing direct quotes rather than paraphrased statements. Above all, when there's a choice to be made, rely on your writer's sense.

One thing is certain. Whatever style you adopt for a particular article, you cannot afford to ignore the elements of good writing. Just because an editor likes fifty-six-word sentences doesn't mean that your modifiers can dangle or that you're free to disregard punctuation. Singular verbs with plural nouns (strata, phenomena, media, and data seem to cause the most problems) won't do the job even if your article is loaded with the kind of picturesque writing the editor adores.

Remember that a sentence expresses a complete thought. Even though some of your potential buyers show a tolerance for sentence fragments, those incomplete sentences have to make sense. Otherwise, they will appear to be syntactical or punctuation blunders. And be sure to say exactly what you mean. I once edited a report about a program through which teenage mothers could continue high school while their babies were cared for in a nursery. The writer, trying to explain the program, said, "The girls are able to continue with their education while their babies are cared for until they have graduated from high school."

Use definite, specific language. Avoid superfluous words. Pay special attention to adjectives. Are they the most effective, descriptive modifiers you can use? Avoid clichés and overworked words, but take care in coining your own words and phrases. Even if the editor seems to buy articles full of newly minted expressions, yours can't be obscure or inappropriate. Orthodox spelling (night, not nite; through, not thru) is important, too, unless you are writing for the rare editor who prefers the shortened forms.

With a little bit of help from my editor friends, I've collected the following excerpts from articles that fall into the "least likely to see publication" category:

"As a mother of six, and pregnant to boot, my washing machine is always full."

"Salads, tossed, cut or wilted are the byword this year by the diet the customers at the _____ Hotel are no exception."

"Striking women three times more often than men, its victims are primarily the young adult in the prime of life."

"A senior citizen that I talked to recently recounted to me the reason. . ."

"Get up in the morning, look out the window and see the sun rise. And if you don't, it will probably be overcast."

"Relevant to the current mania for computer games, I have made a study into the subject."

Though you can learn from bad examples, you'll profit more by studying the successes. Fortunately for the freelancer, they're easy to find. Just reach for the nearest magazine.

6

The Name Game

A good name is better than precious ointment.

—Ecclesiastes 7:1

In the prologue of John Steinbeck's novel *Sweet Thursday,* his Cannery Row character, Mac, suggests that the author insert a little hooptedoodle in his book now and then. Hooptedoodle, according to Mac, is some pretty words, maybe, or a little song sung with language—not part of the book, really, but an insert.

I agree with Mac. Every book should have a bit of hooptedoodle; a little something that allows the reader to relax and wiggle his mind. So, let's hooptedoodle it up right now with a game.

The following fifteen titles appeared in three magazines. Your challenge is to decide which five go together and were published in each of them. The answers are on the next page, but you won't need to peek.

1. Tiny Village Terrorized by Glowing Spaceship Carrying Bizarre Beings
2. Behind the Classroom Door: What Kids Really Think About School
3. All-New Longevity Test: How Long Will You Live?
4. Cat Sealed Inside Wall Rescued After 3 Weeks
5. New Laboratory Food Made from Fungus is Inexpensive, Tastes Like Fried Chicken
6. Local Suds
7. Pasta Perfect
8. Success Story: Her Million-Dollar Business Began at Home
9 Scientist Performs Amazing Experiment by Growing Teeth of Chicken in Mouse's Mouth

10. Secondhand Chic
11. Goals: How to Set Them, Achieve Them, Enjoy Them
12. Sodium: The Hidden Menace to Your Health
13. Doctor Amazingly Cures Man by Exploding Bomb in His Body
14. Inner Space
15. Food Crazy

You're right! Titles 1, 4, 5, 9, and 13 go together. They appeared in *Weekly World News*. Titles 2, 3, 8, 11, and 12 were in *Family Circle:* 6, 7, 10, 14, and 15 in *San Francisco*. I could have substituted heads from hundreds of magazines and the game would have been just as simple to play. Editors are incredibly consistent as far as their title choices are concerned—a fact avid article analysts can use to good advantage.

Why bother? Titles aren't that important, you contend. Editors always change them. Wait a minute—they don't *always*. If your title is compatible with the publication's personality, fits the layout, and the editor can't come up with one she likes better, she'll use it. Even if the title is changed, you score points by coming up with a good one—good, in this case, meaning one appropriate to the publication. And add another plus for *perfect* titles. Editors, like readers, can be hooked by them. A title that catches the editor's imagination will make her want to like the piece, make her visualize the title printed in her magazine.

If you can devise a just-right title at the time you're querying, your chances of a sale escalate. An editor who hasn't worked with you before has no evidence of your ability. It's difficult for him to decide whether to take a chance that you're reliable, that you'll deliver an article suited to his magazine. Upon first glance at your custom-designed title, he'll see you're on his frequency, and that's the best of all editor-writer beginnings.

In the course of your analysis, you'll see that titles (or head or headlines, as they're sometimes called) fall into four major categories—label, interrogative, imperative, and statement. Use the following definitions and examples as a guide to identifying them.

The *label.* I can't count the number of times I've read that label titles are somehow second-rate, last resorts to be avoided.

Be that as it may, editors choose labels for their pieces more often than any others. The label can consist of only a noun ("Gold"), a noun with modifiers ("Delectable Ice Cream Desserts"; "Giant Wave") or include verbs ("Traveling Without a Man"; "Backpacking in the Canadian Rockies"). When a verb is included, it's usually in the present progressive tense as in the preceding examples, but it doesn't have to be ("How to Buy Running Shoes"; "Diets that Work").

Another favorite is the *imperative*. It's a stronger title than the rather passive label in that it urges the reader to action ("Don't be a Windup Parent"; "Stop Selling Yourself Short"). Imperatives are often used to title how-to pieces such as "Learn to Bake Perfect Bread" and "Make Your Vacation Dollars Travel Farther."

Editors who like the *interrogative* title believe that by asking a question, they elicit reader response to the article before it's even read. Titles like "Can Your Kitchen Pass the Food Storage Test?" and "What? Exercise and Lift Weights for Cycling?" can hook a reader even if she's casually flipping through the magazine.

The *statement* title is exactly that—a short sentence stating the theme of the article, such as "Legends Lend Magic to Hawaiian Adventures" and "The Gentleman Is a Cook."

Often two title types, or two of the same type, are combined in what I call the *two-parter*. It's a cinch to recognize because it always contains either a colon or a dash—"Kachinas: A Heritage in Miniature"; "Garage Sailors—On a Budget Cruise" (about people who drive from garage sale to garage sale seeking bargains). Although both parts of a two-parter are usually labels, they can also incorporate the interrogative, imperative, or statement. Actually, the two-parter is much like the label title/blurb combination. The words before the colon or dash (usually two to four of them) name or describe the article's subject. The words following the punctuation summarize the article's slant.

Although most titles fall into these four groups, there's wide variation in the devices used to construct them. You'll notice that articles' names are often alliterative, most of their words beginning with the same sound—"Six-Shooter Serenade," "Handy Hints on Hosting," "People—the Perfect Party Mix." The last one also illustrates another device, the play on words. Some editors go overboard with these plays on words and phrases; others shun them entirely. One magazine that uses a lot of them is *The Country Gentleman,* with such titles as "Mules of the Game" and "Born Toulouse" (a story about Henri Toulouse-Lautrec). Some editors like plays on abbreviations, too, as shown by two titles in an issue of *Camping Journal*—"Portland: Nugget of Ore" and "MN for all Seasons."

A few years ago, *Smithsonian* ran a story about a nineteenth-century paleontologist who had willed his body to his university. A present-day faculty member later discovered the old fellow's skeleton in storage. Thinking a storage room not a fit resting place for a distinguished man of science, the professor took the bones and gave them a place of honor in his office. He decorated them with tinsel at Christmas and drank toasts to old Dr. So-and-so's memory. The title was "Not Alive, but Well."

Popular vehicles for wordplay and parody are well-known slogans, book titles, and quotes or words from a song or poem. "Curds and Why" was the name of a piece about cheese; "The House that Jack Smith Built," "What A Difference a Decade Makes," and "Knee Deep in Crocodiles" were all takeoffs on lines from rhyme and song. The article title, "To Tip or Not to Tip," was followed by the blurb, "No Question about It." You'll notice that these last four titles can stand by themselves—a fact important to keep in mind when you're constructing a parody title. Those of us in the age group my hairdresser refers to as elderly (over 45) must take care that the phrases we think everyone's familiar with really *are* widely known. It's fine to parody a pre-World War II song title if you're writing for a retirement publication or one whose audience is in the over-forty age group, but chances are teens and young adults won't appreciate your efforts. By the same token, young writers, when putting together articles for an audience encompassing all age groups, will leave many of their readers mystified if they base titles on recent rock hits.

Another title-making trick is to rhyme words: "Hot Slots" (a piece on antique slot machines); "Spy in the Sky"; "Finger Lickin' Chicken." Using a word or phrase that has a different meaning when spelled differently can also be effective if it's done well. Among those I've thought especially clever were "Bone Appetit: Rating Pet Foods" and "Fete Accomplie," a story about entertaining. As you can see, in order for them to work, there must be an association between the phrase you've taken off on and the article's subject.

Coining a word, such as "Habersplashery" (a fashion article in *Esquire*,) or playing off a better-known aspect of a place, are two other techniques. A good example of the latter was "The Other Tables of Las Vegas," a label title for an article on dining out which was printed in *Bon Appetit*.

Although on occasion you may find a sensational headline in a general interest magazine, they're generally used only in tabloids and detective magazines. I've never sold an article with a sensational title, but I love reading the more outrageous ones. Pick up any issue of *Star, Midnight/Globe, Weekly World News, Official Detective,* or *Inside Detective* and you'll find titles like "Was the Virgin a Victim of White Slavers?" "Murderous Ordeal of the Women in the Motel Room," and "Terrified Family Claims: Ghosts Killed Our Pets."

First cousin to the sensational title is the shocker/terrifier. You'll find this type in general circulation magazines like *Next*—"Terrorism's Monstrous New Age"· "All Aboard the Doomsday Plane."

Paradox is popular, too, and not difficult to construct. "Why Hollywood's Rich Producers Are So Poor," "Dive to the Top," and "Spend Dollars and Save Money" are effective titles born of contrast. Double entendre—using a phrase that has a double meaning, one of them usually indelicate—is tricky. Although a few publications thrive on sexual innuendo, profanity, and four-letter words, most magazines consider that kind of writing taboo.

Actually, other than blue language, most anything goes in titles. You *will* want to take care, however, that your title doesn't either put the reader down or scold him.

Title Tailoring Tricks
Once you know what kinds of titles an editor likes, there are several tricks you can use to come up with just what he wants. First, examine your capsule sentence to see if it can be para-

phrased and shortened. Consult your thesaurus for synonyms.

If you're searching for an imperative title, ask yourself what you are trying to get the reader to do. Then start your urge to action with a verb you know the editor goes for. Strange though it may seem, certain words are repeated over and over again in magazines during the course of an editorship.

This leads us to another technique: fill in the blanks. Take titles from similar pieces in the publication and substitute a word or two. Remember the *Reader's Digest:* "I Am Joe's Stomach" and "Liver" and "Bladder" and on through your biology textbook? The results often aren't ultra-original, but the method works.

When parodying, rhyming, or using any of the other creative devices, it's a good idea after you have your capsule sentence well thought out to push the whole matter into your subconscious. You'll find that a malleable phrase will pop into your mind at the most unexpected moment—when you're filling the car with gas or walking down the supermarket aisle—and will need only a bit of polishing to work. (Be sure to keep paper and pencil handy.)

Sometimes naming an article happens quite another way. Your article idea may first appear as a full-blown title, flashing through your brain like a streak of summer lightning. When this happens, you'll work from the top down, contriving a lead and capsule sentence that are complementary and in the publication's style.

Paying attention to title length is a must. Most are six words or less. Don't fall into the trap of thinking they *all* are. True, you won't come across many like this one, which appeared in *Panorama*—"How I Became a Supporter of and Appalled by Docudrama, and a Fan of the Talented, Frustrated, Confused Men and Women Who Would Like to Make Television Better if Only So They Wouldn't Have to Apologize for What They Do—Write and Produce the Stuff America Loves." But you will see the six-word limit exceeded with regularity, especially in tabloids, whose features often span several columns.

To determine the ideal title length for a particular magazine, copy down those from three to six back issues. A look at the contents pages from four issues of *New Mexico Magazine* (see

Table 1.

Date	Title	Type	Word Length
10/79	History's Forgotten Town	Label	3
	The Arabians Come to Town	Statement	5
	The Manzano Maples	Label	3
	Socorro Cook-off	Label	3
	The Great New Mexico Haunted House Mystery	Label	7
	High Sun & Deep Powder	Label	4 or 5
	A Closer Look: The Ski Areas	Label (two-parter)	6
	Ski Touring	Label	2
	Gold in the Hills	Label	4
1/80	Keeping Well—Medicine in New Mexico	Label (two-parter)	5
	Life at the Top	Label	4
	Country Doctor	Label	2
	Medicine Arrow	Label	2
	In Search of a Curandero	Label	5
	The Patient's Advocate	Label	3
	New Hope Department	Label	3
	A Problem-Oriented Solution	Label	4
	A Tribal Feeling	Label	3
	Navajo Medicine Man	Label	3
	Tucumcari's Doctor from Afar	Label	4
	Telehealth	Label	1
	A Matter of the Heart	Label	5
	Resolving the Cuban Crisis	Label	4

(Place names counted as one word)

Table 1 (cont'd)

Date	Title	Type	Word Length
	Taking Medicine Back Home	Label	4
	A Hospital Made for Kids	Label	5
	Self-Respect in Carlsbad	Label	4
	A Sore That Never Heals	Label	5
	A Touching Mural	Label	3
	The Rent-a-Granny Lady	Label	5
3/80	In Praise of Mr. Longears	Label	5
	The Miracle Workers	Label	3
	Cow-Country Legacy	Label	3
	Images on Stone	Label	3
	Amonett's Saddle Shop	Label	3
	A Special and Mysterious Gift	Label	5
	Focus New Mexico—Willard Clay	Label	4
	A Spring Tradition	Label	3
	How to Build a Library	Label	5
	Archeological Advance Man	Label	3
	R.C. Talks About Gorman	Statement	4
	Billy the Kid Turns Up	Statement	5
4/80	A Hundred Years of Railroads and Railroad Towns	Label	8
	Six Shooter Siding	Label	3
	The Second Albuquerque	Label	3
	When the Railroad Came—Las Vegas	Label (two-parter)	5
	The Last Frontier		3
	Raton and the Northeastern Plains	Label	5
	Riley's Switch	Label	2

Table 1 (cont'd)

Date	Title	Type	Word Length
	Steel Trails Westward	Label	3
	One Yard Wide, 100 Yards Long	Descriptive (a type occasionally found)	6
	Short Trip on a Long Train	Label	6
	Highballing West on No. 5078	Label	5
	Fred and his Girls	Label	4
	The Great Grants Train Robbery	Label	5

Table 1 above; note title types and word length) will show you how it's done.

Tallying up the results, we find that of fifty-four article titles, all but four (more than 86 percent) are labels and forty-two of them contain only three, four, or five words. Though state and regional magazines have an unusually consistent title flavor, staffs of most other publications also have readily discernible title preferences.

Soybean Digest is a case in point. A look at the contents page of just one issue tells you a lot about coming up with a perfect title for that editor. "Puzzled about Storage?" "Computerize Your Combine," "Which Way Will a Sideways Market Move?" "Super Solar Storage," "Looking for Money?" "Pyrethroids Blast Insects," "Line up Your Target Pests" and "Shave Harvest Losses" were the titles in a typical issue. Right away, you'll notice that three of the titles are interrogative, three begin with an imperative verb, one is a label and the other a statement. You will also see that the editor is not averse to alliteration.

A second look reveals that three-fourths of the titles have

three words in them; one has five and the other seven. Your best title choice, therefore, would be a three-word interrogative or imperative, and chances are you would want to begin with a verb, since five of the eight title examples do.

Title/Lead Compatibility

Deciding what to read first (or what to read later or whether to read the magazine at all) is like impulse buying. We choose whatever strikes our fancy at the moment. I'm sure that if you surveyed magazine readers, you would find few who begin reading at the front and go straight on through the book. Most of us, after glancing at the cover and/or contents page, proceed to turn pages until a title or illustration catches our eye. If it's compelling, we say to ourselves, "That's one I want to read." If it's irresistible—a real grabber—we say, "I've got to read this *right now*."

Therefore, a cardinal rule: The title and lead must be compatible. It's not fair to the reader to promise to tell her about "Money-Making Careers to Start at Home," then not get to the subject until halfway through the piece. Since the title tells what an article is about and the lead introduces and capsulizes that subject, there has to be harmony between the two.

An excellent example of the title/lead tie-in is this one, which appeared in *Weight Watchers:*

SINGLE AND DIETING?
7 Ways to Make it Easier
by Freda Kramer

"You don't have to be single to be fat," sighs Muriel, a 42-year-old divorcee, "but it helps. The urge to binge when alone is much, much greater than when you're married."

Steve, a textile designer and bachelor who has lived alone almost 20 years, wonders if he would have gained as much as he did—130 pounds—had he married.

And Kay, a television production assistant, says, "I used to come home every night to an empty apartment, I did what came naturally—eat. But it was junk food, like cookies, peanut butter and ice cream—it *wasn't* food I would have eaten if I had had company around. I'm sure married people don't have such poor dinner habits."

Like Muriel, Steve and Kay, there are 15 million people in the United States who live alone, and 75 to 80 percent of them go on a diet at some point in their lives. Does that mean that singles are more likely to be overweight than their married peers? Not necessarily. It may even mean that they're more weight-conscious than the rest of the population. But one thing is clear—the single lifestyle does present special problems to dieters.

Each of the three paragraphs in the lead points to the title—people living alone and eating improperly, eating more than they needed, munching junk food, gaining weight. The fourth paragraph, after examining the enormity of the problem, further amplifies it with the capsule sentence: "But one thing is clear—the single lifestyle does present special problems to dieters." And that's what the article's title says it's about—the single dieter's problems and proposed solutions.

As you analyze articles, you'll see a strong correlation between title/lead compatibility and well-crafted articles. You will realize that whatever styles and structures editors prefer, they're not buying many articles that lack some sort of title and lead tie-in. Since leads are usually no more than one to two hundred words long, don't fashion the title from material that's buried on the fourth page of the piece (for more on lead lengths, see Chapter 8).

"Most people's titles aren't lively enough" for Bruce Finson, editor of *Pacific Discovery*. "A good title gives the reader some information and leads that reader on," he says as he points to two of his favorites "Island of Ghosts" and "Staircase through Time." "The reason I like 'Island of Ghosts' is that you know it's about an island, but you don't know quite what it is about, you see. It's not so obscure that you don't know what the subject's about; and yet it's not so explicit that you've got the whole story in the title." Referring to "Staircase through Time," an article about geology, he says, "In a science magazine if a title says something about time, it's almost got to be geological. But staircase? It turns out that it is literally a geological staircase in terms of geological forms. But the reader doesn't know that. The title says just enough to pique his curiosity."

Speaking of pique, one of *Travel & Leisure* editor Pamela Fiori's favorite titles uses that word—but in a different context. It's called "Pique Season" and is about the travails of traveling during the peak summer months. Fiori believes that what a title says depends a great deal on the marriage of words and pictures.

She cites one of her magazine covers which pictured "a beautiful woman wading up to her gorgeous neck in the Caribbean sea. Her hands were behind her head, as if lounging in perfect tranquility. Her expression was sublime. The cover line was 'The Art of Doing Nothing.' " She goes on to say that neither photograph nor cover line would have been as effective on its own.

Seventeen's executive editor, Ray Robinson, says, "If you can't come up with a decent title, perhaps you can't come up with the piece." Robinson looks for titles that draw his readers into the article, and by analyzing the pages of his magazine, you'll realize he means what he says. Among his favorites are "Auto-Mated" (on computer dating) and "How to Catch the Eye of the Guy Who Won't Date." Robinson notes that there's a move toward discursive titles, as opposed to the literal or definitive. An example is this one he used in a recent issue—"How to be Happy Even if You Don't Make the Cheerleading Squad or School Play or Swim Team or Student Council or   ."

Since there are trends in title fashion, the article designer should update his title research periodically, noting whether his target editors are following trends or continuing their established patterns. No editor will go overboard and abandon the old completely, but the more innovative among them will react positively to your not-quite-traditional efforts. David R. Legge, editor-in-chief of *D*, lists a rather unorthodox title among his favorites: "Guess Who's Not Coming to Dinner: What if You Opened a Restaurant in Dallas and Nobody Came? It Happens. A Lot." He says he likes it because "the title is clever, explains the story, and sure sold us a lot of magazines on the newsstands." Another he likes is "Tempest in the Ivory Tower," subheaded "The University of Dallas slept through the turmoil of the Sixties and Seventies. Now it has awakened to a controversy that is shaking its foundations." "Again," he says, "this title comes at its subject matter obliquely but not so cleverly that it obscures the description of the story that is to follow."

It sometimes happens that writers fall in love with their titles. They may become so enamored, in fact, that they don't construct solid stories to go with them. Clever titles without good writing backing them have never sold manuscripts. Writers with the titlemania may also want to protect their article's names with copyrights (which isn't possible because titles cannot be copyrighted) and are devastated when editors rechristen their pieces. There's one sure cure for this affliction—the realization that selling your article—whatever it's ultimately called—is certainly better than no sale at all.

The addition of blurbs to many titles poses a question for both beginning and experienced writers. Will it hinder or help their chances if they write blurbs for their pieces? Although this is traditionally the editor's job, there are occasions when you can give him a hand. If I can contrive a *really good* blurb, constructed to fit perfectly into the editorial mold, I type it below my title. When I can't dream up a first-rate one (or if the magazine rarely uses blurbs) I don't produce one.

Following the same rule, never include subheads—the segment titles that break up blocks of text—if you haven't seen them in your target magazine. When they're used, subheads are usually written by the editor. If you can provide good ones in his preferred style, the editor won't have to bother, adding more points in your article's favor. The same analytical tools used in dissecting titles can be applied to subheads with the same results—satisfied editors.

And that's the name of the writing game.

7

Analytical Countdown

The best asset a writer can have is some native talent. The second-best asset is a capacity for sustained drudgery.

—Jack Alexander, Writing From Idea to Printed Page, 1949

The above quote isn't there to discourage you. Honest. It should give you comfort, in fact, for very few writers are convinced they have talent. We're all terrified when we begin a major article or a book. What if our mind freezes and the muse fails? What if we have to call that editor and admit we're not up to the job? But those of us who succeed have one common ingredient in our make-up—an element that's often confused with talent, or even genius. It's the ability to work hard.

So this is the "roll up your sleeves and don't put it off any longer" chapter. By this time, you've found that studying covers, mastheads and editors' pages gets to be intriguing; that coming up with appropriate leads and titles provides a puzzle-solving sort of pleasure. Analyzing ads and photos is almost fun. *But,* analyzing words, sentences, and paragraph lengths is *not* exciting, and I certainly won't predict it will replace tennis or golf as your favorite leisuretime activity. It *is* the surest method I know of separating the published writer from the also-submitteds. And if you spend time counting words, you'll have more chance of counting money from your article sales.

This awful toil *is* necessary. You'll be tempted to short-cut. Don't. There is a direct relationship between this kind of labor and writing success. The English language is so versatile, and the ways to express a thought so varied, that there isn't *one* single formula for putting words together that works. Through word analysis, you can construct articles in any magazine's image.

Ready, Set, Go!

The first step is to gather together the past year's issues of the magazine for which you wish to write. You'll be able to get many of these magazines at the library. Back copies of in-flight and company-sponsored magazines are often available from public relations people. Have friends save old issues of fraternal, professional, and other non-general-circulation magazines. In many cases, the editor of a publication will send you several back copies upon request, especially if you've gotten a go-ahead on assignment or speculation.

Ideally, you'll want the whole year's back issues. If that's impossible, try for six and settle for three or four if you must. The more back copies you have, the easier it will be to find articles like those you're going to write.

Select the six articles that parallel yours most closely. Whenever feasible, I clip out or photocopy these pieces, eliminating the hassle with bound pages and their maddening propensity to flip over. You'll also save space in your filing cabinet (or cardboard box) by inserting articles rather than whole magazines into your dossiers.

Your next job is to read each of these articles with an analyst's eye. Total concentration is vital. In fact, one freelancer I know types parallel pieces from magazines she wants to write for to be certain she's concentrating on the material. She reports that it's an effective means of becoming totally absorbed—unless you're a typist who has to look at the keys.

As you read, use the following checklist and note the answers:

1. What is the purpose of the article? Your answer may be to guide, inform, advise, entertain, shock, inspire, incite to action, warn, or a combination of purposes.

2. How broad is the article's focus? Ask yourself if the piece deals with a single theme or a theme with variations.

3.   How deeply does the writer delve into the subject? Note how many points the writer makes and how extensively she goes into each of them.

4.   How are the various points substantiated (by examples, reinforcing quotes, statistics)?

5.   Does the writer take an advocate's stand or does he simply relay the facts and let the reader come to a conclusion?

6.   What were the probable sources of the writer's information—interviews, historical documents, government pamphlets, other magazine articles, reference books, on-the-scene observation?

7.   What person is the article written in (first, second, third, or a combination)?

Research indicators.   Most stories, unless they're in-depth looks at a person, place, or process, don't require lots of on-the-scene research (and the need for astronomical travel expenses that the majority of magazines don't reimburse writers for). You can estimate the amount of face-to-face exploration or interviewing you'll have to do by reading parallel articles. For example, an article on robots with quotes from five experts in the field doesn't mean that the author traveled to the NASA Jet Propulsion Lab at Cal Tech, Silicone Valley, and to the three other locales in the East and Midwest where those experts work—unless there are detailed descriptions of manufacturing facilities. Even then the writer may have obtained most of the information by doing background research at the library and from interviews by letter, telephone, and/or cassette tape.

One of the easiest articles I've ever collected material for was on unusual museums in the United States. It highlighted eight of these repositories of the quaint, quizzical, and downright bizarre, only two of which I'd visited. Information for the others was gathered by mail and phone. Roundups are usually done this way.

You'll notice that editors usually want a "geographic mix"

(whether of the whole country or a region thereof) for these articles, so if attendance at each of the featured events or attractions were mandatory, not many writers could afford to bankroll the research. Also, most national magazine articles with quotes from the experts demand that those experts be from different areas of the country—not just from your hometown. The type and quantity of research required varies from publication to publication, but analysis of their back issues will tell you just what kind and how much you will need to please their editors.

Figuring the Figures

When you've completed this part of your research, it's time to come up with some figures—averages of the number of adjectives, adverbs, words of more than two syllables; quotes, anecdotes, and statistics that your target editor likes in the pieces he buys. This is *not* to say that if six articles from a publication average 10 adjectives per 100 words, you must duplicate the ratio exactly in your article. It means that you want to be close (say 8 to 12, rather than 4 or 15).

This doesn't mean, either, that you have to count every adjective, adverb, and the like in each of the six pieces. I usually work with 500-word segments. The quick and easy way to come up with these segments is to count 100 words in a typical column (most magazines today use a three-column-per-page format). After you've counted 100 words, measure the vertical length of that block of type, then multiply those inches by five. If 100 words measures 2⅛ inches, the 500-word samples you'll use in that particular magazine will each be approximately 10 inches long. Obviously, if the magazine uses a variety of column widths—2-inch and 3¼-inch columns are the most common combination—you will have to measure accordingly, but the method remains the same.

I've found that it works best to take adjective, adverb, words of more than two syllables, and statistic counts from one 500-word segment of each article. Shorter segments are often not representative of the whole, while analysis of longer portions involves unnecessary work. Choose these segments at random from the body of the article. It's not important, for example, to analyze the section beginning with the fourth paragraph, or the seventh, or the ninth. You needn't be consistent in examining segments from the same exact placement in each article. I've discovered, though, that analyzing the lead or final paragraphs makes for a less representative sampling.

The 500-word-segment analysis also works well for getting an idea of average sentence length, while a determination of the approximate number of words in each paragraph of an article doesn't take much time if you use a ruler, even if you do the whole article. It may seem a bit weird to you, or at least picky, to craft your sentences and paragraphs in a magazine's mold. Perhaps it is weird and picky, but it helps produce sales. Editors are very busy people. Like writers, they never can squeeze quite enough hours out of a day. When they look at a manuscript that they can tell won't take much of their blue-pencil time, you've given them an extremely positive feeling. A manuscript with 72-word sentences they'll have to chop into two or three or five, paragraphs they'll have to divide and provide transitions for or join together, make them wonder if the piece is worth the effort they will have to expend.

Before you begin counting, set up a group of symbols you can recognize at a glance. Here are the symbols I use:

A	-	*Adjective*
Av	-	*Adverb*
Anec	-	*Anecdote*
Sy	-	*Words of more than two syllables*
S	-	*Statistics*
Q	-	*Quotes*
1/Per	-	*First person*
2/Per	-	*Second person*
3/Per	-	*Third person*

When I'm counting sentence lengths, I put the number of words at the end of each sentence. A circled number at the end of each paragraph tells me the approximate number of words in it.

Above all, don't neglect to count the number of words with more than two syllables. There are several readability formulas based on such criteria as length of words and sentences. These have as their foundation the belief that the more difficult material is to read, the fewer people who will want (or be able) to read it. My studies have shown that publications vary widely in the number of polysyllabic (more than three-syllable) words, and even those with more than two, which are used. There is also a highly positive correlation between a magazine's circulation size and the absence of "hard" words. This is not to say that small-circulation magazines are always more difficult reading than the big books. But as a general rule, you'll find that the top-circulation magazines use a simpler vocabulary because they're aimed at a cross-section of the population with a wide range of reading skill levels. Although in computing the fog index (mentioned in Chapter 5), words of more than two syllables that are capitalized are not counted as difficult words, I include complicated names of people and places in my more-than-two-syllable count. It's true that words like Massachusetts and Kissinger have a high recognition factor, but not all people recognize the same words.

Speaking of quotes. To determine the number of quotes an editor likes, skim each of the six pieces, placing a *Q* symbol in the margin opposite each one so it will be easy to add up the marks. Then divide the number of quotes into the article's approximate word length, if you like, to get the ratio of words to quotes. When I did a study analyzing articles in travel publications, I needed a consistent basis for comparison, so I determined the number of quotes per 500 words:

$$\frac{(\text{number of quotes}}{x} = \frac{\text{approximate word length})}{500}$$

While reading the pieces, take note for your files on the kinds of quotes and their placement in the articles. Did the quotes come from interviews? From books of quotations? Lines from fairytales, songs, and folklore? Perhaps they are "blind" or anonymous quotes. They may have come from news items or historical journals such as diaries, or maybe they were excerpted from speeches. Note, too, the kinds of people who made them— the famous, the infamous, the man on the street; the chief of police or the cop on the beat. Some editors prefer contemporary quotes. Others go for pearls of wisdom uttered many years ago. Their length varies also; some are one-liners, others paragraphs long. You'll find that their presentation differs. Editor A may like a quote prefaced by "according to _____", Editor B may prefer "_____ said."

Some editors are partial to quotes in the lead paragraphs. Others love them in endings, while some like them sprinkled evenly through the text. Still others don't like them at all.

Determine how many anecdotes are needed by the same method you use for quotes. And, again, pay special attention to the kinds of stories the editor likes. It's disillusioning, but true, that some of the anecdotes we read aren't about things that actually happened (at least not in exactly the way the writer says they did). One well-known freelancer in the social science area admits that many of his anecdotes are fabricated, based on information he has gathered from authorities in his specialty. Others will tell you they rearrange their stories a bit to fit in with the articles they write. I'm still convinced that you cheat your audience when you present fiction as fact; but be that as it may, if an anecdote is well-crafted, it's impossible for the reader to know whether the incident really happened or not. However, since it is difficult to make up anecdotes, the article analyst makes her writing life easier by knowing in advance how many and what kinds of anecdotes she needs to write a successful piece. That way, while she's doing on-the-scene or library research, and especially while conducting interviews, she can be on the alert for the right kinds of anecdotal material. During an interview, for instance, when the interviewee is making an important point, she can probe for illustrative stories.

Write by number. Statistics are those facts that can be stated in numbers—1,000 people, a 450-foot tower, one-half of the world's food supply. You'll find that they're used liberally in certain magazines and types of articles (especially historical, technical, and business), absent in others. I use 500-word segments to find out how many a particular editor will find pleasing, and figure my ratios as I do adjectives and adverbs.

Not only is it vital to know how many statistics you'll need, you'll want to know how to present them in palatable form. There are editors who like to disguise them completely. Instead of saying that an island has so many thousand square miles, for example, you must liken its size to that of another geographical entity, "Shivering in the North Atlantic just below the Arctic Circle, Iceland is only slightly smaller than the state of Kentucky." Instead of giving a city's population, the editor wants that fact presented as a relationship to the size of another city, state, or country.

For example, one editor might like you to say that Luxembourg has a population of about 77,000, while another would prefer that you write "About three-fourths as many people live in Luxembourg as in Twin Falls, Idaho." The latter is not statistical, strictly speaking, so while not including it in my statistical count, I still would make a note as to how the size of any geographical areas mentioned should be treated.

After analyzing the words that make up your selected articles, you will have a well-defined pattern to follow. This list of writing specifications should cut your typewriter time in half while doubling or tripling your chances of sales. Once you've sold an article or two to a magazine, you will have absorbed its editorial requirements and won't have to repeat the analysis for that publication.

Counting words is sustained drudgery, no doubt about it. But it doesn't take analysis to find out it's lots more fun than counting rejection slips!

8

Great Beginnings and Happy Endings

The beginning is half of the whole.
—Plato, *Laws*

The p'int of good writing is knowing when to stop.
—L. M. Montgomery, *Anne's House of Dreams*

A successful freelancer remarked some years ago, "I look at the lead as my first chance. My last chance. My only chance. A mediocre article can make it if you have a great lead but a great article with a dull lead will come boomeranging back for one basic reason. The editor won't bother to read beyond the first dreary paragraph."

I won't go so far as to say that editors never buy articles with dull leads—I've read too many of them. But to my mind, those beginning paragraphs are the writer's best chance for making an editorial conquest. It's like the first lick of an ice cream cone. If that tastes good, you'll be set up to enjoy the whole thing. Of course, the rest of the article can't deteriorate into a mishmash of vagaries or a blob of poorly crafted prose. Chances are, though, if you can write a compelling lead, you'll do a competent job on the rest.

As we've learned, what's good so far as an editor is concerned may not be our own first choice. That goes for leads, too. We might, without analysis, think that one type of lead would be perfect for an article and use it. But if we have learned that the editor in question goes for a different kind of lead 50 percent of the time, a second type, 30 percent, and never *ever* uses the type of lead we have in mind, we won't play our favorites, but his.

It's hard enough, you say, to come up with a lead anytime, let alone when you're restricted by editorial preferences. We've all been brainwashed with the stories about the journalist who put paper into his typewriter, stared at the blank page for two or three days, then, when he finally decided how to begin, wrote the article in half an hour. I have a suspicion that the mystique that has grown up around writing leads, like writer's block, is often used to rationalize our unwillingness to get on with the show.

Lead analysis eliminates that excuse. By knowing what an editor wants, you'll have no reason to stare at that empty page for more than five minutes—nor will you want to.

But first you have to know exactly what a lead is and what it should do. It's the curtain raiser, the attention grabber, usually one to three paragraphs long, which sets the stage for your *capsule* or *nutshell* sentence. This sentence is the statement of the article's theme. It sets forth, in synopsized form, what the writer is going to spend the next five or fifteen hundred words detailing.

The purpose of the lead is to interest, entice, and intrigue. It must persuade the reader that the article is more important to him at that moment than shoveling the sidewalk or watching Monday Night Football. It's your entree to the reader's time— an entree you gain by letting him know that what you have to say is important or pleasurable or vital to his well-being.

As you read the leads of the articles in several back copies of your target publication, put an asterisk next to those you find especially effective. Effective or not, note the kind of lead in the margin opposite each one. You'll want these notes for future reference.

I also find it helpful to identify the tone of each lead, what-ever its type. I ask myself whether it's low-key or hard-sell; whether the editor likes a lot of razzle-dazzle or prefers a more restrained approach. The tone of a lead should establish the mood or feeling created throughout the entire article. The kinds of leads you are most likely to find are:

1. Summary. One of the most popular leads (and perhaps easiest to write), the summary usually is only a paragraph or two in length. It tells, succinctly, what the article is about. Tabloids like the *Star* and *National Enquirer* make extensive use of the short summary lead. Look at an issue of any one of them and you'll find it is filled with articles which begin with one summarizing sentence.

The tabloids aren't the only publications in which this type of lead is popular. You'll find summary leads in almost every magazine on the newsstands today. This one appeared in an article called "Fire Island" in *Sierra:*

> If environmentalists' current efforts are successful, New York state will soon have its first designated wilderness area. In early April, the National Park Service (NPS) proposed that 1347 acres on Fire Island be designated as wilderness.

And *Nation's Business* printed this one in an article called "Ex Post Facto Fix," which told about the fund for cleaning up toxic wastes:

> Government's term for it is the Comprehensive Environmental Response, Compensation and Liability Act of 1987.
> Generically, it is called the "super-fund."

Although most summary leads are much shorter, you will occasionally come across one that's quite long, like this lead from an article in *Prime Time:*

> There are many good reasons for attending a university, especially during the middle years of life. It is a way of pursuing new interests; it can lead to professional advancement, open up new career opportunities, bring adults into contact with others who have similar interests, and may even bring back fond memories of former student days. But before enrolling in any courses, be careful about the institution you choose. Many of them are eager to receive your tuition, and are ready to exploit the fact that you are a ripe candidate for their marketing effort.
> Furthermore, it is important to know your own goals before choosing a college or university. If you take courses simply to meet other people, to entertain yourself, or to gain personal satisfaction, it makes sense to first investigate the costs involved and the ease of getting to classes. If, on the other hand, you take courses because of a serious personal commitment to greater knowledge and understanding, or as part of a program for professional or career advancement, then you are also making an investment decision. In that case, the qualitative considerations set forth here should be taken seriously.

2. Interrogative. The interrogative lead asks a question. Its purpose is to make the reader wonder, and in wondering, proceed to read the article.

A series of questions also can be an effective lead as illustrated by this one in *Nevada Magazine:*

> Have you ever had your favorite TV program suddenly interrupted by an unscheduled commercial flashing momentarily on the screen, accompanied by garbled, off-track voices? Or did you ever receive a substantial bill for refrigerator repair, only to find that your unit runs worse than before? What about the attendant who cannot properly service your car, or the switchboard operator who gets you Chicago instead of New York?
>
> Domestic hazards such as these are symptomatic of our country's most pressing educational dilemma: the tragic lack of trained technical people to run and maintain the complex industry of the world's most technically advanced nation.
>
> On a barren, rocky desert mesa overlooking Las Vegas stands a striking answer to this acute occupational problem— Southern Nevada Vocational-Technical Center.

The questions in this lead are used to dramatize a problem— using situations all of us have encountered at one time or other. Next, the problem is restated in a summary sentence, and the third paragraph points to one solution and the topic of the piece. The capsule sentence in articles with question leads often involves an answer or partial answer to the question or questions posed.

An especially effective interrogative lead is this one, which began an article called "Dressing Up with a King Size Flat" in *Sun Magazine:*

> Would the soundest sleeper, a few decades ago, ever have dreamed a sheet could go out of style? Or stranger yet, into high fashion?
>
> Not likely. Yet both are happening today.

3. Narrative. This lead sounds like a storyteller beginning a yarn. It can be crisp or gentle, depending on the subject. Sometimes the narrative lead sounds a bit like the opening paragraphs of an essay. Other times, it provides background material leading up to the subject. One of the most beautifully crafted narrative leads I've ever read appeared in a *National Geographic* article called "The Magic World of Hans Christian Andersen":

> There's a world, just around the corner of your mind, where reality is an intruder and dreams, the bad along with the good, have a disconcerting way of coming true.

You can get into this world in many different ways: by tumbling down a rabbit hole or climbing up a beanstalk, by riding a Kansas cyclone over the rainbow—or opening a book of fairy tales by Hans Christian Andersen.

Of all the travelers who have journeyed to that enchanted realm of once upon a time, none—to my mind—has come back with treasures more glistening than this unlikely Dane, who wrote, "Life itself is the most marvelous fairy tale."

Another well-crafted narrative lead is this one from "Michelstadt: A Special Joy" in *Aloft:*

Once upon a time there was this romantic little road linking several romantic little towns dating back to medieval times. After properly exhausting several vocabularies in their hunt for romantic little words to describe the ancient walls and turrets, tourism promoters dubbed it the *Romantische Strasse* and stood back for the rush of humanity which inevitably came.

So today in the peak seasonal months, there's hardly room to breathe amidst the souvenir stands in towns like Rothenburg and Nordlingen. Visitors are branching out to discover less well known but equally romantic smaller villages to satisfy their craving for a prowl through history.

Thus, consider Michelstadt, a tiny village often overlooked by the non-German tourist because he has to work a bit to reach it.

4. Anecdotal. These mini-stories are effective ways of introducing a subject, since we all like glimpses into other peoples' lives. In order to *be* effective, they must relate directly to the topic by illustrating it, amplifying it, dramatizing it, or by proving a point.

In profiles, the anecdote often serves to illustrate a characteristic of the subject, give the reader a glimpse into the person's early life or, in the case of a celebrity, tell how he or she got the big break. Travel anecdotes frequently relate a travel incident or give insight into the lives of the subject locale's inhabitants. Whatever its subject, the anecdotal lead gives a human-interest quality to the piece, as illustrated in this article called "Brace Yourself," a piece on orthodontia that ran in *Sky:*

Chris S. studied the information form in the dentist's office. Surrounded by squirming children and their weary mothers, he rapidly filled in the blanks, until one question stopped him cold. "When did the patient reach puberty?" Chris could not contain his laughter, for *he* was the patient, a 31-year-old freelance photographer who shoots for magazines such as *Time* and *Newsweek*. It had been a long while since he went through puberty; and it had been a long time since he'd had a straight smile.

This anecdotal lead supplied an excellent first paragraph for "We're Having a Baby," a *Lady's Circle* article:

One day, when I was nearly four years old, my grandfather asked me if I'd like to go for a ride with him to get my mother who had been away for several days. I hopped into his car and we went for a short ride downtown where Grampa drove the car to the entrance of a huge brick building. My mother came out with a bundle in her arms, and I was ecstatic to see her. Before Grampa started up the car again, my mother said she had a surprise for me. She opened the pink bundle and introduced me to my baby sister. That was the first I knew of the whole event. . .So, when I had my own family, I decided to handle things differently.

5. Case history. The case history is like the anecdotal lead in that it, too, tells a story, or part of one. Case history leads, you'll find, are most often used to introduce articles related to medicine or the social sciences. The following lead, typical of the case history, appeared in an article on depression in *McCall's:*

Nancy is the kind of woman other women envy. At 37, she is strikingly attractive. She has a successful and attentive husband, two smart, pretty daughters, and a blossoming career as an advertising copywriter. She gives the impression of being outgoing, optimistic; the adjective people most often use to describe her is "sunny."

But there is another side to Nancy. For several years she suffered from a black depression—what doctors call "spectrum depression"—an anguishing ailment that robbed her life of all but anxiety, dread and sadness. Nancy says that her mood began to darken in her late 20s, when her two girls were small. The horizons that had once seemed so limitless now appeared to end at the edge of the playground. For three years, from about the time she turned 30, she was in constant psychic pain. Then the black mood started to lift, and by 35 the worst was over.

What were those years like? "Mercifully, I don't really remember a lot of it," Nancy says now. "It was like carrying around a heavy weight that I could never put down. Sometimes it felt like anxiety, sometimes anger, sometimes misery. But it was always there. I was never seriously suicidal—I guess I was too much of a coward for that. But I do remember that there'd come a time in the late afternoon, especially on those dark winter days, when I'd stand at the living-room window of my apartment and wish I had the courage to jump out. Luckily, it was a third-floor apartment overlooking a large garden—but I've often wondered what might have happened if I'd lived on a higher floor."

The article goes on to tell about Nancy's treatment and then launches into the article's topic—clinical depression.

A shorter case history began the lead for an article called "The Time Clock in Your Genes," which appeared in *Marathon World*:

Late in the evening of May 4, 1975, two Royal Air Force pilots succumbed to heart attacks. Twin brothers, the men had been taken to separate hospitals in the same city and the grieving families were unaware of what was ensuing in the other emergency room. Later, sharing their bereavement, the families discovered the "coincidence"—the sort of eerie parallelism that had haunted the brothers' entire lives. Not only had the two men died of the same cause, but they had died at approximately the same time.

A common variation of the case history is the series of case histories (usually three), all of which illustrate the article's main thrust.

6. Statistics. This type of lead is effective only if the statistics are big enough, show contrast, are shocking, or are far different from the average reader's preconception of them. You'll see that statistical leads vary from a short paragraph with only one statistic to this rather long statistical lead which was used in a *Family Circle* article on car maintenance:

"Taxis in New York City are frequently driven 150,000 to 200,000 miles before they're taken off the road," says James Gillen, executive director of the Minute Men Taxi Co. in Long Island City, N.Y.

E.V. Bjurman, national service manager of the Buick Motor Division of General Motors, agrees that cars can be economically driven a minimum of 100,000 miles.

"Our cars can usually be driven a minimum of 150,000 miles," says Richard Hurdelbrink, national service manager of Checker Motors Corp., a leading taxi manufacturer.

The U.S. State Department operates about 2,000 vehicles at overseas embassies and consulates. According to L. Curtis Smith, chief of vehicle procurement, "We have no trouble running our cars 75,000 to 100,000 miles, if they get proper maintenance."

Now, compare these figures with the mileage that the *family car* is driven:

"The average American driver gets rid of a car after she or he has driven 30,000 to 45,000 miles," says Stanley Rowe, director of statistics of the Motor Vehicle Manufacturing Association.

If you think that basic structural differences between taxis and State Department cars on one hand, and the family car on the other, determine this significant difference in performance, forget it!

Taxis are the same as your basic family car, painted fancy. Checker cabs, for instance, are outfitted with the same Chevrolet engines and transmissions put into Chevys sold by your local dealer.

State Department people drive the same kinds of cars you do. They're built by American car makers and are basically no different than your Ford, Plymouth, Pontiac, Olds or whatever.

Why, then, do fleet cars, which receive more abuse, last twice as long as the family car? The answer is *maintenance.* Fleet cars get the maintenance they need *when* they need it.

This leads us to two questions: Exactly what *maintenance* will help double—maybe triple—your car's life, and how often must it be done?

Although that lead was much longer than you'll ordinarily find, it is an excellent example of the stage-setting aspects of beginning paragraphs.

Here's a shorter lead in which statistics are vital. It's from an article called "The World's Smallest Baby," which was printed in *Family Circle:*

When Chaya Snyder of the Bronx, N.Y., entered the world last August 2nd at Albert Einstein Hospital in New York, she weighed 15 ounces and was not even 15½ inches long. Dr. Lawrence Skolnick, head of the hospital's Department of Neonatology (which deals with newborn babies), vividly recalls the delivery of this extraordinary infant.

7. Conversational. This kind of lead is effective because of the informality of its approach. It makes the reader feel, "Hey, this guy is talking to *me.*" You'll find the conversational lead most often in articles dealing with personal relationships, the outdoors, humorous articles, and some how-to's. The following, from an article called "Two-Time Losers" in *Prime Time,* makes good use of the personal, I'll-tell-you-all-about-it approach:

Let me begin by being very personal. I'm not just a writer covering some provocative subject matter, I'm also a human being who can himself look back on the bittersweet experience of two marriages and two divorces. My first marriage began when I was 21 and ended before I was 22. It came to an abrupt halt mainly because my then-wife and I discovered we had nothing to say to each other across the breakfast table or anywhere else in our small apartment. In retrospect, we probably married each other mainly to escape from our parental homes, an approach to separation from one's family which was not uncommon in the 1950s.

My second marriage began when I was 32 and ended when I was 47. My second wife was (and is) a lovely woman; our problem was that our rhythms were very dissimilar. Let that be shorthand for a number of serious personality conflicts that marred and ultimately irrevocably damaged our marital relationship. My net gain: some rich times, some pain (the fodder for growth), a daughter.

As an entry in the columns of marriage and divorce, I do, of course, have plenty of company. There are roughly one million of us "two-time losers," as some people judgmentally call us— or "redivorced persons," to use the U.S. Census Bureau jargon. And our numbers are growing.

If you can't find the traditional capsule sentence here, don't worry. Conversational leads frequently state the article's theme in a group of sentences rather than in a single phrase.

Another conversational lead I like sets the tone for an article called "Seaside Fantasies" in *Geo:*

Imagine yourself sitting on a beach with the sun on your back and your bare feet half buried in the sand. Dig your hands into the sand and let it dribble out between your fingers to form a tiny mound—but think of it as a towering mountain. The sand feels good and invites you to squeeze it, to mold it—and perhaps make a whole range of mountains all around you, each no bigger than your fist. Undoubtedly, it was in just such a scene, uncounted years ago, that the first sand castles were built. All they required then and all they require today are sun, a beach and a dream.

8. Descriptive. This is a favorite with many travel editors. It works especially well if the writer is able to evoke enticing images. Descriptions also can lead off articles on processes or inanimate objects, and personality pieces. This descriptive lead appeared in *Music City News:*

> The sweltering Texas sun had only been working a couple of hours when the gates to Willie Nelson's Pedernales country club swung open to admit the first rolling wave of a sweaty throng that would, by noon showtime, swell to 60,000. They rushed to stake their claims for precious space on the 20-odd acres of trampled golf course spread out in front of an enormous outdoor stage; they erected tents, staked up beach umbrellas, hung room-size canopies, spread blankets, or simply wedged themselves into a standing spot somewhere in the crowd. They had come for the annual Texas holiday ritual, the Willie Nelson Fourth of July picnic, a 12-hour-plus marathon of marijuana, booze and country music.

In "Get it All Together at Canyon Ranch," from *Phoenix,* the descriptive lead does have a capsule sentence:

> A young couple play a strenuous set of tennis against a backdrop of desert mountains. A matron from St. Louis, determined to lose 50 pounds, takes quickly to a beginning belly dancing lesson. A single professional woman from Phoenix soaks blissfully in a Jacuzzi after a vigorous bout with the weight equipment. An older couple from California take a leisurely stroll, enjoying the morning sunshine.
>
> Such are the scenes and the "typical" players at Tucson's Canyon Ranch, which, since it opened at the beginning of the year, has become quite the spot for adults looking for a health-oriented retreat and/or a scenic, relaxing playground.

The conversational lead is a favorite of (and is often abused by) beginning writers. Their problem seems to stem from the inclusion of too much irrelevant detail, and the results sound amateurish. It is possible, however, by studying good examples, to learn to separate necessary information from that which clutters up the prose.

9. Quotation. If good quotes are available, these leads almost write themselves. Usually there is a bit of explanatory prose between the quotation and the capsule sentence, but that sentence can also come directly after the quotation, as it does in the following example from an article in *US*.

> "I was brought up with the idea that if you wanted to give someone a gift, you didn't go out to the store and use your credit card. You made it. You spent hours putting it together, with love and care."

True to her upbringing, Susan Richardson, 24, a star of ABC's "Eight is Enough," has been delighting her friends with presents she makes herself—whimsical, multicolored rag dolls, "some of them as big as people and all of them crazy."

Though most quotes used in leads are attributed to a specific person, occasionally you'll find those that are not. Here's a case in point. It's the lead from "Special Effects: The Devil's Magic" in *Flying Colors:*

Gleeful audiences have two reactions when a stage magician saws a pretty lady in half. "What fun to be fooled" and "How did he *do* that? He didn't really saw her in half, did he? *Did* he?"

We all know it was just an illusion, and we love it. But no self-respecting magician will ever tell how he did it. The illusion must remain illusion, or both layers of audience reaction are ruined.

Another lead you're likely to come across is the **shocker.** It is usually a one paragraph summary-type lead that contains information calculated to jar the reader, to make him react with a "Really?," "I can hardly believe that" or "How terrible!" Use of the paradox and of negation are often used in the shocker lead— "It's common knowledge that the more sleep you get, the better you feel. Right? Wrong."

Never use the shocker when your material doesn't warrant it. If you set up your readers to expect thrills, chills, and spills, don't give them something that's about as exciting as reading last month's garden club minutes.

Tying your subject to a recent development that has been reported by the media, the **news peg,** works very well with some publications. Other leads you'll find less frequently are the **biographical** and the **definition.** The biographical lead is most common in magazines devoted to history, beginning with the birth of a person or construction of a historic site, then going on to relate important incidents in that life or lifespan. The definition is used to introduce articles whose subjects may not be completely understood without an explanation.

Editors' Choice

Although all editors don't favor the same kinds of leads, it's interesting to hear what some of them have to say about their favorites. Jane Offers, editor of *National Motorist,* points to this first paragraph from an article called "Oregon's Volcano Vistas," which appeared in her publication:

> Friday the 13th was an unlucky day for Portland, Oregon, residents last June. Since March, Mount St. Helens had rumbled and quaked, bullying our northeastern neighbors. Ash spread eastward across the continent, but Portland lay safely forty-five miles to the west. We gloated over our good fortune, and enjoyed the excitement of the mountain's fury. Ignoring Portland's vulnerability, we watched the news about the volcano from the safety of our living rooms.
>
> Then Friday the 13th arrived.

Offers calls this "an emotional 'feeling' lead, helped by the Friday the 13th, which in a sense is negative, but still appeals, because readers tend to be curious about adversity and hard times."

Alan Rosenthal, who edited *Discovery* for nine years and now freelances full-time, is a past master at identifying compelling leads. He maintains that effective ones do three jobs: "Attract the reader's attention; use simple but active prose or a twist; get the reader into the theme of the article quickly, without excess verbiage." One of his choices is this lead from an article titled "Abracadabra: It's Magic and It's Everywhere":

> One stormy evening recently, an Alabama attorney, masquerading under an assumed name, thrust six sharp sabers through the body of his young wife. He was in full view of more than 300 onlookers, yet not one person, including a policeman standing nearby, tried to stop him.
>
> The attorney, Donald Spurrier—or Starbuck, if you prefer stage names—is an amateur magician. Within the past few years he has trussed his spouse in straitjackets, locked her in boxes, chopped her in half—all in the name of entertainment. And each time she has emerged unharmed.
>
> Spurrier's interest in the ancient art of deception is shared by millions, and the popularity of magic acts has climbed to its highest point since the days of Houdini.

Lead Writing Magic

There are all sorts of ways you can trigger your typewriter to produce editor-approved leads. I like to start by putting together my capsule sentence. It may not be written exactly as it will appear in the finished draft, but it will be a concise, one-sentence statement of what the article is about. If you can't write such a sentence, it's possible you're going to have trouble writing a satisfactory piece. One writer I know has a sign over his desk, "What in hell are you trying to say?" That question, I've found, is the key to writing. If you aren't *completely clear* about what you want to say, if your ideas are only vaguely formed, the article is going to flop.

After I've settled on the best capsule sentence I can write, I begin asking myself the following questions. In most cases, the lead is written before they're all answered.

1. What leads does this editor like best? Few editors go with the same type of lead for every article, and most of them seem to like two or three kinds particularly well. If you have a choice of two or three types, go with the one that your subject best lends itself to. If none of the editor's favorites seems compatible with your material, write the kind of lead she uses once in awhile.

How do you know which leads dovetail best with your subjects? Check over your material for anecdotes, quotes, and statistics. Ask yourself if the subject can be introduced naturally by description or narration or conversationally, and so on down the list of possible choices. The word *naturally* is most important, for in order to be effective your lead must seem like an integral part of the article—not some words that were tacked onto the front because every piece has to have one. Fortunately, almost all editors print articles with summary leads, at least once in awhile, so after you've gone down the list of an editor's pets and all else fails, you'll have one workable option.

Incidentally, if you can't write a summary lead about your subject, you don't have your article well enough in mind to begin writing it.

2. How long are most of the leads? The importance of this answer varies from publication to publication, but it should never be ignored. Woe betide the writer who sends an article with a fifteen-paragraph lead to a magazine that gets into its subjects quickly, say two paragraphs maximum. *Never* write a lead longer than any you've seen in back issues.

If you have a choice—perhaps the magazine uses leads that vary from one to six paragraphs—opt for a length in balance with the length of your piece. If you can avoid it, don't use a five- or six-paragraph lead on a very short article. You can afford to use more words getting into your subject, however, when the piece is one of the magazine's longer articles.

3. What makes this story important? Since, as we've said, the lead is the grabber, you'll want to do that grabbing as forcefully as you can. What better way to capture the reader's attention than by indicating early on why she must read the story?

4. What is the most interesting facet of the subject? Along with alerting the reader to the subject's importance, you might want to incorporate some fascinating aspect of it in your lead. You probably will touch only briefly on that interesting angle, elaborating upon it later in the text, but the allusion will help snare the reader (and the editor).

Winding Down

Though to many editors they aren't as important as leads, you must give your best effort to constructing endings, too. It's possible to grab an editor with a terrific lead, then lose her with an ending that fizzles. Like the stand-up comic's routine, there has to be consistency in the presentation. If the end of his act goes over like the proverbial lead balloon, the audience won't recall that the first joke was really funny. If your ending has the bounce of a dead tennis ball, your readers (and the editor) won't remember the lead that attracted their attention in the first place.

Most writers find that the midsection of an article is the easiest to write, but report they have as much trouble making graceful exits as they do planning grand entrances. Here again, the editor's past choices can come to your rescue.

By studying the kinds of endings your editor prefers, you not only devise patterns to follow, but learn how to write them by a sort of writer's osmosis. Whenever you see a particularly effective one, you'll begin asking yourself why it's so good and what the writer did to make it that way. In the process of studying closings, you'll come across these most popular types:

1. Split anecdote. In order to end in this fashion, the article must begin with an anecdote. Only part of the story is told in the lead, with the end of it used to wrap up the piece.

2. Summary. This is the closing you'll find most often. It neatly ties the article's contents or conclusion into a synoptic paragraph.

Not only do I like the title of the piece—"For sale—brand new genuine fake antique!"—which appeared in British Airways' *High Life,* but I like its snappy summary ending as well. The second-to-the-last paragraph continues a quote:

> As for anyone considering taking up collecting seriously, "Buy a good handbook on the subject that interests you, go round the museums and get used to looking at the genuine articles, attend sales and get some idea of prices, then gradually start buying.

Setting the reader up for the close:

> And if you should get caught, which is increasingly likely these days, take heart. Some of the best fakes are acquiring values not far short of the originals.

An effective variation of the summary is the full circle, in which the article begins with a summary lead and then reiterates the lead in a summary ending. In this article from *Pace,* Piedmont Airline's inflight magazine, the author begins her article "Nostalgia Lives!" by repeating the two words of her title:

> "Nostalgia lives!"

The next thousand or so words enumerate and describe some of the items, fads and fancies of the past and discuss nostalgia of the future. The piece ends with a simple full circle summary:

> "Nostalgia not only lives—it prevails."

3. Urge to action. Sort of a pep talk, this ending prods the reader to do something about the situation related in the preceding paragraphs and usually tells him how most effectively to take this action.

This closing appeared in *Sierra* in an article called "Alaska in the House: The Last Act?", which discussed legislation to protect wilderness areas:

Unfortunately, this is more than a soap opera. We are not dealing with fictitious plots or imaginary characters. The Alaska issue is not only real, but the most important conservation opportunity of our lifetimes.

We cannot be simply viewers of the soap opera, either. We must be active participants in this drama—or lose the whole show.

While many urge-to-action endings play upon the reader's sense of duty, others, such as this from "California's Top 25 Attractions" in *National Motorist,* persuade him that the action will result in a good time:

And there you have our choices of the Top 25 Attractions in California. National Automobile Club is offering some valuable admission discounts at many of these attractions, so why not take advantage and have some fun?

4. Quotation. Pearls of wisdom pertaining directly to the article's theme can be uttered by an authority on the subject, the person written about, an associate in a personality piece, or a sage of yore. But to keep this type of ending from sounding like a tacked-on whimper, the closing quote must be a strong one.

"Executive Playthings," printed in *enRoute* (Air Canada's inflight), which told about special toys for businessmen, ended with this quote from a Toronto psychiatrist:

"There's a logical use for these toys. The idea is to induce a temporary twilight state, where you turn off the stream of facts and allow this shuffling (of the unconscious in a natural way) to occur. That's an essential part of decision making—allowing the mind to wander. It doesn't matter what form the game takes—it only matters that there be a distraction."

In "Gasohol: Fuel from the Farm," printed in *Auto Club News,* the quote ending gets its strength from summarizing gasohol's attributes as previously stated in the article:

It's still too early to do much more than guess about the future impact of gasohol, but for the present it has found some faithful followers, particularly in the Midwest. One Iowan explains it this way: "I get a premium fuel for a cent less than unleaded. My car runs smoother and I don't have to worry about gas-line freeze-up. Besides, it helps the farmers."

5. For further information. The freelancer's favorite, for obvious reasons, this ending is used most often in informational, service-type articles and how-to's.

You'll often find endings such as this in travel articles:

For additional details and descriptive brochures about India's beaches and resorts, as well as flights, contact the Government of India Tourist Office, 3550 Wilshire Blvd., Suite 204, Los Angeles 90010, and Air India, 3250 Wilshire Blvd., Suite 1206, Los Angeles 90010.

It'll Save Energy. . .But Will It Save You Dollars?" in *Consumer Life* closed with the following paragraph:

There is literature available on solar systems—some free, some costing a nominal fee, others more expensive. A selection includes:

This was in turn followed by a listing of five publications and the telephone nmbers one could call to order them.

6. End of a sequence. Some topics lend themselves to a series of points or instructions, the last of which is a natural place to end the article.

Whatever kind of ending your analysis indicates is right for a piece, it must be a logical conclusion and an integral part of the whole. Carol Amen, whose articles have appeared in dozens of publications including *Ford Times, Modern Maturity* and *California Living,* says, "One thing I try to do, and remind my students of this also, is to go back to the beginning and see what I promised, or implied or hinted at, and then be sure to check if I have delivered, and to tie up the loose ends. If there was a person with a problem in the opening, I may put that same person, and some workable solution or way to live with the problem, in the final paragraph. The aim is to provide resolution."

Freelancer Helen Bottel's goal, too, is to tie things up in her last paragraph, relating back to the beginning, using a pithy comment or quote that may add a dimension, and, she hopes, make people think. She illustrates her point with excerpts from an article called "Helping Your Teens to Handle Today's Sex Freedom," which first appeared in *Family Circle* and was later condensed in *Reader's Digest.*

The lead began,

"Too many adults view the New Morality as the New Immorality and fear has driven them into a square box where they either cower or fight blind. . .What CAN we, as parents, say to our progeny about sex, especially premarital sex?"

And the ending reads,

"Put your arguments as questions. . .Don't force discussions. . .Just be there—and let your child know that no subject will ever be off limits. His ideas may clash with the old way, but if you have raised him with honesty and affection, stop worrying. He may not choose exactly the route you hope, but he will be true to your standards for his time and place."

Through my writing years, I have collected leads and closings which, like Bottel's, are especially effective. You may want to also. To keep them in simple-to-use form, just divide a three-ring binder into sections, with tabs indicating the different types of beginnings and endings. When you find good examples, clip them out, write the publication's name and date and then scotch-tape them to blank pages. Filed according to type, these "patterns" will guide you when the time comes to write your own. In all probability, you'll actually enjoy writing the first and last paragraphs of your pieces. For by using analysis, those beginnings and endings will lead to the beginning of gratifying editorial relationships.

9

Wrapping It Up
with Analysis

Little do such men know the toil, the
*   pains,*
The daily, nightly racking of the brains,
To range the thoughts, the matter to
*   digest,*
To cull fit phrases, and reject the rest.
—Charles Churchill, *Gotham*

The only argument I've heard against analysis is that it "kills spontaneity." I can counter that one. Spontaneity, as far as my experience (and others I've talked with) is concerned, hasn't sold many articles. In fact, doing what comes naturally is what keeps many writers—especially nonfiction writers—from selling.

Instead of producing spontaneous creations, you want to put your material into analytically on-target, rejection-proof form. You have your subject and markets well researched—perhaps there's even a go-ahead on speculation. Your title and lead are firmly in mind, and you have culled every possible clue to the editor's preferences from previously published articles. What remains to be done is to get the article together—written from beginning to end, prepared for submission, and shipped off to the magazine.

Just as each editor has favorite styles and title, lead, and ending types, so does he or she have preferred structural patterns. To say that all any writer needs to know about article construction is that there must be a beginning, middle, and end is a statement of omission. And to believe that the writer, as long as he constructs the beginning, middle, and end, can do anything his fancy chooses within that structure, is a form of rejection-wish.

Since every article poses different problems, your organizational techniques will of necessity vary from piece to piece. One thing is certain, though: in order to work efficiently and achieve success, article construction cannot be a hit-or-miss proposition. The whole job goes more quickly and smoothly, I've found, if my material is in good order.

Getting It Together

The only hard-and-fast rule in organizing your material is that it should be assembled in one place. I like to take my notes in spiral notebooks, consolidating all the research for a piece in one book. Other writers favor steno pads, file cards, ruled legal tablets, or bits and pieces of scratch paper. But unless we can lay our hands on all those notes when we're ready to write, we'll have chaos, whatever method of note-taking we use.

As I read over my notes, I evaluate the importance of each bit of information. If it's vital to the piece, I circle a number 1 in the margin opposite. I identify all my material with either a 1, 2, 3, or 4, depending on the necessity of its being included. When, upon review, I find a particularly strong quote or an impressive statistic, I mark it with an asterisk. As I'm reading over my notes, I coordinate the various pieces of information by writing key words in the margin. These indicate which point the material pertains to. As I'm flipping the pages, I often think it would be easier to use cards, but when I've finished the piece, I'm thankful I can file that notebook away (contents clearly marked on the front cover) and not have to worry about losing any odd pieces of paper that might come in handy when I write another piece on a closely related subject.

Many of the tidbits we gather in the course of research are so fascinating that we hate to leave them out. But unless these little gems are germaine, unless they contribute to the basic theme of the article (or unless the editor is one who likes a touch of the not-exactly-extraneous-but-almost), you'll find that they should be eliminated. Deciding what research material to include isn't difficult when you study published articles to see what information was important. If an editor has shown a preference for government statistics, use them. If he goes for statements from corporate executives, you'll want to include some, too. Perhaps he likes lots of facts in a sidebar.

At some time during the research-evaluating process, I may put together a rough outline, which includes a list of ingredients. Both the outline and ingredient list follow as closely as possible the format my boss of the moment favors. It might look something like this:

I. Lead (two paragraphs—interrogative, first choice; summary, second; quotation, third—likes quotes from government officials)

II. Two paragraphs of general information on the subject (Substantiate with statistics from the Department of Labor)

III. Sub point #1 (Illustrate with anecdote)
   A. Paragraph of explanatory text about subpoint
   B. Substantiating paragraph with quotes from two authorities
   C. Contradictory information from business sector with quote from corporate head

IV. Sub point #2
   A. More government agency statistics with rebuttal from business sector containing statistics they have compiled plus some hard-hitting comments from a second business executive
   B. Analysis of these conflicting stats by an economist

V. Closing (one paragraph summary, first choice; quotation, second; for further information also possible)

This outline illustrates only a few of the structural details you should be on the alert for when analyzing an article's structure. Determine at what point the basic questions—who, where, when, what, why, and how—are answered. If the writer is established as an authority, take notice of the part of the article in which this is done, and how. Look at the pacing. While there are editors who delight in copy packed with information, they have colleagues who want to give the reader a rest now and then.

Ask yourself how the theme is developed (remember, that's the succinct capsule sentence which ended the lead). Perhaps it's in the *New York Times* style (expository statement beginning each paragraph, followed by supporting information). Or it may, in the case of historical articles or accounts of contemporary history, be developed in a chronological sequence. Another technique you'll find is the dramatic-incident opening, followed by an explanation of events leading up to the episode, then an elaboration on the dramatized incident.

Check for facts, explanations, and opinions, noting where they are located in the text. If the article involves controversy, in what part of the article is it introduced? Where are negative and positive concepts set forth? If the writer wishes her reader to empathize with her subject (or feel antipathy), when does she insert information calculated to achieve this aim? How many points should be covered and what proportion of the article should be devoted to each of them?

If you've done your research well, you will have far more information than you can possibly use. Beginning writers try to include everything. But it's like struggling to pack clothes for a six-week trip into an overnight case. Everything won't fit where you'd like it to. The successful writer, like the experienced designer, learns to fashion his material so there's enough to cover the subject properly but no more than the customer (alias editor) demands.

Once you've done most of your research and drafted your outline, it's possible to begin writing the third paragraph, the eighth—any place in the article that seems easiest. There's no rule saying a writer must begin a piece by writing the lead. Some writers find it simpler to start in the middle or final paragraphs. I have written articles that I began with the ending, chipped away at the body, and finished with a lead; other times I've worked the "proper" way. There are occasions when one good sentence pops into your head. When that happens, start with that sentence and flesh out your article in whichever direction is easiest for you.

I type bits and snatches of what I'll need, then fill them out until they become paragraphs without worrying at all about the way what I'm writing will fit in—only knowing that it is essential to the piece. I leave about four spaces between each paragraph. Then, when I have typed perhaps one-half or three-fourths of the material I know will be necessary, I start cutting the paper between paragraphs. Though more often than not I've typed the material sequentially, there are paragraphs that will fit better in other places than where I had originally intended them to go. I insert these paragraphs into the appropriate spots, attaching them with transparent tape (staples and rubber cement work, too), and add a few inches of plain paper when I decide that additional material should follow. This cut-and-paste technique saves hours of retyping and allows you to do all but the final draft without having to redo complete pages.

Sometimes you'll find that you have to perform major surgery, cutting and taping several times until you get a piece flowing just the way you want it to. The virtue of the cut-and-paste method is that you can work your material in jigsaw-puzzle fashion, interchanging the parts until they fit.

Keep It Rolling

No matter what sort of structure he uses, the successful writer must have a feel for copy flow. His articles have to be written in such a way that they pull the reader smoothly along. To accomplish this seemingly effortless journey from lead to final paragraph, the writer has to have a way with *transitions*. They're the phrases that take the reader from one paragraph or subject to another: the continuity words.

Not all editors share the same favorites for smoothing out their readers' paths, so again, you'll want to find out which transitions your editor likes best. Some of the most common ones you will find in the course of your analysis are:

1. Words or phrases that move the action forward, e.g., *secondly, furthermore, besides, another;* or that connote the passing of time—*on his next visit, the following day.*

2. Repetition of last point. Paragraph ends with the sentence, "Thousands of people today are jeopardizing their careers because they are unable to make decisions." First sentence of the next paragraph begins, "Not only are thousands of people suffering from the inability to make decisions. . ." and goes on to make the next point.

3. Repetition of key words. A paragraph ends with the word *anxiety.* The first sentence of the next paragraph begins, "That same look of anxiety was on her face the next time I saw Nancy."

4. Summation of last point and bridge to the next: "While there are times when you will need to assume a passive role, it's a good idea to express a conflicting opinion if your convictions are strong" could be the sentence following a paragraph in which assumption of a passive role is discussed.

5. Question referring to the last paragraph, i.e., "Why is it that...," "How do you...?"

6. Option to reader, e.g., *Whether, If you choose to...*

7. Chronological. These transitions seem to fall into place naturally. Paragraphs begin with words and phrases like *Next year, After he had moved west, Following months of backbreaking toil.*

8. Numbered steps. Many how-to articles need few transitions if the steps in the procedure are numbered. When transitions are necessary they are usually of the "in order to," "after you have," and "before you..." variety.

9. Location or method of transportation. Most commonly used in travel pieces, these include such phrases as "Around the corner from," "A few blocks away you'll find," "On the other side of the city," "You can go by bus to..."

10. Naturals. In some articles, material can be arranged so well sequentially that actual words of transition aren't necessary. These pieces are like old buildings whose stones fit so precisely that they were constructed without mortar. Skillful crafting is required to make one paragraph flow neatly to another, but the effect gives a continuity to the reading that results in superior articles.

However skillfully they're constructed, some articles require many more transitions than others. There are editors—particularly those with newspaper backgrounds—who prefer short paragraphs in order to break up columns of type with white space or to facilitate reading. Others don't bat an eyelash at graphs of 150 to 200 words. No matter how much paragraphing you have to do to conform to the editor's wishes, make each transition as smooth as you possibly can.

If you have trouble coming up with a perfect transition, look at that problem as a warning flag. An analysis may reveal that the material isn't arranged as logically as it might be. Or perhaps the problem stems from a gap—a whole paragraph or two of information that's needed to expedite the flow and give continuity to the piece.

Dots and Dashes

There are editors and writers who look at punctuation as an adjunct of style. It is. But it's also an element of structure, since punctuation not only contributes to the way words read, but to the mechanics of the article as well.

Look at the dash, for instance. It's a stylistic device, to be sure. In some publications, however, you'll never find one of them. Some editors prefer semicolons instead. Or they might want writers to confine their pause symbols to commas. You can easily discover punctuation preferences by reading what has been published.

And then there's the much-debated exclamation point. Editors seem to either adore or abhor them. I've come across pieces where virtually every other paragraph ends with an exclamatory mark. I've gone through a year's back copies of other magazines where there's not one to be found. As a general rule, editors feel that if the sentence is constructed correctly, there's no need for the mark symbolizing enthusiasm at its end—the enthusiasm is in the placement of the words.

If you're not convinced yet that editors have definite punctuation prescriptions, listen to what John Shuttleworth, editor-publisher of the *Mother Earth News,* says:

"At *The Mother Earth News,* we have a general rule of thumb (which, as might be expected, gets bent out of shape daily...but which at least *does* give us a 'known point' to work from): *In a complex sentence, use a comma or commas once...then switch off to dashes, parentheses, quotations, an underline, or an ellipsis.* Then come back to a comma or commas.

"Commas and colons are all right...but it has been our experience that the great portion of the reading public has a deep-seated and unyielding grudge, hate, and/or fear of semicolons. I don't know why...except that scholarly (or, usually, pseudoscholarly) authors always seem to try to impress their audiences with turgid prose that runs on and on and on and is frequently punctuated by what seems to be two-thirds of the world's lifetime supply of semicolons˙ 'Ordinary' people get turned off by semicolons. Whatever the reason, we don't use semicolons very often here. If you want to sell to our magazine, you won't either.

"An additional hint: The 'and/or' is another valuable piece of 'punctuation' that is too seldom used but which can add appreciated pace to a chunk of copy. And don't forget the word-coined-by-hyphenations and/or the 'word created with quotations.'"

Shuttleworth's views on punctuation aren't shared by all editors. But you can be certain that each one of them has his own clearly defined rules as to how material should be punctuated. Since you'll rarely find this information in a magazine's guidelines for writers, the only way you will uncover it is by reading the publication.

The Finished Product

When your punctuation is just what the editor ordered and all your material is taped in perfect sequence, you're ready for the final draft. Though your first through umpteenth draft-in-one may look like a survivor of battle, that finished manuscript must not. I am convinced that the marginal manuscript that sells does so because it is legibly typed in the prescribed fashion.

Why, you ask, should you spend all that time painstakingly typing a manuscript the editor is going to mark up anyway? First of all, contrary to rumors, editors don't buy manuscripts scribbled on the back of cereal boxes. Even if the editor has agreed in advance to buy the article, until that check is in your account, you're still a salesperson and you'd better have your shoes shined.

Secondly, a neat manuscript projects a successful, professional image. A sloppy, unorthodox presentation tells the editor you're an amateur at best, incompetent or really weird at worst. It may seem unbelievable, but I have seen submitted "manuscripts" handwritten on both sides of several sheets of 4x7-inch note paper (complete with garlands of flowers at the top) or typewritten in red on fluorescent green pages.

Finally, you're looking for repeat business. It's much easier to edit an article without typos, with proper margins and spacing between lines of type. If an editor finds your material easy to work with, it's an incentive to buy more in the future.

Your paper should be standard-size typing paper (that's 8½x11-inch, with 20-pound bond recommended and never the erasable kind, which smudges and is difficult to read). Your typewriter ribbon must be new so that the print is easy to see. In the upper left-hand corner of the first page, single-space your name, address, and *telephone number with area code.* The phone number is terribly important, as we who have analyzed the publishing world know. Many editors detest dictating letters (or writing them themselves), and they often don't have time to wait for correspondence to make the round trip. If those editors have a telephone number so they can pick up the phone and finish their business in minutes, your chances of a sale skyrocket. Jonathan Miller, editor of *Flighttime,* and *Texas Flyer,* maintains that he and lots of other editors he knows act on impulse. And what's the greatest impulse tool around? The telephone.

In the upper right-hand corner, type *about* or *approximately,* followed by your word count (rounded off to the nearest ten). One-third of the way down the page, center your title in capital letters. Whether you underline it or not isn't important. Just as double- and triple-spacing allow room for editing, that third of a page of white space at the beginning of the article leaves room for the editor to write type specifications for the printer (and a new title if yours isn't the one she wants). If a magazine often uses blurbs between titles and articles, you may want to put one there—provided it is a strong one and in the magazine's style. Two spaces under the title or blurb is your byline as you wish it to appear. The article itself should start three spaces below the byline.

The general rule in typing manuscripts is to double-space. You'll want, however, to check the writer's guidelines for that publication to be sure. Some magazines specify triple-spacing or three spaces between paragraphs. Others ask for a certain number of characters on each line. Whatever is asked for, supply it.

Caroline Hadley, of *Nevada Magazine,* feels that even if an editor doesn't ask for a specific number of characters per line, setting up your manuscript that way "is super for an editor if you do it right." Ninety-nine percent of the national and special-interest magazines published today use a three-column format, she says, and while the type size may vary—publications for children and the elderly are printed in larger type—it's usually constant, or predominantly so, in a particular publication. Just count the number of letters and spaces in a line.

Although left-hand margins of one inch and right-hand and bottom margins of $1^{1}/^{2}$ inches are suggested in most instructions for manuscript preparation, editors I've talked to say that they prefer more white space. So when you're typing, set up your margins so that they're at least half an inch wider than the rules prescribe. What you want to do is produce pages of copy that are as easy as possible for the editor to read, edit, and mark for typesetters.

On succeeding pages of your manuscript, type your name in the upper left-hand corner. On the next line under that, type an identifying word or slug—say *Norway* in a piece called "Norway—Scandinavian Delight"; *Backpacking* or *Bicycle* for an article titled "Bicycle Backpacking." The reason for the two-choice slug is that if the article were submitted to a backpacking publication, *Backpacking* wouldn't be definitive enough to set your piece apart from hundreds of others the magazine publishes, whereas *Bicycle* would. On the other hand, if the piece were submitted to a bicycling magazine, the *Bicycle* slug wouldn't serve to identify a sheet of paper as part of your piece if dozens of manuscripts accidentally were mixed together. Following the slug, type a dash and the page number.

Move the carriage down at least four more spaces before you begin the manuscript typing on these pages. Two or three spaces below the final line of your article, use some symbol to indicate that there is no more. I use a series of spaced asterisks (* * *). You can write *The End* if you wish, or - 30 - (newspaper shorthand for the end of copy).

Package your color transparencies in the plastic pocketed sheets available at photo supply stores. Protect black-and-white glossies with sheets of cardboard. And on the manila envelope containing photos, write in impossible-to-miss large, legible printing, *PHOTOS—PLEASE DO NOT BEND.*

To further project your image as an experienced writer, include a cover letter with the manuscript and/or photos. You can use typewriter paper, but your letters will look more professional if they're typed on businesslike letterhead. The cover letter can be a short paragraph and shouldn't be longer than three, unless some unusual circumstance warrants it. Refer to the contents and why you're sending them: "In response to your request of May 23 that I submit "Bizarre Bazaar Bargaining" to you for consideration, I have enclosed the manuscript along with a selection of color transparencies. I hope it's what you have in mind." Be *sure* to spell the editor's name correctly. Many editors state flatly that if an article is sent on speculation or is unsolicited, they will reject it if their name isn't spelled right. This isn't as egotistical or arbitrary as it may seem. After all, if a writer hasn't spelled the editor's name correctly, there is no reason to assume that the other information—names, dates, statistics, directions—is accurate either.

When a manuscript bounces back with a rejection slip (or is held eleven months by an editor before she decides she doesn't want it), send the query out to another magazine that very day. *Don't send the manuscript.* There are certain changes, minor or major revisions, that need to be made before it will be just right for your second, third, or fourth market choice. Whenever you send a manuscript following a go-ahead on speculation, be sure to include a self-addressed envelope with adequate postage attached.

When your article is forced to make the rounds, retype every page that looks less than virginal. There's no point in letting an editor know he's getting merchandise another editor turned down.

Account Book Analysis

Picture yourself down the writing road a piece. Analysis is paying off. You're coming up with more ideas and selling more articles than ever before. As a producing writer with articles in all stages of completion—from queries awaiting editors' responses to finished manuscripts in the mail—you've encountered a new problem: keeping track of your work.

Since recordkeeping is vital to the professional writer's business, you'll want to analyze not only magazine articles, but your bookkeeping procedures as well. Time is money when you're self-employed, so you'll want a system that's the most efficient for you. It may not be the one the freelancer across town uses; it might be one nobody else in the world is comfortable with. But if it suits your working habits and does the job, that's enough.

Many writers use ledgers, entering submission dates of articles and results, expenses, and income in the columns. One writer I know uses a daybook, making entries daily and attaching receipts to the appropriate pages. Those systems simply do not work for me. My system may not work for you, but some variation of it might.

I prefer a filing system that allows me to keep all my records in two metal recipe card files and a larger accordion-type file. One of the recipe card files has dividers which read QUERIES, WORK IN PROGRESS, SUBMITTED MANUSCRIPTS and IDEAS.

Most of my articles start out with idea cards. Whenever I have an idea for a piece, I jot the idea, the article's working title, and any snippets of information I may have on a 3x5-inch card. It's impossible to remember all the wisps of inspiration floating through your brain, so it is imperative that you write them down before they're lost forever. When I have collected enough material on a particular topic in a file folder with the corresponding working title on it, I write the query. The name of the article appears at the top of a 3x5-inch card that I place in the QUERY file. Under the title, I write the publication submitted to, and the date, leaving room for the date I will receive word of any action (acceptance, assignment on spec, rejection) on the piece. If the query is rejected, I resubmit it to another editor, making appropriate entries on the next line of the card.

As the article idea progresses from query to acceptance on assignment or speculation, the due date is added and its card is moved to the WORK IN PROGRESS section. When the piece is in the mail, the card moves to SUBMITTED MANU-SCRIPTS, with the date of submission duly recorded. When I am notified by the editor that the article is acceptable, with no rewriting or additional information required, I jot that date midway down the card, along with the amount I'm supposed to be paid. When I receive the check, I mark "paid" next to that figure, along with the date.

The second recipe card file is my favorite. In fact, when I need an ego boost, I take it out and look at the cards it contains. This is my success file. Separating it into sections are alphabet divider cards under which I file my sales. Sometimes I get a bit premature and move a card into this file when I've been notified of acceptance, but before I've been paid. This, sadly, is a mistake. Magazines stop publication or change hands overnight, at which times it is questionable you'll *ever* get paid. A new editor may come on the scene, and unless you have a written agreement, you won't have made that sale if he or she doesn't like the piece.

My larger, accordion-type file measures about 8x10 inches and has twelve compartments. Originally, the tabs between compartments said things like Dental Bills, Utility Receipts, and Car Maintenance Records. I covered them over with gummed package tape and made my own—POSTAGE, OFFICE SUPPLIES, RESEARCH MATERIALS, TRAVEL, GASOLINE, PHOTOGRAPHY, TELEPHONE, ADMISSIONS, LODGING, DINING, PHOTOCOPIES, and INCOME RECEIPTS. Whenever the spirit moves me (usually when the pile is so huge that my desk becomes inoperative), I file all my receipts in the appropriate slots. It makes the job of recapitulating income and expenses an easy one at income tax time (I put a 3x5-inch card listing publication, date, and amount in the income compartment for any article sale whose check doesn't have a receipt portion).

What expenses you can charge off are a matter for you and your accountant to decide, and your labels might differ from mine. Whatever they are, be scrupulous about keeping receipts for every expense that might be deductible. At year's end, you can put the file's contents into a manila envelope, label it with the year, and start filling it again. (A book you may find helpful in dealing with the business side of your writing is *The Complete Handbook for Freelance Writers* by Kay Cassill. Regarding taxes, consult *The Writer's Legal Guide* by Tad Crawford or *Law and the Writer* by Kirk Polking and Leonard S. Meranus.)

Even if you aren't in need of an ego trip, it's a good idea to analyze your productivity every now and then. Like many other writers, I keep track of how many hours it takes to do each piece. I include time spent interviewing, researching, traveling, writing and for concentrated thinking. I don't count the minutes my brain is wrestling with the article while I'm stirring spaghetti sauce or knitting a sweater, since the piece isn't my primary project during that time.

What constitutes profitable allocation of time will change as your success quotient and reputation grow. You will find that some articles are virtual money-losers because they take so much time that you otherwise could spend putting together articles for more lucrative markets. Other pieces, even though they may bring only $35 or $50, are winners because you may be able to research and write them so quickly. I recently did a mini-profile for $50 that took half an hour for the interview (ten blocks from my home) and forty-five minutes to write. If you're working on a big writing project, these short pieces often provide a welcome change of pace plus the reassuring sight of checks coming in every once in awhile.

Your life circumstances will also dictate what is profitable to produce. If you have the time for extensive research and interviewing, big pieces may bring you more money and gratification. Writers who hold full- or part-time jobs often find that doing several short pieces in lieu of a few longer ones works in best with their schedules. But long article or short, you'll utilize your time most efficiently if you let analysis help you with the writing.

10

Hints on How-To's

There once was a writer named Pruett,
Who when he played handyman, blew it;
Though his projects were messes,
His words brought successes,
For he knew how to tell how to do it.
—Anonymous

When the do-it-yourself craze began in the 1950s, few of us dreamed that thirty-plus years later it would still be going strong, much less that it would spread epidemically into a do-it-yourself mania. Today we not only construct our own solar houses, teach ourselves Swahili, and brew our own beer, we also keep down our stress levels, use positive motivational techniques in business, and plan the month's activities by charting our biorhythms. There isn't anything we won't attempt to do if we have instructions from a book or magazine article to follow.

If we write for a living, we know that catering to this craving for self-fulfillment and self-accomplishment means money in our pockets. There's always room for improvement, and if we can write articles telling the American public how to build a better hot tub or save money at the supermarket or use yoga to enrich their love lives, our freelancing lives will be enriched—at least financially.

Most of us know how to do many things, and if we don't, we know where to go to find out. The housewife/writer doesn't have to leave her kitchen to write how-to's dealing with recipes and homemaking chores. The handyman can build dozens of woodworking how-to's while standing at his garage bench. I've sold how-to's on fighting inflation with your freezer and stretching travel dollars, making clothes for fashion dolls and needlepointing the Nevada State Seal, sewing patio skirts and beach cover-ups. They were among the easiest articles I've ever done, and I didn't even have to leave home to do the research.

How-to writing, especially in presenting a project, is straightforward and doesn't demand great literary skill. It does, however, require an ability to explain processes clearly. It is easier for many writers to describe a lovely spring day than the steps involved in tying one's shoe. But all writers can learn to explain processes easily if they will study the how-to's previously published in their targeted magazines and adapt the terminology to the procedures they're writing about.

Not only are how-to's a snap to write, they're in demand. Of the magazines listed in *Writer's Market* that print nonfiction articles, more than 60 percent state specifically that they are looking for how-to-do-it material—and almost as many trade publications want it, too.

Another bonus of the how-to article is that ideas are limitless and easy to think of. In fact, they're rather like bananas, coming in bunches. One idea suggests another, which in turn...until you have pages full of them. Perhaps you will begin the idea wheels turning by reviewing your own interests, problems you've solved, projects you've been involved in, items you've made. You can gather ideas from hundreds of books in the library. The best way I know of generating how-to ideas sure to fit a magazine is to find out what projects and problem solutions have been printed in the past.

As an example, let's look at the how-to's in *National Enquirer*. Tabloids are loaded with how-to's and, as we will discuss later in this chapter, are simple to analyze and write. "How Wives Can Make Their Husbands Feel More Masculine," "Famed Astronaut's Exercises to Make You Look and Feel Better," "10 Vital Ingredients for a Happy Life," "Slimming Secrets of Town That Went on Crash Diet," "How to Spot and Report Child Abuse," "How to Use Body Language to Win Friends and Find Romance," "How to Keep Economic Stress from Destroying Your Life," "Touching a Person You Love Improves Your Relationship," "How to Match Your Makeup to

Your Clothes and Coloring," "Be an Optimist & Improve Your Life" and "How to Discover New $$-Making Ideas" are the titles of the pieces appearing in just two issues. All but one, you'll note, are aimed at self-enhancement and are very much "you"-oriented. Only the child abuse piece deals with a subject in which the welfare of others is paramount. Examining the titles further, you'll discover three predominant themes—the body and its covering, money, and personal relationships. If you had more back copies to study, you would find a fourth theme—one you might call the "occult"—with such articles as "How to Use ESP to Communicate With Your Pet" and "How to Tell the Future with Dominoes."

Working within the framework of these four basic themes, you can get a lifetime's supply of ideas by slanting your approach ever so slightly. "Be an Optimist & Improve Your Life" could just as well be changed to "Be a Realist," or "Learn to Enjoy the Simple Pleasures," or "Don't be a Sucker," and improve your life. Instead of telling female readers how to make their husbands feel more masculine, you might tell those husbands how to make their wives feel more beautiful, successful, loved, or important.

Like the *Enquirer,* each magazine has its pet themes for problem-solving how-to's. They may be personal, family, or employer-employee relationships; improving your mental health; glamorizing your body or making it stronger. Other publications focus on business techniques, á la merchandising, marketing, promotions, and packaging. You'll find that how-to's on helping others, as well as articles about deepening personal spirituality, figure heavily in religious magazines. Your job as a freelancer is to zero in on the kinds of how-to's used most often by an editor and then, by the process of association, come up with similar ideas.

Analyze magazines featuring project how-to's the same way. If a publication runs ethnic recipes, think of an area they've not covered, or different kinds of food from an already familiar region. When a magazine's how-to's are 75 percent knit items, your chances will be best if you query about a knitting project that's different enough to make it interesting, but not so far-out that it will be inappropriate for the readership. Don't submit a metalworking project to a magazine that has printed material only on projects made from wood or send an article on steam-cleaning car engines to a publication that never uses articles on automotive repairs.

The How-to Lineup

For the purpose of analysis, how-to articles can be categorized in three groups— the *personal problem solution,* the *miscellaneous problem solution* (how a community, agency, business met a challenging situation) and the *project.*

Sorting out personal problems. Personal problem solution how-to's, in turn, usually fall into five types:

1. How a certain person solved his or her problem. By telling one person's story, the writer gives readers information they can use to solve a similar problem.

2. The case history. This technique is used most often in articles dealing with psychological or health problems, and is frequently authored by an expert in the field (or cowritten with one). The names of the people in the case histories are usually fictitious, but their stories should be true. (Some writers admit that not all their case histories actually happened, that they are composites created from information obtained through experts.) Several case histories with accompanying comments are also popular.

3. Point-by-point advice. A few paragraphs of prose, followed by points that are numbered or bulleted •, make this format easy to duplicate. Even if numbers or bullets aren't used, you'll find that each point is covered before going on to the next. Though it's not an infallible rule, most editors don't care for more than a dozen points and rarely use articles with less than five.

4. Advice from an expert or celebrity (either by the expert or celebrity, coauthored or as told to). When Bessie Brown who lives down the block goes on a diet, it's not news—unless Bessie weighed 534 pounds and lost half of it in six months. But when Cheryl Tiegs takes off thirty pounds, the story sells to *Family*

Circle. One would think that diet articles (or those dealing with children from previous marriages or a hundred other beaten-to-death subjects) would sell about as well as bicycles in the Himalayas, but if you have access to a celebrity or to an expert, it's a good bet you'll not only sell the article, but make better than average money doing it.

Speaking of experts, maybe *you* are an authority and don't realize it. If you have had a great deal of experience in one particular area—raising ten children, serving as a surgical nurse for fifteen years, handling one thousand personal injury claims as an insurance agent—you're as much an expert in your field as if you had a string of letters after your name.

5. Anecdotes in series. These are a sequence of little stories, each amplifying a point or group of points pertaining to a single subject. The anecdotal approach differs from the case study in that it is less clinical. In fact, anecdotes can do a lot to lighten an otherwise somber subject. The writer cements these anecdotes together with reinforcing quotes from experts, statistics, and expository material that moves the piece from one story to the next.

Other problems. Miscellaneous problem-solving how-to's are usually written along the same basic lines as the first four of the personal problem solution types. Trade journals, in particular, request case histories of businesses. They believe readers can learn by reading about successful or unsuccessful operations. You'll see articles about a community that provided entertainment for its teenagers, a government agency that eliminated waste, a business in an out-of-the-way location that attracts more customers than its better-located competitors.

When writing the expert/celebrity-advice piece on other than a personal problem, you should in most cases focus on some connection between the expert/celebrity's field of endeavor and the problem he or she has solved. You could do a piece about Milton Friedman's gourmet favorites or Julia Child's opinions about America's balance of payments problem—perhaps. But keeping Friedman in the sphere of economics and Julia in the kitchen will give you much better chances of success. Once in awhile, though, you can score by finding an expert/celebrity who really is knowledgeable in another area—and when you do, an article evolving from that not-so-well-known talent or expertise is even more salable than advice on the obvious subject.

Perhaps the most stylized how-to format in contemporary publications is that used by the tabloids. There are minor differences between how-to articles as presented in the *Star,* the *National Enquirer, Info,* and *Globe,* but you'll find the formula is essentially the same. Each article begins with a block of text—one to five paragraphs usually—and the lead is *always* in the first paragraph, often in the first sentence. In each of the *Enquirer* articles mentioned earlier in this chapter, a single-sentence lead sets forth the theme. The form of these sentences, and almost all other how-to leads in the publication, is identical—a declarative sentence followed by the words "say experts," "say psychiatrists" or "say leading experts."

That parallelism continues in the *Enquirer,* with direct quotes from the expert or experts mentioned in the first paragraph, followed by eight to twelve points, each preceded by a bullet. The structure of how-to articles in other tabloids varies after the opener. Not all use quotes, and some have a summarizing paragraph following the bulleted suggestions.

Variations of style and structure in problem-solving how-to's are greater among publications other than tabloids, but after you study them carefully, you will find that each magazine is just as consistent in following its own how-to pattern issue after issue.

One of the quickest ways to make money (and get published in a major magazine) is to whip off a one-paragraph how-to. Any problem you've found a simple or clever approach to solving—sibling rivalry, keeping kitchen utensils in order, cutting costs on fertilizer, or face cream, or fish food—can be converted into cash. *Family Circle, Woman's Day,* and other general circulation magazines publish a page of these tips in almost every issue. Top publications pay about twenty-five dollars per item, which isn't a lot of money. But when you consider that they take only minutes to write, your dollars per hour ratio is terrific. I got twenty-five dollars for these sixty-seven words that appeared in the "Readers' Idea Exchange" in *Family Circle:*

Our vacation mementos used to end up in boxes, packed

away and forgotten—a jumble of postcards, menus, brochures and other souvenirs. But not anymore! Now we bring along a large manila envelope for each day of the trip and put the day's accumulation of remembrances inside. Once we're home again, it's an easy job to slip them into plastic-paged albums, along with any photographs taken.

That paragraph took fifteen minutes to put together and type. Oh, that I could find markets for sixteen of them each four-hour writing day.

Another bonanza for the writer who has not yet been published in a magazine is the department that uses under-500-word how-to's, such as "The Better Way" in *Good Housekeeping* and "Right Now" in *McCall's*. They're virtually the only way a nonname writer can break into these magazines unless her idea is an absolute blockbuster. Once published in a department, chances increase that the editors will be receptive to your ideas for longer pieces. Every writer who has an ounce of perception can find possibilities for these articles—new ways of saving energy, providing or improving services (usually at the community level), breakthroughs in scientific fields—are the kinds of ideas editors of these departments most often go for.

Prospects from projects. Much of the project how-to material in magazines (especially food, fashion, and home decoration) is staff-written, but don't be deterred. Food, fashion, and other department editors spend much of their time putting their sections of the magazine together and can't be out in the field gathering ideas as often as they'd like. Therefore, they're interested in innovative ideas and will seriously consider good ones from freelancers. Even *Sunset,* which claims to be completely staff written, will buy ideas and/or articles from freelancers if they're particularly strong ones, according to a department editor.

Any action that can be duplicated by following a tested process is the raw material from which project how-to's are fashioned. There's no end to subject possibilities—barbecuing a lamb, building a sailboat, root cellar, or a radio transmitter.

The project how-to is rarely more than 1,000 words long; usually it's much shorter, 300 to 600 words being the most-often-purchased length. The same format used in the personal problem point-by-point advice article can be applied to the project as well, and most project how-to's are written that way.

The other popular project how-to you'll encounter is the step-by-step in photos. Here, a photograph of each procedure is presented in sequential order, with a few sentences of text explaining each step. The trick to producing successful articles of this type is to provide uncluttered pictures that clearly show what the person is doing. This is more difficult than you might think, so if your camera skills aren't as complete as you'd like, see about having a professional do the job (on speculation if you don't have a definite assignment). Arrange to pay him a percentage of your fee when the article has been assigned.

Another requisite of many project how-to's is that you send the completed project to the magazine, even if you have excellent photographs of it. The item is usually, but not always, returned to you when the art department has finished with it, so be sure to make arrangements prior to selling the article if you must have it back.

Though the form may vary slightly, point-by-point how-to's almost always share several elements. The problem or project is described in the first paragraph, or at least an allusion is made to it, followed by more explanation in succeeding paragraphs. After that, you'll find at least one sentence encouraging the reader to tackle the project or spelling out the advantages of doing it, and another reassuring him that it is not hard to do. The instructions come next.

The procedures for most project how-to's are broken down into consecutively numbered steps. Other techniques include the use of bullets instead of numbers, and beginning each step with **boldface** type. Each step is explained at the time it is introduced. How fully each of these steps is explained depends on the readers' skill and experience levels. The way to determine these most effectively is to note how much detail is inserted into the how-to articles that have been published before.

Notice that there's never any backtracking. Steps are presented in the order in which they are performed. You'll lose a lot of readers—in more ways than one—if you write a piece that says, "Oh, I forgot to tell you back there when you were hooking up wire B to terminal A that you'd better unplug the electricity unless you want a thousand-volt jolt."

Since time sequence is vital, be especially careful when you're writing a piece on a project you've done so many times that you do the smaller steps unconsciously. To be absolutely sure that I have every procedure in proper order and haven't missed a step, I like to do the project and write the piece simultaneously, even though I've made the item a dozen times before. It's easier to measure a piece of fabric or lumber before you have joined it to another, to determine just how long you've simmered the stock or let the glue set *while* you're doing it. It takes twice the time to bake an exotic dessert or build a birdhouse this way, but the article-writing process is shortened considerably and the results are far more accurate.

Be sure, too, your writing is precise. You don't want to tell the reader to "measure the picture frame molding lying flat on the workbench." He would probably assume you meant that the *molding* should be lying there, but who knows?

It is also important that you pay close attention to the magazine's preference in terminology. Are they directions or instructions? Materials or supplies? And where is information such as the amount of time needed, necessary equipment, and component size listed—all in one place or scattered throughout the article?

If you are giving directions on more than one project in the same article, or the project is multifaceted, look closely to see what transitions have been used in similar articles to link the various pieces together. Often only subheads are needed. Another popular device is a paragraph or two of prose with general statements about each point that follows.

Generally, when the last instruction has been given for a project, the writer's job is over. Some editors, however, like one last paragraph, either urging the reader on, reinforcing the "you can do it" pep talk at the beginning, or telling about variations and adaptations of the project he can try.

After I have completed the rough draft of a project how-to, I consult my checklist to see if I've followed the magazine's format exactly and included all the information that's necessary. The checklist looks like this:

1. Approximate number of words in prose form at beginning of article.

2. Terminology. (Before I begin a project how-to, I jot down the words the editor of that magazine likes to see writers use, then check to see if I've used them.)

3. Are all the ingredients, materials, supplies listed and are they in the proper order?

4. Are any steps missing?

5. Are the steps in sequence?

6. Is there any way the process can be simplified or shortened without changing the end result?

7. Would the process be easier to understand if more instructions were added?

8. Is each word precise or might any of them be misinterpreted?

9. Are there any sketches, line drawings, or illustrations that should be included? (The magazine's art department usually takes care of the finals on these, so your sketches usually need only to be clear, with some sort of scale indicated.)

Harry Wicks, Home and Shop Editor of *Popular Mechanics,* is one of the editors who often requires artscrap to show how the pieces of a project go together. Pencil drawings are fine with Wicks, and they don't have to be in scale, but they must be complete and readable, he says.

To write for *Popular Mechanics,* Wicks advises, "Study the magazine and submit only articles in keeping with the magazine's philosophy. *PM,* for example, is not looking for articles on needlepoint, or lengthy human interest stories."

"But," he adds, "we do run many pages of projects, and we always show the how-to-do so that readers can duplicate the items if they choose to. *PM* is a very visual magazine. How-to articles with professional quality photos, with captions, stand the best chance of being accepted. However, on occasion, a reader who is incapable of producing good photos sells us a piece because his idea is so on-target. In such cases, we rebuild the project shooting photos as we go. This is done with exceptional projects only. Snapshots are okay but the negatives should always be included. Photos should be keyed and the captions typed on a sheet (using that key)."

Another tip Wicks gives to writers for improving their chances of selling *Popular Mechanics* a piece is to "keep your correspondence brief and to the point. If your letters are windy it's a good bet that your manuscript will be wordy." Manuscripts should be to the point, according to Wicks, and not a repeat of the information contained in photos and captions.

Rebecca E. Greer, Articles Editor at *Woman's Day,* says most of her magazine's how-to articles are staff-written. The others are generally written to order by freelance writers who have queried first. To get that assignment, Greer says a writer must study the magazine, produce good, fresh ideas, and demonstrate the ability to write well. She stresses that what the writer must know to sell to *Woman's Day* cannot be learned by reading a paragraph or two in a market book—that studying the magazine is the only way to find out what will please the editors.

Sales Tips

You'll not often find picturesque writing in how-to pieces, be they about projects, personal or other problem solutions. Since their function is to provide patterns—for living as well as for making things—the primary goal of the writer is to get the message across. Adjectives should be chosen with special care. You will find that sentences in general tend to be less complex than those in other kinds of articles. Human interest plays a big part in personal problem solution how-to's, and you will observe a larger than usual proportion of anecdotes in these pieces. Many of them are also written in what might be called a sympathetic tone, even if the problem the reader is hoping to find a solution for is of his or her own making. Though the imperative "don't" is used fairly often, you'll notice that suggestions are phrased positively as well as negatively, and it's a rare how-to that scolds its readers.

Present tense makes how-to's more exciting; it gives them more of an "it's happening now" feeling. Although it is impossible to write some of them this way, you'll find editors who show a definite preference for that form whenever it is workable. Many of them, too, lean toward first- or second-person accounts. "He," "She," and "They" make the idea more remote, editors reason, while "I" and "You" give the reader "I can do it, too" encouragement.

Not all how-to articles are identified by a how-to in their titles. "How to Solve Your Own Energy Crisis" might just as well be called "Solving Your Own Energy Crisis," or "Solve Your Personal Energy Crisis," or "Ten Self-Energy Saving Tips." When you are writing a how-to piece, construct the title to say exactly what problem/project is being addressed. Then manipulate the words into the form the editor has shown in the past that he prefers.

In any how-to, the writer has an obligation to whomever may read the article. Some people take every word they read as gospel—"if it's in print it has to be true." It would be exploiting their naiveãe to tell them that a beginner can learn a skill it took the writer fifteen years to master, or to intimate they'll be financially secure the rest of their lives if they follow the article's advice. I have received more mail about project how-to's than any other kind of article I've written. The knowledge that readers trust your counsel makes you check all material for accuracy (and consult an expert!) if you are unsure of any point.

As far as payment is concerned, personal problem and miscellaneous problem solution articles are generally more lucrative than project how-to's. Though I have received five hundred dollars for a project, I have found that there are compensations for even the under one-hundred-dollar articles. The writing is fast, you often have a usable object when you've finished, and you can charge off the materials involved in its construction as a business expense. Doll clothes patterns and finished garments that bring you thirty-five dollars can do double duty as a little girl's birthday gift; that handy workbench you designed and dreamed of having will cost less if you can sell an article telling how to build it and charge off your materials.

How Nots
Decades have passed since divorce and cancer were spoken of

only in whispers (and then never in front of children), but many magazines still have definite ideas about which personal problems ought to be aired openly. By reading descriptions of the magazines in *Writer's Market,* writers' guidelines, and studying back issues, you should be able to evaluate the subjects that will be shunned. The more conservative religious publications, for instance, specifically state unacceptable subjects in their guidelines for writers. Topics having to do with tobacco, alcohol, abortion, and divorce are the most common taboos you'll encounter there. But even more liberal publications, religious and secular, have limits they will not go beyond. Though the editor of one of the more open-minded women's magazines may welcome articles with new twists on living arrangements, she may not feel her readers are ready for financial detailing and chore-sharing in a ménage a trois. How-to's dealing with homosexual relationships are another realm into which editors tread lightly, if at all.

As far as non-personal problem how-to's are concerned, you'll find there are fewer prohibitions. The only taboos usually will be those resulting from advertising and sponsoring organizations' influence on copy. Obviously, a how-to for a project requiring ambergris won't sell to a conservationist publication, nor will those requiring the use of animals in what the readers view as a less-than-humane capacity. But other taboos aren't apparent unless you are familiar with a magazine: the National Wildlife Federation, publishers of *Ranger Rick's Nature Magazine,* discourage the keeping of wildlife pets; *Exploring,* sponsored by the Boy Scouts of America, does not print articles on hang-gliding or the martial arts.

When planning a project how-to, it's a good idea to check out your target magazine's advertising, as this could influence your acceptance or rejection. You'll notice that magazines featuring articles on outfitting yourself at rummage sales and creating your own originals don't run many clothing manufacturers' ads—unless the magazine's circulation is very large and cuts across all segments of society. Publications with pages of advertisements for expensive tools don't run many how-to articles that decry sophisticated equipment and advocate a back-to-pioneer-days approach to building. Editors, though most say they are not influenced by their advertisers, are practical people. They know that if they lean too heavily toward do-it-yourself construction of products similar to those their clients advertise, those clients will soon decide there are better magazines in which to promote their wares.

Yes, editors are practical people. Writers, to maximize their potential, must be practical, too. You may not want to devote all your time to writing how-to's, but then again, you might—they're today's hottest sellers.

11

Information Please

We do not know one millionth of one percent about anything.

—Thomas Alva Edison

Whenever two or three writers gather together, the conversation at some point turns to unsold manuscripts. While every prolific novelist has one book his publishers won't touch with a ten-foot blue pencil (the story is that Arthur Hailey's was *Airport*), productive nonfiction writers have an even more frustrating pile of unsold typed pages. Theirs are folders of 1,000- and 2,500-word pieces that must be marketed individually.

I used to call my file of unsold manuscripts "Dead Horses," but now I've relabeled it "Resurrectables," for I've found that most of the pieces—especially the informational ones—hadn't sold simply because I hadn't found the right markets. Most successful freelancers I've talked to agree: you can sell any well-written informational article, since *some* segment of society will be interested in learning about whatever subject you've researched—if you know where to sell it.

Informational articles have a bigger market than any other. In fact, it would be difficult to find a magazine that doesn't print these articles in every issue. City magazines and regional publications are full of them, for they are information advance men. Their job is to tell readers about the city, state, or region—where to buy the biggest pumpkins, the best second-hand clothes, the most delicious hamburger; where to see magnificient rock formations, catch enormous fish, or get away from it all.

Travel magazines' subscriptions depend on telling readers about places and travel pleasures around the globe. Business magazines without informational articles would leave thousands of frustrated subscribers and plummeting sales. Women's magazines, natural science and outdoors publications, sports, theater, and children's magazines, Sunday supplements and newspaper features, depend heavily on pieces that give their readers the facts. Without informational articles, the raison d'etre of technical and trade journals would vanish. Collectors, whether they specialize in coins, antiques, bottles, or barbed wire; people who want to improve their health; car lovers, cat fanciers—all want to know more about their special interests.

Info on Informationals

An informational article's primary function is to transmit knowledge. This is not to say that the informational piece can't be entertaining or humorous. But whatever its style, the article must, if it's a good one, leave the reader feeling that he or she has learned something.

There are five basic types of informational articles—expository, investigation, evaluation/review, exposé, and doomsday.

Expository pieces explain their subjects in detail, without extensive controversy or criticism. The conversion of tropical forests to cropland, the role communication plays in our lives, scientific discoveries, manufacturing processes, the functions of government agencies—almost any topic that people are curious about can be given an expository treatment. Like the news story, an expository article answers who, what, where, when, why, and how.

Investigative articles focus on the how and why aspects of a subject. They look into an event to find out how and why it happened, or at a certain practice to determine why it exists. They also may expose the pros and cons of such controversial subjects as antidepressants, chemical fertilizers, faith healing, or the use of divining rods to locate water. In order to make the investigative piece work, you must choose a subject open to debate.

Evaluations/reviews examine the attributes of a work of art, performance, place or product, either objectively as in some consumer magazine articles, or subjectively as in the case of book reviews. "How Good Is Our Juvenile Justice System?" "Rating the Washing Machines," "Do California Wines Measure Up?"

and "In Search of the Best Taco in Town" are the sort of titles that tell readers at a glance that the article will give them an evaluation or review of the subject.

Exposés are the stuff weekly tabloids are made of. They're the "look at how bad it is" pieces. Graft, corruption, cheating, false claims, fraud, and public hazards are all grist for the exposé writer's mill. Though the tabloids devour them, you'll find well-crafted articles of this kind in an increasing number of magazines.

Doomsday articles are the exposé's first cousin. As times become more threatening, demand for these pieces grows. Instead of exposing a questionable practice or situation, they call attention to some deplorable facet of contemporary society—inflation, pollution, nuclear annihilation—that readers fear. The doomsday pieces, after explaining the dangers to a terrifying point, usually then offer measures the readers can take in order to avoid disaster.

An important quality of most informational articles that bring top payment, make the cover, and/or fill the prestigious pages in the middle of the book is timeliness. Most of the really big features are about subjects of current relevance. You'll certainly see informational pieces on lost civilizations, historical events, art, and artifacts, but for the most part such articles deal with current trends, new developments, and the latest advances in subjects of interest to great numbers of people.

Though depth of treatment varies from article to article and publication to publication, the most successful informational articles are those that include a good deal of "meat." Whether the thrust of the piece involves one point or several, each of them is shored up with specifics, examples and substantiating information, assembled by the writer's diligent research.

Many writers find this kind of painstaking research tedious. But if you want to produce first-rate informational pieces, it's imperative that you analyze previously published articles to find out how much research the editor likes, then dig even a bit deeper. Since there will always be lots of lazy writers who skimp on their research, you'll score editorial points by doing a thorough job of yours.

Clarity is vital. In order for information to be communicated, it must be understood. Therefore, top informational articles, whether they be written for technicians or readers with an average eighth-grade reading ability, must be presented in language those readers are comfortable with. With the ever-increasing technological gap, one of the greatest areas of opportunity in writing today is for freelancers who can take scientific or technical subjects and translate them into laymen's terms and simple language. Good organization is essential here, since getting facts in the right order makes for understandable copy.

The first rule of writing about anything is that you yourself must clearly understand the subject. Don't attempt to write for a magazine if most of its articles are over your head. You'll be less frustrated and more productive if you concentrate on subjects and publications that don't stretch your abilities too far.

Getting Your Foot in the Editorial Office Door

Any query letter should be exciting, intriguing, and the writer's best effort, but the query for an informational article must be *particularly* so to sell an editor. While the how-to promises solution to a problem and the personality piece can almost sell itself on the basis of that personality, the informational article has the built-in potential of being dull. If the editor hasn't worked with you before, he has no way of knowing you can make a revolutionary method of carpet cleaning sound as exciting as sky diving—unless you give him a foretaste of your magical prose in the query.

Since editors worry, too, that the informational piece won't be anything more than a rewrite of materials readily available in books and other magazine articles, the promise of original, primary source research is one of the writer's most valuable sales tools. That's because so many of the articles that come cascading over editors' transoms are poorly researched rehashes without any creative investigation of the subject. If information for your article comes from the results of five hundred questionnaires or from the professional observation of two hundred people, tell that to the editor in your query. Reassure him that your piece will contain new material by naming the authorities you'll interview. If the field is a technical one, editors will want to know that you are competent to handle the subject, so tell about any credentials you might have, including the names of publications in which you've published technical articles. Be sure any facts you use are accurate. Editors have nightmares about sloppy research, and few have staffs large enough to check out every point in detail.

What do query letters have to do with analysis? Plenty. If an editor has shown in past issues that he likes anecdotes, include one in your letter. If she goes for quotes, use a terrific one in your first paragraph. Scan your accumulation of editors' pages to see what phrases and concepts he especially likes. Get familiar with the magazine's philosophy so your slant will be in perfect harmony. When an editor publishes articles heavy on adjectives, when she shows a preference for action verbs or present tense, use those devices to illustrate that you're the ideal writer for the magazine.

It's not a bad idea to write the first one to three paragraphs of the query as you see them appearing in the actual article's lead. You won't be able to dash off the letter in half an hour, perhaps, but you will have taken the opportunity to showcase your approach in a manner that will give the editor the edge of a security blanket to cling to. The extra time you spend will also mean less time spent when the go-ahead comes and you begin to write the piece.

I like to use a four- or five-paragraph query. The first two paragraphs tell about the subject in a style closely approximating the magazine's. The next paragraph or two briefly tell which aspects of the subject I'll be writing about and what information I'll utilize. The concluding graph contains information about availability of art, when I can have the piece done, and my pertinent credits. To further entice the editor, I sometimes add a final sentence—"If you would like additional information on how I will develop the subject, I will be happy to send you a detailed outline."

After the Editor Says Yes

When the editor lets you know he likes your idea and the way you plan to treat it—at least well enough to look at the manuscript on spec—you'll want to redouble your analysis.

Naturally, you will include in your story those elements that your research has shown were successful in past pieces. You'll be most successful in identifying these elements if you study stories of about the same length as the one you are going to write. The length requirement you will find most often in market listings is from 1,000 to 2,500 words. Articles of more than 2,500 words are becoming less popular each year, but certain magazines such as *Playboy* and *National Geographic* buy them regularly.

In the past decade there has been an increasing demand for short-shorts (from about 350 to 1,000 words). The success of these pieces depends on development of a single theme—you just don't have enough words to expand to corollary ideas.

Though some magazines include a certain number of short articles as a part of each issue, others use them only occasionally, depending upon space requirements. They're easy to squidge in when the editor finds he is short of copy, so many magazine chiefs keep several on file. These short articles demand tight writing, but a well-written article, such as this, "Collecting Postcards," which ran in *Travel & Leisure,* can contain a lot of information.

A real friend, according to *Farmers' Almanac,* is someone who takes a winter vacation on a sun-drenched beach and *doesn't* send a card. Chances are that friend is buying cards all right; he's just not mailing them. Like hundreds of other Americans, he may be a deltiologist—a serious card collector, a social historian, an image junkie or simply a postcard nut.

For some, the lure is nostalgia or popular culture; for others, the acquisitive urge or investment. Whatever the reason, postcards are now the third largest category of collectibles in the world (after stamps and coins) and, in the words of an antiques dealer who's been in the business fifty-two years, they are the cheapest forms of art you can buy and among the fastest-rising securities on the market.

"Some cards have appreciated 5 to 10,000 percent in just two to three years," says Stan Simmons, Los Angeles postcard dealer, "but when all these old cards are out of the attic trunks, that's it, no more."

Not surprisingly the arts, politics, world news and celebrities play a role in supply and demand. The touring King Tut exhibit, for example, revived interest in Egyptian cards. The Panama Canal Treaty boosted values of the 1915 Panama-Pacifc International Exposition cards. Giveaways promoting the Beatles' only Las Vegas appearance skyrocketed to $12 each following the rock group's breakup. And newly-opened travel areas, such as China or Cuba, offer deltiologists a rare opportunity to acquire stamped and dated cards—21st-century collectors' items.

Like anything else, collecting postcards has its fads and specialities. With over 1,500 categories to choose from, neophytes are almost always astonished by the seemingly endless variety—everything from rare silks to dime-a-dozen scenics; from miniature art treasures to Kewpie dolls; puzzles, mermaids, French glamour, military history, transportation, greeting cards, politics, comics, and early advertising cards like the Coca-Colas, today worth $100-$200 apiece.

The story begins with a romance. According to legend, the 2nd-century Athenian statesman, Pericles, worried that his beloved Aspasia might not guess the source of gifts he was sending and enclosed his name inscribed on a card, a small wooden writing tablet known as a *deltion*. Thus the term deltiology coined in the early 1930s.

Though controversy surrounds the invention of the postcard as we know it, a young Austrian professor, Dr. Emanuel Herrmann, is generally honored as the father of the modern card because of his 1869 proposal for a small lightweight correspondence card costing less to send than a letter. At first, the new stationery met with some opposition. But within two decades beginning in Europe in 1871 and America in 1873, the picture postcard caught the fancy of the civilized world and, with no room for long flowery phrases, revolutionized its writing habits.

By the turn of the century, collecting postcards was a vastly popular hobby. Journals and exchange clubs proliferated, and Queen Victoria herself was said to be a parlor deltiophile. By 1904, at the peak of the craze, Americans were mailing 2 million cards daily, and no Victorian drawing room was complete without a bulging album, the more flamboyantly exotic the better.

Many pioneer cards are still in mint condition. Early Continentals now qualify as antiques, and collectors prize the pre-World War I albums, not only for their pictures but the messages of bygone days as well.

The beauty of deltiology is that there's a card for every taste and pocketbook. Over-sized fruits, circa 1910, start around 35 cents; photographic stereo cards, same era, $3.50-$7.50 each. The most valuable of the European cards, the Raphael Tucks and artist-signed Art Nouveaus, can escalate as high as $800 for an Alphonse Mucha four-card set. Among the rarest postcards—those novelties with real hair or fabric, movable parts, revolving discs, composite sets—are transparencies which, held to the light, reveal new scenes. Those from the 1900 Paris Exposition Universelles start at $18; from the 1904 St. Louis World's Fair, around $20.

"Postcards are definitely a good investment for the small collector," says antiques author and editor John Mebane. Beginning collectors, he suggests, should avoid a willy-nilly, hit-or-miss approach and concentrate instead on one or just a few postcard types, gathering together as many different versions of that type as possible to round out the collection. "Watch market trends to see what types are rising in value most rapidly," he says, "and compare prices of several dealers before shelling out any cash."

Shopping for old postcards can be as easy as frequenting auctions or local flea markets. But most deltiologists prefer dealing directly or through the mail with other postcard fanciers. They often belong to postcard clubs or societies like the International Postcard Collectors Association or Deltiologists of America, which maintain large libraries on the subject, promote research and supply information on sets, series and various dealer offerings.

For postcard buffs or tourists selecting "wish you were here" view cards, a tip: skip the Bank of America or Eiffel Tower. With towns and citites changing overnight, the most collectible postcard is one providing an historical record of the way it was years ago or a current scene, method of transportation or life style that easily could be wiped out with the next highrise, factory, autobahn or political coup.

"Remember," advises Stan Simmons, "when it comes to postcards, today's existence is tomorrow's nostalgia."

Let's say, hypothetically, that you received a go-ahead on speculation from *Travel & Leisure* to do a short piece on collecting some other kind of item such as paperweights or souvenir spoons. With the postcard piece as a pattern, it would be an easy matter to construct your article.

First of all, you might list the various questions the author has answered—why people collect postcards, what their investment value is, when they originated, what kinds to buy, what they cost, where to shop for them. You will want to answer similar questions in your piece.

Notice that the piece contains many more statistics than most articles of its length—a clue that you should check out other articles in the publication to see if lots of numbers are a requisite. Note, too, that the writer has quoted two authorities on the subject, giving the reader some of the article's information in quotes rather than expository statements.

Details that Clinch Sales

Analysis of informational articles will reveal other factors that will influence your chances of selling the manuscript. Adopting the correct publication viewpoint is a must. Do the magazine's writers take an advocacy stand? Are the pieces strongly positive, decidedly negative, or balanced between the two? Do the writers sound like instructors, experts, or friends? And how much controversy does your particular editor encourage?

Tracey Karsten Farrell, editor of *San Francisco,* allows writers to tackle controversy head on, while just a few blocks down Market Street, Jane Offers, *National Motorist*'s editor, will only publish pieces on controversial subjects when both sides of an issue are presented and no stand is taken. Down the street or even in the same office building, editors eschew controversy in varying degrees, and a miscalculation on the writer's part is almost certain to result in rejection.

The informational piece also succeeds in relationship to its reader appeal. Subject matter has to interest at least half a magazine's readership, according to editors I've talked to, and the more diverse the publication's audience (say *TV Guide* or *Reader's Digest),* the more difficult it is to come up with an idea that's strong enough to satisfy this criterion. Seventy-five percent or more of the readers of an offroad vehicle magazine published in the West may be glued to the pages containing the latest information on offroad use of government lands, but that kind of topic would have slim chance of selling to a general interest publication distributed nationwide. Baby magazine subscribers want to hear about the most recent developments in burpless baby bottles and baby-safe playpens, but those just aren't the sorts of subjects most Americans want to read about. In sum, the informational article with the best chances is one which thoroughly covers a topic that has the potential of touching all our lives.

As far as informational article taboos are concerned, these pieces are published in such a wide range of magazines that you can only determine what's verboten by studying your target closely. One general hint—if you don't see liquor, cigarette, or casino ads in a magazine when those ads regularly run in other magazines of its type, you can be assured that the publisher or sponsoring organization prohibits their solicitation. That's an indication that you should send articles dealing with or containing heavy reference to any sort of spirits or gambling to another market. A few of the anti-liquor, -cigarette, and -gaming publications will take a story briefly mentioning one of their forbidden subjects, but only when it's essential to the article's content. If that's so, be sure they're *not* presented in a positive light.

Paragraph punch is an asset to any article, but even more so in the informational piece. The easiest way to put pow in your prose is to have a dynamite subject, but you can make less than grabbing topics more interesting by emphasis in the right places. Variation of sentence length helps, especially when you keep the longer ones to the point and avoid rambling. Another technique is putting your most powerful sentences at paragraphs' ends, with the most important words just before the periods. After you've written your rough draft, experiment with word and sentence positioning. Perhaps you'll have written something like:

> Most shops in Acapulco close between the hours of two and four in the afternoon, so you might as well forget about shopping at that time. Instead, be like the Mexicans and take a *siesta.*

Pretty prosaic, isn't it? But a few minutes' thought and creativity can inject more pizzazz:

> What if you want to hit Acapulco's beaches between 2 and 4 p.m., but you're out of sun cream? Better forget about your *siesta* in the sun. The Mexicans will be taking their *siestas,* too, so shops won't be open.

Your analysis will show that there are some editors who don't go for sparkling writing, but they're few and far between. Anyway, after trying to work up enthusiasm for just one article for a dull publication, you'll most likely be looking for more exciting markets to analyze.

The Big Idea

We've talked a good deal in this chapter about choosing your topic, but the question is how you, the freelancer, can get your idea mechanism regularly to spew out these article nuclei.

Reading the newspapers with an eye for the intriguing is one way. Listening to people's conversations, tuning in on their interests and concerns is another. You can also talk to the movers and shakers in your community to find out what's happening, or twist topics in magazine articles to produce satisfying results. Take a look at the following article titles and think about them for a moment:

"Where the Rich and Famous Shop Abroad"
"Why People Make Mistakes"
"Computers at Home"
"How Long Can We Cope With Inflation?"
"The Land Fraud Is Back"
"What Is Our Nation's No. 1 Enemy?"

They all are titles of pieces that have sold to editors of leading publications. And why not? Their subjects are ones that people want to know more about. That's the good informational idea's magic—a topic readers will find too compelling to resist.

As an exercise, take each of these titles and see how many variations on their themes you can think of. The one on computers could become "Computers in the Classroom," "Computers on the Farm," "Computers in the Next Decade," "Are Computers Taking Over Our Lives?" By deleting the word *inflation* from the next title, you could insert a dozen or more different ideas—crime, terrorism, high interest rates, increasing taxes, unemployment, lowered productivity.

You will be able to generate more ideas than you'll ever have time to use with this method, focusing on subjects popular at the moment. But the most effective freelancers are those who hit on a subject before it's in the news or in the conversational buzz. What separates the ordinary informational piece from the one that becomes an issue's lead story is often the writer's ability to get in on a subject trend early in its editorial life. It's like catching the big wave before it crests in order to maximize the full potential.

Editors, whose job it is to spot trends, advise the freelancer to think in terms of the future, of concepts and innovations that will influence society during the next few years. Bruce Finson of *Pacific Discovery* suggests symposia on technical subjects at universities as a great source of new ideas. "If a university or one of its departments chooses to have a symposium on a special subject, that's usually because a fair amount of active research is going on in that field. Something is beginning to stir. It's at this point when the subject might hit popular interest," he says.

Other editors suggest reading future-oriented magazines such as *Omni* or *Next,* and studying *Forthcoming Books in Print* and *Publishers Weekly.* The former editor of several magazines recommends reading *W,* the *Women's Wear Daily* publication for trends in living styles, and sees the gay community as definite trend setters.

There are other ways you can zero in on trends just as they're beginning. Go to nurseries, home furnishing stores, and hardware dealers to find out about new varieties of plants, styles of furniture, and tools. When there's a convention in town, find out who the speakers are and arrange to attend if you feel they may have something new to say (I've never had any trouble gaining admittance to a convention program when I've phoned the person in charge in advance to make arrangements). Trade shows are the place to find out about new products. If you can talk to the manufacturer, ask him what he sees as future developments in his field. Follow up any promising leads and you're sure to find that some of them are big enough to develop salable articles around.

Top informational article writers may not realize it, but they are continually analyzing the world around them. While reading a two-paragraph item in the morning paper about an off-the-wall invention, part of the alert freelancer's brain evaluates the wisdom of finding out more about the subject. An eavesdropped conversation at the stockbroker's is weighed for its article potential. The flyer announcing a university lecture is considered regarding writing possibilities. Finding exciting article ideas not only makes for more and bigger sales; it makes the writer's (and the reader's) life more interesting.

12

The Well-Developed Personality

People have one thing in common: they are all different.

—Robert Zend

Did you ever wonder what Robert Redford fantasizes about? Why George Brett decided to become a baseball player? Where Princess Caroline shops? Writers who specialize in personality pieces don't wonder for very long. They find out.

They satisfy not only their own curiosities, but those of millions of readers as well. For we all seem to have an insatiable desire to know how America (and the world) lives.

Editors capitalize on our busybody natures. There are few magazines in circulation today that don't include some kind of personality piece, at least occasionally. The popularity of two relative newcomers in the gossip magazine group, *People Weekly* and *Us,* has been little short of amazing. *People,* which first came out in 1974, now has a circulation of 2,300,000, while *Us,* established three years later, has figures approaching 850,000.

Although those two magazines focus primarily on celebrities, readers' curiosity doesn't stop with the famous and infamous. We will read anything and everything about anyone, it seems, from the newsboy on the corner who wins the Irish Sweepstakes to the seventh-grader who works as a part-time disk jockey.

So if you haven't access to any celebrities—those people who have achieved the outstanding—don't give up. Look instead for people who have interesting jobs, unusual hobbies, or inspiring philosophies. You'll see in the listings that publications like *Grit* want pieces on folks who have gone from rags to riches. People who have overcome handicaps are other interview possibilities. Tabloids, especially, go for personality pieces about the notorious. Though dozens of big-time entertainers perform each year in Reno, where I live, and an equal number appear an hour away at Lake Tahoe, I like best to interview people who aren't well-known—the manufacturer of the diving boards used at the past six Olympic Games, a thirty-year-old art dealer with a national reputation in auctioneering, a saloon owner who played with the big bands.

Every writer can find his own local "celebrities" to write about, and almost every regional and city magazine editor waits eagerly for this kind of piece. Antiques magazines feature stories about interesting collectors—and you'll find them in the most isolated hamlet as well as in big city penthouses. Trade magazines profit from profiles of successful small-business owners. Religious magazine editors pray for pieces about people who will provide inspiration for their readers. Retirement magazines are naturals for stories about people who have made the transition from career to fulfilling retirement. Your problem won't be in finding people to write about, but finding time to get all those query letters about them into the mail.

Before you start writing queries, though, you'll want to do some compatibility studies. While magazine editors may be curious *personally* about the same people you are, their professional curiosities are limited to the kinds of personalities that will round out their publications' images. Obvious examples are athletes for sports magazines, corporate executives for business publications. But analysis will show you that your champion discus thrower will have a better chance with some sports magazines than with others, and your electronics wizard or movie-theater mogul might sell more readily to a business magazine other than the one you first had in mind.

More fun, and often more profitable, to pursue are the less obvious personality/publication go-togethers. Magazines published by auto manufacturers look for pieces about people who use their vehicles in unusual ways (I'm trying to track down a magician who advertised on the back of his VW Rabbit "Have Rabbit. Will Travel."). Trade publications often buy pieces featuring personalities who do out-of-the-ordinary things with their products—an artist who works in peanut butter; a woman who has papered her walls with can labels—and/or articles about people in their particular trade who have uncommon avocations or skills, such as a truck driver who makes bobbin lace or a secretary who teaches her pet chimp sign language.

Pairing up personalities with publications is easy if you know what signals to heed. Notice what percentage of the pieces center around men and how many feature women. Age is also important. The subject's lifestyle and philosophy are other determinants. Membership in a specific organization is imperative if you're hoping to sell your personality to some fraternal magazines. Church affiliation often counts with religious publications.

Personality Traits

Personalities, according to the Emerson system, can be divided into five types—*profiles, question-and-answer interviews, a day in the life of, roundup,* and *group.*

The *profile* is distinguished from other personality pieces by its depth. Comments from business associates, family, friends, employees, fellow workers and other people acquainted in varying degrees with the subject, who relate to him on various levels, give rounded, total personality coverage. The profile is also closer to biography than any of the other personality pieces.

Reading previously published profiles will give you a blueprint to follow. Titles alone will give you inspiration and insight into magazine staffs' minds, resulting in perfect personality matchups. For example, after finding that *Modern People* goes for "Incredible Woman Lives on 35 Cents a Day," "Meet the Weirdo Who Makes Millions Being the World's Ugliest Man," and "Greta Garbo Was a Spy for the British During WWII," you'll realize that your subject will have to do something more than a bit out of the ordinary in order for that magazine to be interested in buying.

You'll also know, once you get the assignment, which people to interview in order to give your readers a multifaceted profile of your subject. If the porter and the waiter and the downstairs maid contributed their impressions of celebrities in previously published pieces, you'll want to contact people who serve your subject. If fellow board members, adversaries, or government officials have been quoted in past profiles, get people in similar positions to tell you how they feel about your star, tycoon, or politician.

When you've discovered what kinds of people you'll need to interview, it's time to turn your attention to the questions you'll ask. A writer friend confesses that when she was a journalism student, she would always decide *after* an interview how to write the article. She says, "I was forever having to call the subject back to get more information because I never had the right stuff for the story I decided on. And the subject had always just left on a fishing trip."

By analyzing parallel articles in your chosen publications, you'll be able to ask the right questions first time around. When you're dealing with important people, time will usually be of the essence. They don't have that much of it to spare, and you don't either if you want to keep that ratio of time spent/dollars earned in good balance. By determining the exact questions you will need to elicit the responses required, you'll not only save time preparing for your interview, but win your subject's gratitude by keeping the meeting short.

Not only will you be able to tell what questions to ask the celebrity, you'll know *where* to conduct the interview as well: The interviewee's meeting places are surprisingly consistent in a particular publication's profiles.

For instance, *50 Plus* profiles tell early on in the piece where an interview was conducted—"So I was sitting around in [Art] Carney's suite, on the 28th floor of the Aladdin Hotel. . ." ". . .he [Walter Cronkite] answered slowly, leaning back in his office chair. From the adjacent CBS newsroom came the clacking of typewriters and wire service news machines." "And yet I think the most unexpected of all my encounters took place in Phyllis Diller's bedroom recently."

The interview site served as the lead in one of *50 Plus'* pieces:

> I turned right off Palm Canyon Drive in Palm Springs, a peaceful resort city in the desert, 100 miles east of Los Angeles. It had been raining hard when I left Los Angeles, but the rain ceased near Palm Springs. The air was clean. The sky was cerulean blue. Floating clouds made it a Tiepolo ceiling requiring an angel. The San Jacinto mountains seemed so close. I found the

angel, but it was not overhead. It was in a ranchstyle California Spanish villa almost at the foot of the mountains.

With the stage set, the rest of the article goes on to tell about the angel—Mary Martin.

You can shortcut your library research by analysis, too. There is no point in leafing through *Who's Who* to find out how many children your subject has if profiles in the magazine never mention that sort of family history. You might want their names, though, if your targeted magazine's profiles include quotes from the children. In any case, you'll be more efficient with your time if you know in advance which information is needed and which is extraneous to your purpose.

Your analysis should tell you also if it's necessary to interview your subject in person. Almost every profile worth the stock it's printed on comes from face-to-face interviews with the central figure, but often quotes from associates have been obtained by letter, tape, or phone conversation. When the article contains a physical description of the personality as well as of his or her surroundings, it's almost certain (if the writer is ethical) that material for the piece has been obtained by a personal interview. Lines like these from an article about Bette Davis in *W* are almost impossible to manufacture without a face-to-face meeting: "Genteelly erect in a straight-backed chair in her suite at the Sherry Netherland, Bette Davis seems unusually demure as she discourses on the subject of women. . . .she says, narrowing her eyes, . . .a phrase she delivers with such malignant gusto that you temporarily believe it."

Reading a publication's past personal histories can also tell you a lot about the structure its editors prefer. In *50 Plus,* which runs a profile each issue (usually the cover story), the featured personality's age almost always appears in one of the first five paragraphs. A large part of the article is devoted to telling about the person's career, and the last paragraphs always deal in some way with the subject's philosophy on growing older. These paragraphs may also emphasize what good physical shape he or she is in and include retirement plans (or the decision never to retire).

The staff at *People* have a penchant for personalities who have overcome some sort of setback or problem, and this adversity usually is set forth in the first paragraph, as in this article called "Howard Fast's Many Sides: A Born-Again Yankee."

Most people survive; Howard Fast endures. In the past 50 years he has written nearly 60 books, and though many have sold well, like *Freedom Road* and *Citizen Tom Paine,* the critics were usually cruel. In 1950 Fast, an admitted Communist, was jailed for three months for refusing to disclose the names of Spanish relief fund contributors to the House Un-American Activities Committee. For eight years he was blacklisted: No American publisher would even read his manuscripts, he says. Only European royalties kept him from the poorhouse. In 1951 he managed to get the best-selling *Spartacus* into print by starting his own publishing house, a venture that later went broke.

Eight years ago the book that Fast considered his master-work, an antiwar novel called *The Hessian,* was virtually ignored by the critics. It got a lukewarm review in the *New York Times.* Fast swore he would never try another novel and stomped off to California to write screenplays. "In L.A.," he says, "you work like hell because there is nothing else to do, unless you're cheating on your wife." Only two of his TV scripts were ever produced, however.

Now, at 65, Fast is back on the East Coast and, paradoxically, more popular than ever.

You will also want to satisfy the editor's length requirements. The non-analyst who's an admirer of *New Yorker* profiles—and they are the profiles par excellence as far as most writers are concerned—might go so far as writing a 15,000-word piece, for after all, that's how long the *New Yorker* pieces often are. But, to my knowledge, it is the only magazine that prints such lengthy profiles. Most editors like 1,500 to 2,000 words.

Most editors, too, prefer the anecdote, quote, descriptive, and/or summary lead. The descriptive lead is usually one that tells about the subject's physical appearance, work, environment, or a combination of all three, as illustrated by these opening paragraphs from a *Cosmo* profile on Hollywood director Steven Spielberg:

Steven Spielberg looks like he's facing a disaster. He's hunched forward in his chair, his boyish brow furrowed with worry, his chin resting on the ball of one fist. Dressed in Levis, cowboy boots and a Western shirt, he could be mistaken for a ranchhand who has just been fired or a college senior who has just flunked French. His curly dark hair is rumpled, and behind his aviator glasses, his eyes look bleary.

It is late September, 1979, and Spielberg has been logging

fourteen-hour workdays for months now, trying to polish up his latest movie, *1941,* for a December release. In a room only a few feet away are dozens of cans of film representing two hectic and difficult years out of his young life and $31 million in production costs. *1941* is the most expensive film Spielberg has ever directed, hence the riskiest. In order to merely break even, it will have to attract some $70-million worth of paying customers in theaters around the world. Toward this end, both Columbia and Universal, joint backers of the venture, are banking on Spielberg's stunning record as the most successful director in Hollywood (and, also on the popularity of two of its stars—the former "Saturday Night Live" zanies, John Belushi and Dan Aykroyd).

Family Weekly profiles, you'll find, often begin with a short summary lead like this one about Jackie Gleason:

The great one is back. But he's not the man he used to be.

And another—about the late Richard Rodgers:

Composer Richard Rodgers, who was 76 last June, has written more hits than his age—as a matter of fact, a recent list of his song hits adds up to 108.

In *Family Weekly's* profile style, the reader knows right away what aspects of the subject's life will be emphasized: Gleason's changed lifestyle and Rodgers's songwriting career.

When an anecdotal lead is used, the story is always about the person in profile. Quotation leads come from what either the personality or an associate has said. But just *any* anecdote or quote won't do, even if it fits those qualifications. It must also pertain directly to the angle you've chosen. Via advance analysis, you'll know when a magazine prefers one of these kinds of leads and will be able to angle for the types of stories and quotes you'll need during your interviews.

One of the most popular endings for profiles is a quotation, either from or about the personality. This windup of the piece on Howard Fast is typical:

Fast spends four hours each day at his typewriter. "If I miss a day," he explains, "I lose the thread." His great success after so many personal crises has left Howard Fast with little bitterness. "I'm disenchanted with Communism and most other things," he says. "I'm cynical but not a cynic. I'm cynical about TV, Congress and commercial peanut butter."

The other two endings you'll encounter most often are the anecdote and summary incorporating the subject's plans for the future. You'll see, too, that writers of the most successful profiles have relied on the "full circle," whether they have used a quote, anecdote or summary, to tie the ending to the article's lead.

If you don't feel up to writing a full-length profile or don't have enough material for one, consider doing a mini-profile. They're fun to do and an excellent way to break into print. Short profiles don't pay much, as a rule, but as *PSA California Magazine*'s "VIP" (Very Interesting People) department editor Ellen Alperstein says, "They're like popcorn. You start writing one and soon have sold a whole string." The *PSA* profiles run from 300 to 500 words and pay fifty dollars for the first article; seventy-five dollars for subsequent pieces by the same writer.

Not Quite So Popular Personalities

It's said that Gertrude Stein's last words to Alice B. Toklas's query, "What is the answer?" was "In that case, what is the question?" As a personality piece writer, you had better be sure that you ask the right questions when getting ready to write a *question-and-answer* article. It's not so hard as you might think if you take time to read past articles and formulate the same kinds of questions their authors have asked.

Playboy's interviews are longer than you'll find in most magazines. For example, a typical one, focusing on Malcolm Forbes, began with several hundred words about "The Happiest Millionaire." This was followed by a few hundred more words telling about the places in which the interviews were conducted—on a plane, a yacht, at Forbes's estate—then continued with more than seventy-five questions and Forbes's responses.

Although Q & A interviews aren't that long as a rule, it's a good bet that the interviewer asked many more questions than appear in the article. Chances are, too, that he or she formulated those questions on the basis of evidence gathered from past issues of the magazine.

The personalities who are interviewed and the questions they are asked vary tremendously from one publication to another. Some of the questions asked of Ginger Rogers in a *People* interview, for example, were: "Do you ever get tired of constantly being linked with Fred Astaire?" "Who was the most influential person in your life?" and "What do you think of Jane Fonda?" whereas Forbes was queried on such subjects as capitalism, whether he expected the devalued dollar to make a comeback, and his political views.

Writing an *a-day-in-the-life-of* article can be exhausting, since the best subjects for this kind of piece are fast-paced people. They seem overly endowed with energy, masterminding thirty-five projects simultaneously, then capping off the day with a white-tie fund raiser. Creative types who spend hours staring at the wall don't make exciting day-by-day copy. However, be advised that most of the pieces you read aren't done on the material gathered by their writers in just one day's time. Those writers have followed their subjects around for days—even weeks—and the articles that result are usually composites of what has been observed during that period.

A *roundup* can be a collection of personal opinions on a specific subject expressed by a number of celebrities. Or it can be a group of short biographies of several people, slanted toward an article's theme, such as "1978's Top 25 Influential Americans Over 50." You'll see in studying this type of piece that the writers' questions were constructed to stimulate the featured people and would be difficult to answer with a brief yes or no. If you contemplate writing this kind of piece and can't conduct personal interviews, try to get the answers you're after either by setting up telephone interviews with each one or sending a cassette tape. It's too easy for your quarry to shunt letters requesting information off to the public relations people.

Commonality of interest or purpose is what differentiates the *group profile* from the roundup. In the roundup, the featured personalities can be a diverse lot, grouped together only because their opinions are on the same subject or their attainment levels are similar; people tied together in the group profile must be more homogeneous, sharing such things as profession or philosophical outlook.

Group profiles include insights into, information about, or anecdotes concerning a selection of people who have a common interest or are tied together in some way. *San Francisco* published an article called "Bay Area Playwrights—Five People in the Future of the American Theatre." Subjects of *New Yorker* profiles have included members of a communist cell in Italy and a group of jazz drummers. A natural for *50 Plus* was "Models Who Can Look a Wrinkle in the Eye," which told about five top models over the age of fifty. Another article in that magazine was about the Gordie Howe family and their involvement in professional hockey. The subject's compatibility with the magazine was spelled out in the story's lead paragraph:

> Gordie Howe sat there with an annoyed look on his rugged, 50-year-young face. He had just been asked how long he intended to go on playing the brutal, bone-crushing sport of professional hockey.

Country Club Living occasionally contains group profiles on interesting families throughout the country who belong to country clubs. Often one member of the clan is highlighted (the person whose interests have the strongest affinity with the magazine's image), and less space is devoted to telling about the others.

Common Denominators

As you study a publication's personality pieces, you'll find a great many commonalities. We've talked about some of them in this chapter—age, sex, lifestyle, philosophy. But there are other common denominators such as field of endeavor or areas of accomplishment. By putting all these bits of information together, you will be able to see an article profile emerging. Flesh it out by asking yourself what the purpose of the piece is: to inform, entertain and/or inspire. Determine what themes the writers have developed—hurdles overcome, how subjects developed their skills, what prompted them to become who they are, how hard they work, what makes them tick, their views, their goals. Decide what portion of the article should discuss their family lives, hobbies, religious participation, community involvement. Notice how completely the featured person is described in previously published pieces as far as both externals and internals are concerned.

Another element you'll note in analyzing personality pieces is the writer's creativity. Top personality article writers, especially those who do profiles, excel at forming images with words. They're able to see what makes the person they're writing about different and portray his uniqueness on paper.

Techniques vary. Many personality pieces open by showing

the person in action—on the set of the motion picture she's direct-ing, stopping an out-of-control fire on an offshore oil rig, rehears-ing for a performance of "Tosca" at the Met. When the person-ality has triumphed over some adversity, the article often begins with his or her struggles, then flashes back to the time before the problems began, and rounds off with information about subse-quent accomplishments. You'll rarely come upon a piece, howev-er, that starts with the personality's birth and goes on chronolog-ically through her life. That's biography.

Coping With Interview-Query Conflict

The trickiest part of getting a personality piece off the idea list and into the typewriter is deciding which comes first, the go-ahead or the interview. This depends, in part, upon your writing clout. If you've a reputation for turning out great pieces, editors may contact you with assignments. But most of us have to make that first move, and it can present problems. If you don't know whether the celebrity will grant you an interview, how can you query an editor? And if you don't have an assignment, how can you approach the celebrity? It seems, at times, to be a self-defeating circle.

You *can* query the editor as though you have the interview in the bag, crossing your fingers and hoping the very important person on whom your article's success depends will cooperate if you get a go-ahead. The worst you can do if you're not able to produce what you've promised is earn that editor's undying alien-ation. I've found it works better to be upfront about the situation. Write or telephone the editor (depending upon how much time you have to work with), explaining that a certain personality is going to be in your town (or you're going to be where the celeb-rity is) and asking if the editor would like a piece on him. Say that while you are quite sure you can get the interviews required, if arrangements don't work out as you've anticipated, you will let her know immediately.

Another approach is to contact your interviewee's manager/ agent/secretary and introduce yourself, stating your best creden-tials loud and clear. Say you have a good idea that the editor of _____ (one of the publications you've already mentioned in your credits) would go for a piece on_____ and could the agent arrange an interview. If you're unpublished, this technique won't work, but you might modify it slightly and hope.

Which brings us to the subject of (your) wounded ego: trying to get interviews may be hazardous to your self-esteem, especially when you approach celebrities' interference runners. After all, part of their job involves keeping the boss unharassed. Unfortunately, some aren't too gracious about the ways they do it. One of my students, rebuffed by a public relations person when she attempted to interview a Reno casino owner ("You mean to say you want an interview and you've only been published in one magazine?"), picked herself up, brushed herself off and wrote a personal note to Red Skelton asking *him* for an interview. And she got it. Perhaps the moral of this story is to contact the celebrity directly and don't mess with Mr. Inbetween.

Even if you have the assignment on memo and the interview on tape, the personality piece can present problems. Celebrities are often gadabouts. They're on location in Egypt, closing a protracted business deal in Tokyo, fishing for sailfish in the Sea of Cortez—just when the editor says he likes the piece but couldn't you add a couple of graphs about the subject's early life. If you have enough time and/or the editor is willing to underwrite a phone call overseas, you're all right with celebrities within hailing distance of a telephone. But if they're at some remote, communications-free spot, you'll have some scrambling to do. Don't panic, but instead sit down and think of other people who might be able to give you the information you need—a mother, exsweetheart, fourth grade schoolteacher. If they can't supply it, chances are they will direct you to someone who can.

The classic story of writing a profile under adverse circumstances was that of a writer assigned by *California Living*'s editor Hal Silverman to do a piece on Joseph Alioto, then mayor of San Francisco. The writer was unable to get an interview with His Honor, so she did the next best thing: she camped in his waiting room and interviewed everyone who came out of his office.

Most personality pieces don't require that degree of resourcefulness. But since there are scores of ways to present your featured attraction, going into analysis will go a long way toward making the piece an editorial office hit.

13

Business
(with Pleasure)

The business of America is business.
—**Calvin Coolidge**

I'll never confess it to business publication editors, but I almost flunked Econ II in college. To this day I'd have trouble telling you exactly how the Federal Reserve System operates. But that doesn't stop me from writing business articles. There is such a spread in the degree of expertise required, and so great a variety of magazines to write business pieces for, the writer can fit herself into any of several niches in the market that are compatible with her abilities.

These niches are there because Americans have never before been so interested in things financial. We're living in an age of acquisition obsession. Along with their rising demand for goods and services, people want to know what's new to buy, how they can increase their purchasing power, and how to maximize their assets. According to a recent article in *Quill,* the magazine of Sigma Delta Chi, the journalist should concentrate on business writing if he wants to profit from this growing emphasis on economics.

You don't have to live near the financial canyons of New York or San Francisco to write business pieces. Though Reno has millions of tourists come to town each year, it's a city of only about one hundred thousand—not exactly the commercial capital of the West. Yet I've found business article ideas by the gross, about everything from gold mining to the economics of geothermal energy.

If you live on a farm in Iowa or in a village in Missouri, you're in the heart of America's corn and soybean country—and agribusiness articles are big writers' business these days. The Sunbelt, with its rapidly expanding economy, is full of story potential. The South's commercial renaissance, Detroit's automotive machinations—whatever place you call home can be base of operations for your career as a business writer.

Manufacturing Ideas
In order to launch your business, you'll need ideas. As you are studying the markets, ask yourself the following questions:

1.   What are my state's main industries?

2.   Are there any unusual items produced in my area, or commonly used products made with unusual methods?

3.   Do any outstanding business leaders, inventors, or innovators live (or perhaps vacation) nearby?

4.   What about local and state businesses—do any of them use out-of-the-ordinary sales techniques, distribution methods, training programs, promotions or displays?
   If you don't know what all your state and city businesses are (and in a large, diversified state this is a problem) ask chambers of commerce or the department of economic development for any publications they may have that list them. I obtained a booklet from the San Francisco Chamber of Commerce that gives the names of and information about the top fifty concerns headquartered in the Bay Area, and I've been able to get similar publications from organizations in other parts of the country.

5.   Are there any consumer groups in the area, and if so, are they doing anything that's newsworthy?

6.   Are there any unusual businesses around—cottage industries, co-ops, recycled merchandise outlets—that have had outstanding success?

7.   What are the problems my friends in business talk about and who are the experts I could go to seeking possible solutions?

8.   Is there anything within my experience—either as a busi-

nessperson or consumer—that could be parlayed into an article?

9. Are there any trade shows or business meetings with well-known speakers, or lectures on business at the local university or college that might result in article ideas?

10. Have I heard of any rackets, frauds, or business injustices that I might look into?

Many of your ideas won't be big enough for the national financial publications, but they may be just what the editors of state, regional, and city magazines are looking for. Or you may be able to sell them to airline inflights that serve your part of the country. Well-written rags-to-riches stories are good mail as far as tabloid editors are concerned—and almost every community has its local boy or girl who started out on a shoestring and now could buy diamond-studded ones. Be on the lookout for members of minority groups who have made it big in finance and you'll make it big with editors of ethnic publications. Look for news items with economic implications. They're the kinds of ideas that business articles in general interest magazines are built around. If there's an increase in crime, burglar detection and home protection devices will be of interest to the reading public. When innovative investment opportunities or new concepts in property ownership such as time-sharing vacation complexes are introduced, people who don't read financial publications want to know about them, too.

Any changes reported by the press in our eating habits, clothing design, and auto construction can be translated by the alert freelancer into article ideas. As long as inflation and our energy problems show no sign of abating, editors will be looking for new insights into those predicaments. Watch financial programs such as "Wall Street Week" on television for trends in investments. The Yellow Pages of your telephone book, and classified ads in both magazines and newspapers, will spark still more ideas, as will TV commercials.

It's easy to transform items from newspapers, radio, and TV into income-producing properties for writers. For example, you might read a news release reporting that the number of franchised businesses in the United States increased dramatically in the past twelve months. All sorts of ideas should come to mind. What kinds of franchise businesses are the biggest money makers? Which of them require the smallest outlay of cash and/or experience? Is buying stock in franchise corporations generally profitable for the investor? Which stocks have performed best in the past? What are the pitfalls of becoming a franchisee? And there are dozens of other possibilities—a profile of the head of the biggest franchise operation in the world, franchised businesses in Europe, South America, or the People's Republic of China, tips on how to develop a franchise operation around your own business, successful women who head franchise corporations.

Finding the Buyers

The largest markets for articles on business are financial publications, trade journals, and house magazines. National financial publications include such magazines as *Dun's Review, Barron's National Business and Financial Weekly, Commodity Journal,* and several others. Four of the largest circulation books—*Money, Business Week, Fortune* and *Forbes*—are almost impossible to crack. *Money* and *Business Week* buy no freelance material. *Forbes* and *Fortune* use only a few freelance articles, and they are written by well-established financial writers on assignment. Unless you've established a reputation as a business writer, you'll find better marketing possibilities with the smaller, less-well-known financial publications.

Most-often-used subjects in the financial journals are banking and corporate finance trends, expos, management science, and new trends in management, finance and accounting, taxes, and government regulation. You'll find profiles of company and business leaders; information on stock and bond markets, real estate, commodities; case histories; interviews; economic how-to's; personal opinion pieces, and articles on new industries and products, too.

It's well nigh impossible for a writer who doesn't have a sound economic background to write the more technical pieces that appear in the financial journals, it's true. I would never attempt an article on the economics of installment selling or commodities trading. But most of us are able to conduct the interviews and do the other research necessary to write less complex pieces. Occasionally, financial publications print articles that don't require more than a smidgen of economic knowledge. *Financial World,* for example, ran a piece called "Buying and Cellaring" about making a profit on old wine gains. The same magazine has also published articles on autographs, rare books, and antiques as investments.

The number of business pieces devoured by trade journals and house magazines is enormous. *Working Press of the Nation* lists more than six hundred publications that use articles about new products. In fact, almost every listing in *Working Press* promises the potential for some kind of business article sale. *Business Periodicals Index* lists about 250 financial and trade publications, and you'll find that its rundown of articles is an excellent idea source as well. And don't forget the possibility of foreign trade journal sales—many of those markets are listed in *Ulrich's.*

In addition to new product stories, the big sellers in the trades are successful-technique stories and how-to's. A rundown (by no means exhaustive) of other trade article types includes photo essays, interviews, profiles, humor, personal experience, expos, research reports, nostalgia, and historical development. The finance trade magazines—*ABA Banking Journal, Mergers & Acquisitions,* and the like—generally carry more technical articles than the other trade magazines.

Regionals cover the same topics as the national financial publications, only on a more restricted geographic basis. These magazines may serve a city, as does the *Houston Business Journal;* a state, such as *Alaska Construction & Oil Magazine,* or a region, like *Caribbean Business News.*

Advantages of writing for the regionals are, in addition to less intense competition, easy accessibility to businesses, executives and agencies you need to contact for information, and the day-to-day knowledge the business writer acquires of financial happenings in his area. By clipping items from local newspapers, it's a simple matter not only to accumulate ideas, but to start files on those ideas and eliminate digging through newspaper morgues when time comes to write the story.

The biggest plus in writing for regional financial magazines is the opportunity for personal contact with editors and the chance to get the inside scoop on what they really want for their magazines. If you live in the magazine's coverage area, chances are that a trip to its editorial offices won't be a major pilgrimage and will be well worth the journey.

All is not lost even if no regional financial magazine is published in your area. There are times when living on the periphery is a distinct advantage, since editors often want reports on developments in adjacent states. By writing letters stating your qualifications, you'll let them know who to turn to when they need news about your area.

Editors of nonfinancial regional, state, and city magazines look for articles about successful businesses, industries, and business leaders in the localities they serve. Some magazines, if they're not public relations-oriented, like to liven things up every now and then with an expos.

Agencies that promote a region's economy afford business article freelance opportunities, too. Most of them put out annual reports designed to attract businesses to the area, and often augment staff writing with freelance work.

Other good markets for business articles are airline inflights, women's, and some men's magazines. Analysis will show you exactly what they are looking for. For instance, Delta Airline's magazine, *Sky,* runs a profile of a business executive in almost every issue. Seven issues of the magazine contained profiles on the following: Harry Wetzel, chairman and chief executive officer of the Garrett Corporation; Roy A. Anderson, chairman and chief executive officer of Lockheed; Charles C. Gates, Jr., president and chairman of the board of Gates Rubber Company; Robert Anderson, head of Rockwell International; David C. Scott, chairman, chief executive officer and president of Allis Chalmers Corporation; comedian Steve Allen, and actor Hugh O'Brien. From reading those back issues, the analyst not only determines that *Sky* is a market for business profiles, but that there seem to be three basic profile requisites—the subject should be male, in his late fifties or early sixties, and very successful.

When a magazine's business profiles center exclusively

around men, it may be because the editor never gets any about women. She may, indeed, be hungering and thirsting for articles about females who've made it to the top. On the other hand, men may be featured because the publication's readership is predominantly male. Read the ads. If some of them are directed toward working women, pitch the editor a query on a woman executive even if you've never seen one in the book before.

Analysis will show you, too, that it's in writing for women's, men's and general-interest publications that the writer capable of uncomplicating the complicated can count on big dividends. Insurance policies, guarantees, wills, and lending agreements are confusing documents. Saving money is tricky business when it involves big purchases. Though the man on the street wants to know what makes the financial world turn, he doesn't usually have formal training in economics. Therefore, the articles aimed at him are not complex.

Article specifications, also, illustrate the importance of analysis. You'll find that *Elks Magazine* likes new product pieces, while *Modern People* wants to tell its readers how to get rich and alert them to consumer rip-offs. Tabloids print quantities of material on consumerism. Women's magazines run the gamut from pieces on how to choose the best household appliances to stories about women who have been catapulted from kitchen to corporate heights. How to get a raise, save money or moonlight are topics popular in men's magazines.

The Perfect Product Mix

Just as any businessperson planning to unveil a new product begins by looking at the competition, the freelancer contemplating a business piece must analyze what has gone before. *Mergers & Acquisitions* in its *Writer's Market* listing specifies that "articles should contain 20-60 facts/1,000 words (names, dates, places, companies, etc.)," but most editors aren't so precise when it comes to saying what they want. And since business articles are each constructed differently, it's up to the writer to determine what editors who haven't verbalized their preferences are most likely to buy.

One of the first things to look for is the degree of technicality. You can gauge this by noting the number of concepts advanced (and whether they are familiar to the average layman), the number of facts, statistics, and polysyllabic words.

Notice, too, how specialized or narrow the subject is, how much prior knowledge one must have to understand the content, and how abstract the concepts are.

The most technical pieces are those published by magazines read by professionals in the field of finance—bank presidents, investment analysts and the like. Articles in financial publications like *Forbes, Fortune,* and *Barron's* are for the most part more technical than those you'll encounter in airline inflights, which in turn are more complicated than those in general circulation magazines.

The ratio of polysyllabic words tends to be higher, the number of descriptive words lower in business articles than those on most other subjects. You will not often find picturesque writing, but when an editor likes it, by all means give him what he wants. Counting statistics and quotes is important in business article analysis, too, as the editor-prescribed dosage varies considerably.

A comparison of three publications that use business material—*California Business, Western Cleaner & Launderer,* and *United Mainliner*—for example, points up wide divergences as far as statistics, quotes and words of more than two syllables are concerned:

It isn't hard to estimate the kind and amount of research you'll have to do for a business article in a specific magazine. In fact, patterns are extremely consistent and clearly defined in

Table 2.

Magazine	Quotes per 500	Statistics per 500	Words of More Than Two Syllables
California Business	4	8.4	15.2
Western Cleaner & Launderer	0	.36	18.1
United Mainliner	3	3.9	11.1

most financial publications. The need for such information as yields on certain stocks, a company's annual income (and whether that figure is net or gross) and the number of people employed should be readily apparent. Note, too, if past articles touch on labor/employee relations, whether they talk about the effects of inflation, or make predictions for the future. Cost per unit of production, the amount of money spent for advertising, the percentage of revenues plowed back into plant expansion—whatever kinds of information have been presented in the past will guide you in the right research paths.

As you analyze, jot down possible sources of obtaining the facts you need. If you're in doubt as to where to get some of them, consult a good reference librarian. For a manufacturing success story, your list might look like this:

Opening quote (from longtime business associate)

Second quote (from competitor)

Statistics on growth of industry in general (National Association of Manufacturers, business publications)

Statistics on firm in relation to rest of industry (company officials)

Information on product(s) manufactured (company officials, advertising brochures)

Production figures, including comparison with production ten years ago (company officials)

Number of employees (company officials)

Net worth of company (company's annual report)

History of company, including obstacles, triumphs (company officials, previously published material)

Info and quotes on plans for future (get during interview with top company official)

While you're going through this process, you'll be able to evaluate whether you have the expertise needed to do the piece. If you don't understand the terms used in previously published pieces or if knowledge of the industry that could only be obtained by working within it seems to be a requisite, abandon the project. There will be better business article opportunities for you that require only the gathering of information and putting it in the proper sequence.

Before I begin a business piece, I try to interview a local "expert" (preferably someone I know who is in that particular line of work). That way I can get basic information on the subject before I tackle the unknown, and therefore more formidable authorities, saving them time and saving me the embarrassment of asking stupid questions. The questions I ask my local expert come from reading similar articles in my target publication. It's not difficult then to determine how much basic knowledge of a subject the writer needs before she begins interviewing. That's the knowledge I must obtain from my expert on the scene and from library research. Your local authority can also often clue you in on the reliability of or controversial views held by the people you plan to interview—a real help when it comes to evaluating your material.

Next, you must analyze your magazine-in-mind's perspective. Is its banner consumer advocacy, or laissez faire; for unrestrained trade or government control; pro-labor, pro-big business? Is the point of view conservative or liberal? Are the ideas set forth traditional or ultra-innovative? Is reportage even-handed or highly subjective?

By understanding the publication's personality, you'll be able to pinpoint not only the kinds of information needed, but possible sources of information as well. If all the pieces in a magazine take a free trade posture, for example, you'll need to contact exactly the opposite sources for information and quotes you would if the publication took a proembargo stand. You're never going to get good information for a left-wing publication by interviewing an archconservative, unless you deliberately seek his opinions in order to refute them. Statistics from the Environmental Protection Agency won't carry much weight with readers who argue against government control of the environment, but they will with readers of conservationist magazines.

Art Garcia, one of *California Business*'s editors, says that to make a business piece salable, the writer must do his homework. "Study the publication you've targeted," he says. "Know the kinds of material they do and don't use. Story pitches are most often torpedoed by me, as an editor, when someone calls and asks what kinds of stories are we interested in. Had one the other day. This PR gal said she'd only seen one issue of *California Business*. I advised her to pick up a second, even a third, issue if needed and get the feel of the magazine on her own."

Although most editors share Garcia's aversion to the writer asking questions that he should have answered for himself, they aren't opposed to queries as to specific themes they are planning for future issues of their magazine. It's also acceptable to ask the editor of a publication you have no way of getting your hands on to send you *several* back issues. That's the only way you'll be able to find out, for instance, that *Big* (a magazine for people in the earth-moving business) uses an article each issue about a big contractor, one about a big earth-moving project, and one about a big fixed operation such as a mine or quarry.

Merchandising Techniques

Analysis indicates that there are six best-selling ways to package your ideas when you're writing a business piece—the *how he/ she/they did it,* the *how-to,* the *informational* article, the *expose, hard news,* and *personality* piece.

One of the easiest for the non-business-oriented writer to analyze and write is the *how he/she/they did it* piece. This is the kind of article most in demand by trade publications; it shows how a small-time herb grower parlayed her parsley, sage, rosemary, and thyme into a million-dollar mail-order business, or how a tooling shop proprietor devised a diving board from a discarded airplane wing panel.

Whereas the *expose* and *informational* business pieces often require many interviews and extensive library research, you can usually write a *how he/she/they did it* on the basis of one good interview. That is, unless your advance analysis shows you will need comments from customers, clients, competitors, or others associated with the subject. If the business or company is a small or new one, it may not have been written about, so the only way you can obtain information is via the interview route. Don't be surprised if the person you interview arranges for you to talk to other people in the organization. But don't accept interviewing them in lieu of the head of the business if she's the one you arranged to interview in the first place.

Closely related is the business *how-to*—How To Increase Sales with Indirect Lighting, How to Maximize Space with Mini-Displays, How to Attract Business in an Off-Beat Location, How to Get a Job (or a raise). They're almost as easy to put together as the *how he/she/they did its,* involving interviews with a person or group of individuals who have been successful in accomplishing what you'll tell your readers they can do, too.

Informational articles most often focus on new businesses, new products, new concepts; on the state of the economy or some facet thereof, or such concerns of business as taxes, regulations, or procedures. They can also chronicle the history of an industry or business, tell about inventions, and cover almost any good consumer/industry/problem/product theme.

The business *exposé* is growing in popularity and shows signs of becoming even more important as consumer advocacy and awareness continue. As you read exposés in magazines, you can be sure that the material was checked with an attorney before it saw publication, since the last thing any magazine (or writer) wants is a libel suit.

Hard news for national publications is usually taken care of by stringers. These are freelancers who live in various parts of the country and send items from their territories to the editorial offices. Stringing is an excellent way for writers with only a few published pieces to get additional experience, and such a connection isn't too hard to make. All you need to do is send a battery of letters stating your qualifications to trade journals you'd like to write for. Then, if the editor needs someone in your area and your credentials meet with approval, the submission of copy by deadline and in the publication's style should keep you on the payroll. This doesn't mean that a non-stringer's news submissions will never be bought, but you do run the risk that a person has already been assigned to report your area's news.

You will note that *personality* pieces slanted toward financial figures keep the reader's mind on business. Hobbies, family, and friends are given scant space, with the article concentrating on the subject's financial life and philosophy.

Cranking Up for Production

Interview and research notes at hand, typewriter switch on, there's nothing left to do but write the piece. If you've done your analysis, you'll know that summary leads are used more often than any other in business articles. They are usually short and to the point, as the following lead from an article called "Always Borrow Money Needlessly" in *buyways* illustrates:

> Someday you're going to want to borrow money. Chances are that plans for a new home, a new car or a motorboat will send you scurrying to the bank for help. Building a firm base for credit in large amounts ought to take place when your needs are relatively small. In contrast to the merry little jingle which goes, "Never borrow money needlessly," maybe the best time to borrow is when you really don't need the money.

The interrogatory/summary, as in this lead from "Legal Clinics—Balancing the Price of the Scales of Justice" in *Consumer Life* is one you will also see frequently:

> Lawyers that people can afford?
> If legal clinics do what they claim they can do, nearly all of the people in the United States who don't use lawyers—70 percent—will be able to. The arm-and-leg fee days may be on the way out.

Analysis shows that following the summary lead in popularity is the quote. This one is from a piece called "How Job-Vulnerable Are You?" which was printed in *Flying Colors:*

> "It came like a bolt from the blue". . ."They never gave me any inkling that they were thinking of making a change". . ."Why didn't he say he was unhappy with my performance?"
> We hear it so frequently. Job termination is usually a shock. Apart from the economic impact, there is sometimes a considerable amount of psychic damage. For most of us, the work we do means more than just a paycheck.
> But, in too many cases, firing is not only a shock, it is a *surprise. This should not happen.* There are invariably warning signs that should alert the individual to the danger of losing a job. The trouble is that these signs are often apparent to everyone except the party in peril. We seem to have a built-in denial

mechanism that fosters peace of mind at the price of blinding us to impending termination. "It may happen to the other guy, but it can't happen to me," is about the way it works.

These days it's important for even the most seemingly secure of us to step back and take an objective scan of our job security.

The descriptive lead is most often used in business articles to describe the subject of a profile. But it is also sometimes utilized to tell about a business, as in this *United Mainliner* piece:

The company's world headquarters, tucked away in an unfashionable Manhattan neighborhood far from the boutiques and expensive restaurants, is as unprepossessing as an old warehouse. The lobby is nothing more than a nondescript foyer with a security desk. In the elevator, however, a special magic becomes very apparent.

One is immediately enveloped by aromas—hyacinth, oleander, magnolia, bergamot. On the floors above, perfumers and chemists, surrounded by thousands of bottles, are busily concocting scents redolent with images of romance, adventure, intrigue.

As the elevator rises, one detects jasmine, or perhaps olibanum, myrcia or myrrh, and one's mind is suddenly filled with thoughts of exotic tropical nights, Cossack horsemen or Oriental seductresses, of ancient spice caravans and lusty wines. It is as if some olfactory genie, invisible and mischievous, were manipulating the brain. In the executive suite, the fragrance is more straightforward: it is unmistakably chocolate. "Tomorrow it might be strawberry," shrugs a secretary.

This is the home office of International Flavors & Fragrances, Inc. (IFF), a little-known but highly profitable corporation that creates and manufactures aromas and tastes for other companies' products.

Three types of endings—the summary, quote, and look into the future by an expert on the subject—seem to be endorsed by more editors than any other kinds. Since, through analysis, you've been able to structure the part of your article that goes in between to editorial perfection, all that remains is to give the piece a name.

You will have noticed that titles of business articles run from the straightforward and downright unimaginative to those employing plays on words, alliteration, and other devices to give them zing. The excerpt just given, for example, is from a piece called "The Sweet Success of Smell," an appropriate name for a lively, makes-you-want-to-read-on article. There is no hard-and-fast rule. While *Dun's Review* names its articles "Doing Business in Unstable Countries," "Why Recessions Don't Cure Inflation," and "Long-Range Gold Outlook," *Financial World* often uses titles like "Zenith passes the nadir" and "The Repackaging of Nabisco." "Mineral Water Craze: Sparkle or Fizzle?" "How to Beat the Dealer" (about buying cars) and "Get the Picture?" (on camera purchasing) appeared in a single issue of *Consumer Digest*. If you were planning to submit to that market, you would want your title to be an upbeat one. But if an editor has indicated a preference for the commonplace, stifle that creative urge.

On The Flip Side

Business articles don't have to be all work and no play to read. This lead from an article called "For Sale—or What if We Throw in the Refrigerator, the Blender and the Dog?" which appeared in *buyways* treats a serious subject with anything but solemnity:

> If you are planning to put your house up for sale, the best advice I can offer is—change jobs instead. Or add on. Or cut off. Basically, any conceivable alternative beats selling your house.
>
> It's a lot like taking 44 second graders on a field trip to a museum and finding that the museum's plumbing is out of order. That is, it's an experience you will look back on in years to come and *still* not be able to laugh.
>
> But if you must sell, you must. So, I have a few simple rules that can make it all a little easier.

As Norman Sklarewitz, one of the country's top business and industry writers, says, "Business is no longer a 'dull' or 'dry' subject that interests only trade book editors. The subject matter is every bit as exciting and colorful as any other. You have personalities to profile, fraud to uncover, dramatic tales of high risk and danger to tell, and all the rest of the subjects that a professional magazine writer seeks to mine."

Even when your editor doesn't want the light touch or your subject matter isn't scintillating, business writing has its rewards. There's not only the satisfaction of a made-to-order job well done, but the financial know-how and financial wherewithal that can make your own economic future brighter.

14

Inside on
the Outdoors

The end of labor is to gain leisure.
—Aristotle (384-322 B.C.)
The stereotype of the writer is that of a bookish person who spends days chained to a type-writer or hunched over a towering stack of heavy volumes in the library's reference room And though we do spend a good deal of time as non-writers picture us, it's not all Correct-O-Tape and *Readers' Guide* by a long shot—especially for writers who specialize in outdoors articles.

For scribes whose hobbies are out-of-door pursuits, outdoor writing is a sure-fire way to combine vocation and avocation. The only drawback is that outdoor writers often have a hard time convincing people (including themselves) that they're working. Lucky souls, they don't have to wait until labor's end to have fun.

To add to their joys, the market for outdoor articles has increased by leaps and bounds during the past decade. Since many outdoor pursuits can provide relatively low-cost entertain-ment and in most cases can be enjoyed close to home, editors tell us that we're going to see even more pieces on outdoor activities as the inflation/energy squeeze continues.

Just what is an outdoor article? Most of us, before we analyze the matter, would say that it's a piece about hunting and fishing, for we automatically think of the more prominent out-door articles in *Field & Stream, Sports Afield,* and *Outdoor Life.* Upon analysis, we realize that camping, hiking, boating, birdwatching, bicycling, and nature walking are outdoor sub-jects, too. The outdoor article, we find, is a piece whose subject is any leisuretime activity (other than travel and the traditional "athletic" sports) carried on out-of-doors.

Taking Aim

The rod and gun magazines are the biggest market for outdoor pieces. The big three—*Sports Afield, Field & Stream* and *Outdoor Life*—pay very well. But unless you're an established outdoor writer, hoping to catch one of their thousand-dollar assignments is like trying to snag a big one in a stream where experienced fishermen stand shoulder to shoulder on the banks. *Sports Illustrated,* a magazine most of us don't associate with outdoor articles, has published some bang-up hunting and fishing pieces over the years. It pays even more than the three leading outdoor publications and, as you can appreciate, is even more difficult to break into.

You'll find happier hunting grounds if you seek out some of the smaller, less competitive publications. There are approximately three dozen of these magazines listed in *Writer's Market.* About half of them are regional—*The Angler and Hunter in Ontario, The Carolina Sportsman, Illinois Wildlife, Pennsylvania Game News,* to name a few—so the material they buy pertains only to the areas they cover.

Rod and gun magazines may publish the most outdoor articles, but they aren't the only fish in the stream. You'll see outdoor articles in newspaper supplements, regional and city magazines, recreational vehicle and motor club publications, airline inflights, fraternal and men's magazines, in magazines like *National Parks & Conservation Journal, Wilderness Camping,* and *Outside.*

If you want to sell to these non-hunting and -fishing magazines, you'll have to select your bait with care, keeping your scope broader than for a magazine geared toward experienced outdoorspeople. An example of super angling is an article called "Lures for Women Fishermen," which snagged *California Living*'s editor Hal Silverman. Written by two women, the article began with each of the authors telling how she began fishing, and was followed by a checklist of items the woman angler finds handy on a fishing trip. That four-column article was followed by an 850-word piece by another writer called "Where the Fish Are"—a rundown of fishing spots in the magazine's readership area (northern California and Nevada). A third article in the same issue called "Planning Your Outdoor Strategy," told readers about sources to contact, such as Snow Phone, the U.S. Forest Service, and automobile associations for information on campgrounds, state parks, and road and trail conditions. "Choosing a Sleeping Bag" in *Southern Living,* "Birdwatching in Brigantine" in *Motorhome Life,* and "The Pick of the Wilderness" in *Discovery* are other examples of article topics with broad general appeal.

In analyzing the hunting and fishing magazines, you'll not only find that regional differences set many of them apart from each other, but their audiences do, too. Ed Ow, whose *Angler* is 100 percent freelance-written, says his magazine is read by "the fisherman who *truly* wants to improve his fishing." A. R. Harding, editor of *Fur-Fish-Game,* says, "We aim for the real dyed-in-the-wool sportsman—a lot of them are professionals in the field; fishing guides, trappers." *American Field* is devoted to hunting with dogs. The *Flyfisher, Salt Water Sportsman,* and *Turkey Call* are as different as the fish and game their readers are trying to bag.

Reading the ads will tell you a lot about the outdoor magazines' audiences. Some are slanted toward the sophisticated and affluent, others toward conservationists, devotees of alternative lifestyles, sportsmen whose recreational lives revolve around hunting and fishing, and professionals whose livelihoods do. *Outside*'s ads are for products like Earth Shoes, camping gear and backpacking equipment, wood stoves, DeBeers diamonds, Nikon binoculars, and Eddie Bauer clothing, whereas *Field & Stream* advertisements include those for four-wheel drive vehicles, want ads for live bait and tackle, boat kits, dog food, taxidermy instruction, body building, switchblade combs, and do-it-yourself grandfather clock kits. *Fur-Fish-Game*'s ads reiterate editor Ow's statement that many of its readers are professional outdoorsmen—100 percent wild red fox and coyote urine, pelt fleshing tools, powerful skunk scent, and books on mink raising are among the products advertised.

Angling for Assignments
Before you decide on your ammunition or choose which hunting grounds you're going to explore, it's a good game plan to examine just *how* you communicate with nature. Perhaps you're like

me—bored stiff after sitting in a duck blind for fifteen minutes, but willing to walk for hours in search of wildflowers. You may adore butterflies, but loathe rockclimbing. Wilderness camping may be your idea of a perfect vacation, or you might camp in luxury hotels and conduct your outdoor research watching whales or ambling through rain forests. You will write stronger articles if you're interested in your subject. And since the range of topics is as big as the whole outdoors, you shouldn't have any trouble finding several you're enthusiastic about.

It's necessary, too, to select subjects you have some knowledge of. Some outdoor article readers may be novices, but whatever their experience levels, you have to know more about your subject than they do.

Along with analyzing your outdoor interests and degree of expertise, you will want to zero in on the kinds of articles your target magazines print most often. You will discover in the course of your analysis that there are four distinct types of outdoor pieces. The most often published is the *personal experience,* followed by the *how-to, informational,* and *personality,* in that order.

Personal experience pieces do two things. They let the reader participate vicariously in the writer's adventure/experience and transmit information at the same time. This excerpt from an article called "Bear Attack" in *Outdoor Life* will show you how it works:

> The bear came at me with no warning. Ears flattened, neck hairs stiffly erect, it growled fiercely as it charged, full bore, right at me. I saw its flashing teeth as it came, and knew in an instant it was a grizzly, although I'd never seen one in the wild before. There was no mistaking the hump on its back, the broad face and guard hairs. I've seen a couple of hundred black bears in the woods, enough to know that this one was entirely different from the rest.

Outdoor *how-to's* are usually not presented in the traditional how-to form with each step listed in sequence, but nonetheless give the reader all the information he or she needs to do whatever task or project the article is about. Though you will find the words "How-To" occasionally in titles, you're more likely to come across names like "Build a Packframe," "All About Hiking Boots" (a piece telling readers how to select them) and "Basic Flatwater Paddling Techniques."

It's in the how-to realm that the writer who isn't an ardent outdoorsperson can make the most sales. "Keeping Your Bicycle Rolling," "Cooking in the Wilds" and "Photo Techniques for Hikers" are a sampling of the kinds of subject matter that any competent writer, with the help of authorities and some in-the-field experience, can deal with. And for your reader's sake, don't stint on that on-scene research, as there's many a slip between theory and practice. If you're doing a piece on building a shelter from pine boughs or hunting rabbits with a bow and arrow, go through the process yourself, no matter how much advice you have from the experts.

Picture-taking skills are a big asset in the outdoors field. Though your favorite hiking trail or tidepool may be only a short drive from your home, they can be hundreds or thousands of miles from the publication's editorial office. Other exciting outdoor spots are well off the beaten path and difficult to get to. In these cases, the availability of your professional-quality photos will often be a determining factor in making sales.

Informational outdoor articles for the most part supply facts—about an area famous for duck hunting, or government regulations that affect the sportsman, or environmental concerns, or the latest in outdoor gear. They, too, provide writing opportunities for the non-sportsman.

Though you will not encounter a great many *personality* pieces, they're good sellers with editors who like them. Subject choice is most important, as the central figure must be compatible with the magazine's philosophy. For example, *Sierra* (a publication whose sponsoring group actively seeks to make changes in environmental legislation) carried conversations with Senator Edward Kennedy and presidential candidate John Anderson, both known for their conservationist views. Each of these pieces emphasized, as you might imagine, the interviewees' opinions on environmental concerns. Chances are excellent that the magazine will be buying interviews with other conservation-minded politicians in the future. *Outside,* in its department called "Outsiders," publishes pieces on active nature lovers such as one called "Walking Through Time with Colin Fletcher—The man who invented backpacking." This indicates to the analyst that the magazine's editor is looking for personality pieces on present-day John Muirs.

Telling the Story

The various how-to and personality piece formats discussed in previous chapters can be adapted easily to the outdoor market. But the personal experience article demands different writing techniques. If you've not studied them before, you'll be amazed to find how many personal outdoor experiences appear in print each month. You'll also find that these articles are filled with dialogue. Editors feel it creates suspense, excitement and drama when writers use conversation to tell about rafting through whitewater or the 250-pound marlin on the line. When you're reading, notice where dialogue is placed and how much is used, as this will vary considerably from publication to publication. Generally, you'll discover, conversation is interspersed with description and narration to move the action along.

Not only does dialogue keep a piece rolling, it gives information to the reader in a form that's easy to digest, as in these paragraphs from "Ringtails Don't Come Easy" in *Fur-Fish-Game:*

> "Well, times are tough, I guess," I told the old timer as we pulled into his driveway. And they'd been tough, too. It was admittedly late in the season, but we'd hunted at least four woodlots diligently that night and his solidly built bluetick had turned up just one cold track. That cold track had uninspiringly ended at a den.

> "They just weren't running tonight," he said, as we unloaded our gear and took his dog back to a waiting box, "But darned if I can figure out why. It's a warm night for early December, and we had a good rain. There was a front moving in, too, and plenty of standing corn still around. Them woods should have been swarming with coons. I just can't understand it."

The first person is used more consistently in outdoor articles than in any other kind I've studied. This is because of the preponderance of personal experience tales. Often, too, present tense is used to add excitement.

Leads are usually either conversational, descriptive, written in dialogue or as a summary. The descriptive lead is a natural for the outdoor piece because it sets the stage for the action and gives the reader a "you are there" feeling of participation. The following three examples are typical of the well-crafted descriptive leads you will find. The first is from "Sandstorm," which appeared in *Alaska:*

Outside the battered tent, winds howled and blew in gusts to 125 miles an hour. Torrents of rain poured onto the tent and the sands on which the tent was pitched swirled and blasted the canvas around the three hunters huddled inside.

Earlier on that October day, when Dick Nichols of Gulf Air Taxi, Yakutat, had landed the three hunters on the beach, the weather had been clear and beautiful. Who would have suspected such a violent change in a mere five hours?

Listening to the beating of sand, wind and rain on the fragile barrier separating him from the elements, my husband Joe Shaw remembered the reason for the choice of campsite.

As you'll recall from our discussion of leads in Chapter 8, there's not always a well-defined capsule sentence when the descriptive lead is used. In the second example, the writer comes closer to capsulizing what his article is about, but even so, the theme is not set forth so strongly as when other kinds of leads are employed. This one, "Best Goose Hunting in the West," was published in *Sports Afield.*

The sky was a brassy yellow to the east. The land seemed completely barren. Not even a slight breeze could be felt and the only sound was the howl of a distant coyote. As the sun peeked over the horizon the yellow hue dissipated, and the quiet was shattered by the ever-rising crescendo of 60,000 awakening Canadian geese. In the light of the new day, this land glowed under a blanket of freshly harvested grainfields intertwined with dark strips of green winter wheat.

backhoe in the center of a huge sorghum field, now spotted with a large spread of silhouette and shell decoys. From two miles away I could hear the concentration of lesser Canadas as they noisily prepared to leave the sanctuary of Colorado's Queens Reservoir Refuge on the morning feeding flight. As all species of Canada geese often do just before lifting off, the entire 60,000 became quite still. Then, with an unbelievable roar of beating wings and honked conversations, the morning flight was underway. From two miles away the huge flock looked like a rising cloud of locusts. Circling, the majority of the birds settled back down to the lake, but from that first massive movement a steady, unbroken stream of flocks containing 500 to 1000 birds headed out for the fields.

With those first airborne birds I could feel the excitement grow inside me. When three flocks veered from the main group and turned in my direction, everything else ceased to exist—my entire world narrowed to those incoming geese and me. If there was anything wrong with the decoys or with my pit blind it was too late to do anything about it now—with more than 1000 pairs of eyes scanning my set it had better be perfect or that Thanksgiving goose would be but a dream.

The third example of a descriptive lead appeared in *Wilderness Camping*'s "THELON: Flowing with the Ribbon of Life":

A thousand feet below, the landscape transforms. The tiny trees, shrunken "little sticks," become sparse. Snakelike sand hills slink across the land. Eskers. These glacial river channels remain as hills, ten-thousand-year-old homes for fox and wolf. There is water in lakes, rivers, bogs, and soil. Everywhere water. The permanently frozen ground refuses it passage to the underworld, so this land of desert rainfall stays wet and spongelike. On slopes, the saturated soil slumps downward year by year, bending trees and shrubs into contorted growth. Soilifluction, the geologists call it.

The plane roars on to the northwest. Trees disappear. Tundra!

And ice.

Artillery Lake, our destination, is encased from shore to shore. The locals were right. This is the summer that didn't come. It's already Jully 11. Visions of dragging canoes over half-melted, treacherous ice chill our optimism. Falling through rotten ice seems a poor way to die. We picture ourselves huddled, wet and blue, shaking in a canoe, miles from shore. I try to hide a small shiver.

The conversational lead is most editors' favorite for personal experience pieces, if the frequency with which it appears is any indication—and we analysts feel that it is. Rarely including a theme sentence, this lead serves instead as the beginning of the story the writer is going to tell. I especially like this one from "Bluegrass Bucks" in *Sports Afield:*

It hadn't been a good morning. Since first light, when I'd left my car along a gravel road in the Bluegrass Army Depot near Richmond, Kentucky, rain had fallen steadily, making the hardwoods drip and cutting my vision in half in the darkened woods. The only deer I'd seen were does and a single yearling fawn. The does had hurried by, obviously spooked by another hunter and all wag eared and nervous. The fawn, half grown and somehow separated from its mother, came carelessly walking to within ten feet of me, its black nose steaming in the cold air. Finally it bounced off into a field; bleating like any lost child.

The bucks remained out of sight, using more sense than I and keeping to their beds in relatively protected cedar thickets or brier patches. The rain was beginning to soak through my camouflage jacket and flatten the fletching on my hunting arrows. I can put up with being wet and cold, but wet arrow feathers and the possibility of poor shooting—should a buck appear—made me look for cover."

I don't know about you, but that lead makes me like the hunter and want to read on to find out what happens. Writers who can inject their personalities into the conversational style get that vital component of any successful article—reader involvement—going full bore with the first paragraph.

Running a close second to the conversational personal experience article lead is the use of dialogue. In "The Spice of Life" in *Wilderness Camping,* author Mary Schantz uses this lead to good advantage:

"You folks planning on eating lots of fish in the next couple of weeks?" asked the Fish and Game Officer at the Army-Navy surplus store on Anchorage's 4th Avenue, filling in the necessary forms for five fishing licenses as he talked.

"Sure are," came the confident reply. "For four weeks, to be exact. Coho and silver salmon mostly."

"Well, good luck to you," he called out as we headed for the door, the last detail completed in our preparation for a month-long research and relaxation expedition by Folbot into Alaska's Prince William Sound. "Hope you all like fish!" he chuckled as an afterthought.

Schantz goes on to say that they *didn't* all like fish, but then continues to tell how with the use of spices, fish can provide palatable protein for everyone.

That neat and tidy lead, the summary, is used by outdoor writers, too—especially in how-to and informational articles. Notice how effectively the author gets into "Trolling for Trophies at Pend Oreille," a *Western Outdoors* article:

Lake Pend Oreille (pronounced Ponderay) in north Idaho is well-known for its excellent fishing. Yet even this very favorable rating belies the true excitement of fishing there, for Lake Pend Oreille is trophy fishing water—it has produced three Kamloop rainbow and two Dolly Varden world record trout. The largest Kamloop weighed a whopping 37 pounds and the top Dolly went 32 pounds.

And here's how William Sanders got his *Backpacker* article, "Paddle Your Own Canoe," started:

If you're like most backpackers, you've had moments— camped beside a mountain lake, walking a remote river valley—

when you've wished for some kind of a boat. You could paddle out to that intriguing island. Or get closer to where the fish are jumping. Or even knock off walking for awhile and rest your blisters while drifting down the shady stream.

Well, thanks to modern technology, you, too, can become amphibious with very little strain on back or finances. It only takes a little care and awareness in equipment selection and use.

You'll find that the interrogative lead is also occasionally used, especially in magazines aimed at a general audience. A series of questions begin this piece, "Head for the Hills," in *National Motorist:*

What is it about camping that makes it so popular with people of all ages? Is it the idea of peace and solitude? The change of atmosphere, away from concrete and crowds? Or perhaps the feeling of bravado, of matching wits with the wild? Even the low cost?

Camping is all of that and more.

Coming to Conclusions

Personal experience articles often end with a summarizing statement of what the writer gained or learned as a result of the experience/adventure. Or it may be a summary of the article's subjects as in "Great Plains Gobblers," printed in *Outdoor Life:*

The Great Plains turkey hunter, like the bird he seeks, is a vital and rapidly growing figure in the West. In the wild turkey experience he relishes, there are no swampland dawns, no hidden mountain roost sites, and little mention of the relative merits of No. 2 shot compared to BB shot. Instead he talks of sage, shin-oak thickets and mesas, and of rifles, scopes and cartridges. Wild turkey hunting, it is delightful to report, has at long last come home to the West.

The other popular personal experience ending is a quote from a member of the hunting/fishing/camping party.

Personality pieces of outdoor figures end like those in other magazines—most often with a quote, the subject's plans or goals for the future, or the last answer in an interview. Endings of informational and how-to pieces are usually a listing of sources of further information, campsites, fishing spots and the like. You will note, too, that sidebars are big with certain outdoor editors, so let them know in your query when it's appropriate that you have material that will work well in sidebar format.

Querying Season

For every outdoor magazine there is a season. A time for waterfowl, a time for moose, pheasant, and deer. Pike, bluegill, bass and crappies have their days during spring and summer. Bear articles seem to be published most often during the winter, perhaps since it's the slow time of the year for many of the country's sportsmen. And even though the bears are hibernating, those adventures start the readers dreaming of days to come.

Not only rod and gun magazines are extremely season oriented. Camping and conservationist articles have their own places in the year's time, too. It's important to check a couple year's back issues to determine whether there are issues in which an article on a specific subject is traditionally placed.

Analysis will provide even more help in bagging your editorial game. Since outdoor magazines are heavily male oriented, it will come as no surprise to you that most of their pieces are written by men.

A study of nine issues of *Outdoor Life* showed me that fifty-one of the articles were freelance, by forty-one different people—all males. In fact, only one article in those nine issues was bylined with a woman's name, and she was a member of the staff.

Does that mean that a woman can't write for that magazine? I doubt it. But since there's no way of finding out whether any magazine rejects manuscripts on the basis of the sex of the writer (What editor is going to confess if that's true?), I use initials rather than my first name when submitting to a magazine with 99 percent-plus masculine bylines. I'm not practicing deception, just giving myself every possible break. And if an editor responds to my query with a phone call, he often asks if he can use my given name, since too few women submit pieces to magazines they feel are male territory.

While in recent years virtually all outdoor publications have espoused conservation, the degree to which it is emphasized varies so greatly that the analyst must be aware of this also. Some magazines such as *Conservationist, Environment, The Living Wilderness,* and *National Parks & Conservation Magazine* are totally dedicated to the philosophy, so personal accounts of hunting expeditions or pieces involving the use of animals in any fashion which could be considered inhumane are taboo. On the other hand, rod and gun magazines have taken an anti-gun-control posture, so articles advocating the regulation of firearms are anathema to *their* editors.

Anyone who's a hunter or fisherman, or knows people who are, is aware that many of them cut loose with salty language when they miss a shot or the big one gets away. But most outdoor magazine editors want their writers to go easy on the expletives. Study of a magazine will show you just how accurately you can recount your verbal reaction when that _____ tent sprang a leak during the downpour. You'll be able to tell, too, whether your targeted editor wants you to mention brand names or prefers that you use generic terms. One taboo is consistent throughout—no booze in the boat or the blind. And *never* recount any experience tnat flouts the law or safety rules.

Another bit of time-saving information you'll gather from reading similar articles is how much off-the-scene research you'll have to do. An article on mule deer in *Field & Stream,* for instance, was packed with information and statistics in combination with an account of one of the author's hunting experiences. It's the kind of article that points the way to informational sources the writer would need to contact if he or she wished to write a similar piece for that magazine. The number of deer tags issued in 1979, how many deer were harvested in a certain area, where the various hunting zones are and most of the other statistics, it's a sure bet, came from the California Department of Fish and Game.

Most of all, analysis will dictate the style you use. Even among the big three—magazines the layman sees as pretty much alike—there are distinct stylistic requirements for writers who hope to succeed. Just read the leads from articles from each of them, all on trout, that exemplify what their respective editors generally choose as far as style is concerned. You'll notice the reportorial, fact-filled sort of material *Field & Stream* shows a preference for in this piece called "The Allure of High Trout Lakes":

> Although June brings summer weather to the Northern California foothills and valleys, most back-country areas, which are several thousand feet higher, are still in a springtime mood. Now is one of the most pleasant times for hiking or horse packing into

one of the region's national forest wilderness areas to fish the high lakes.

In this part of Northern California there are four national forests, including Shasta-Trinity, Lassen, Modoc, and Klamath. Together they contain roughly 6½ million acres of public land. Included within the forests are six Wilderness Areas with a total of 651,000 acres. Four of the six have lots of high-lake fishing to offer. The remaining two, the Yolla Bolly-Middle Eel Wilderness and the South Warner Wilderness are different in character. The Yolla Bolly-Middle Eel has very little fishable water. The South Warner area offers good stream fishing but only one major lake—Patterson. At the end of an 8-mile trail it has good fishing at times, and it's visited often.

Sports Afield's editorial staff chooses a preponderance of personal experience pieces, and the alert analyst will discern immediately how different they are in tone from those of the magazine's two major competitors, despite the fact that they contain equally as much information. As in the following example, the conversational lead is a *Sports Afield* favorite:

We had driven more than 400 miles to fish for trophy trout, and after two days of dawn-to-dusk casting hadn't landed a fish larger than 14 inches. The weather, we knew, was to blame. But when I awoke early on the third morning and looked out my motel-room window, my hopes suddenly soared.

"Marv, wake up! C'mere quick," I called to my sleeping cousin and fishing buddy Marv Camper. Outside, snow swirled silently in the cone of light spreading from the streetlamp. There had to be at least six inches of the white stuff on the ground, and the thermometer outside the window registered 14° F.

"Now we'll get some action," Marv exclaimed sleepily.

Contrast the folksy tone, typical of *Sports Afield,* with the style of this third-person article called "Four Records That Won't Be Broken," from *Outdoor Life:*

Wes Hamlet had no real reason to be optimistic as he and his fishing partner motored toward the deep waters off the Monarch Rocks on a cold morning in late November 1947. After all, the Coeur d'Alene, Idaho, angler had fished the sprawling waters of northern Idaho's Lake Pend Oreille a dozen times before and returned home empty-handed each time. A superstitious person wouldn't have given much for his chances on this 13th outing.

But, like most fishermen around that part of Idaho, Hamlet had heard the stories about large Kamloops rainbow trout transplanted several years earlier from British Columbia's Kootenay

Lake. Those early plants had grown fast, thanks to an expanding kokanee salmon population that served as a rich source of food, and the lake had already produced several trout of 20 pounds or more.

The two fishermen were on the water early that November 25, and it paid off. At 8:30 a.m. a good fish smacked Hamlet's trolled Lucky Louie plug, and a short time later he boated a thick-bodied Kamloops. It was his first big Pend Oreille trout, but he and his partner estimated it at about 25 pounds—no larger than some of the others they had seen or heard about, so they kept fishing.

Three excerpts don't make an analysis, but as you read several articles from each publication, consistent patterns will emerge. You will find that *Outdoor Life* is the more adventure/suspense oriented of the three—indicated not only by writing style and subject matter, but also by titles and blurbs. "Knee Deep in Crocodiles—Our scientific study of crocodiles in Kenya's Lake Rudolf almost cost us our lives," "Bear Attack!—from the man who survived unprovoked attack and fight to the death with a 400-pound grizzly," and "Magnum Mankiller: Bull Elephant!—to find out about elephant hunting, try walking up to one with a steel and wood toothpick and the ridiculous intent of doing harm" are three of the more exciting topics, to be sure. But they serve to point out that *Outdoor Life*'s editors want to inject drama into their pieces, whether it be about snagging a bluegill or lighting a fire with wet wood.

Analysis will point up still other subtleties. As Dave Bowring, contributing editor to *Sports Afield*, says, "What sells at one magazine may fail at another. This is due to differences in philosophy and format. For example, some popular mags demand that the writer relating a fishing or hunting trip be successful and include at least one good photo of smiling-man-dead-fish or animal. At *Sports Afield*, we would rather stress what it is like to *be* there, rather than the kill or catch itself. What does the pine knot fire smell like? Relating the eerie cries of a coyote, the aroma of bacon over an open fire. In short, trying to put the reader in the locale by using every sensory metaphor that works."

If you were to talk to other outdoor editors about their writing preferences, no two responses would be exactly the same. It's true, as outdoor writer Norm Strung asserts, that in order to succeed one must be a good and professional writer, who understands theme, tone, figurative language, how to put a meaningful anecdote together, and most important, how to string thoughts and facts together with smooth transitions. Catchy titles, gripping introductions, and satisfying conclusions are also part of this craft. But in order to bring home your limit on almost every writing expedition, reading those editors' minds is imperative, too.

Once you start studying outdoor articles, you'll realize that they're not written by babes in the woods. But even if you don't know a spinner from a sinker and can't tell a centerfire rifle from a 12-gauge shotgun, even if your sheepshanks and granny knots would make a Cub Scout blush, read them anyway. You just might become so intrigued that you end up with a new hobby and another outlet for your writing skills.

15

Have Typewriter
Will Travel

As a Spanish proverb says, "He who would bring home the wealth of the Indies must carry the wealth of the Indies with him." So it is in traveling: A man must carry knowledge with him, if he would bring home knowledge.

—Samuel Johnson

I love travel—sixteen-hours-a-day, see-all-the-sights, never-a-dull-moment travel. It's even better when I can write those trips off on my income tax.

Travel writing is one of my favorites for two reasons. First of all, I enjoy the research. New scenes and new faces are far more fascinating than library stacks. Secondly, I want to be a winner. And right now, travel writing is where a lot of the action is. In 1970, *Writer's Market* listed one hundred thirty-four magazines seeking travel material. Ten years later, their number had grown to more than three hundred.

There are even more pluses. The subject matter is limitless. Variations in treatment are as great as the writer will encounter. And travel writing doesn't necessarily involve jet planes to Singapore or cruise ships on the Mediterranean. You'll find that attractions six blocks from your home or a few miles from the office have all the allure of faraway places to editors in a different part of the country. During my writing career, I've sold more than two dozen travel articles about places less than a thirty-five minute drive away, and I have by no means exhausted the possibilities. For these reasons, and the diversity of writing skill levels required, it is one of the easiest markets for beginning writers to break into.

Analysis helps you travel farther and faster on the road to article sales. Knowing the kinds of articles and the type of treatment an editor wants assures that your queries and manuscripts won't be flying in the wrong direction. So let's talk about what you'll need to know.

Divide and Conquer

The first step along the road to a travel-writing career is an evaluation of marketing possibilities. This can be a formidable task, since the publications that buy travel articles are varied, diverse, *and* plentiful. Study the different publications so you can determine which of them best dovetail with your own areas of travel interest and offer you the greatest chance of success.

My analysis of the twelve categories of travel-buying publications will give you a head start.

1. *Airline inflights.* Like the snacks, meals, and beverages served on board, the purpose of these magazines is to make passengers' flights pleasant and the time pass more quickly. They also are aimed at stimulating the readers' desire to travel. Travel articles deal almost exclusively with destinations along the particular airline's route (most inflights contain a route map, so it's easy to see what cities and countries they serve), although in some cases they may feature places that are near destination cities and require surface transportation, or places that can be reached via a connecting flight on a different air carrier.

Though the majority of publishing companies that put out inflights have only one airline as client, East/West Network, Inc., based in Los Angeles, Halsey Publishing of Miami, Florida, and the Webb Company of St. Paul, Minnesota, each produce more than one airline magazine. A possible bonus of writing for these companies is that your article will be printed in more than one magazine, and you'll receive additional payment.

Rate of pay for most inflights begins at ten cents a word. Many of them pay three hundred dollars and up for 1,500- to 2,000-word articles when they have worked with a writer in the past. Several of the magazines use 500- to 1,000-word destination pieces, which are one of the writer's best ways to break into the travel field.

2. *Food and drink publications.* These are the magazines such as *Gourmet* and *Bon Appetit,* whose primary emphasis is on food. Their travel pieces generally incorporate the points of interest in an area along with material on regional foods, like "Kentucky's Bluegrass Cooking," "Great Restaurant Recipes from Brussels," and "Culinary Legacy of Historic Inns."

I've found the magazines in this group to be deceptive in that much of their material appears to be the work of freelancers. In actuality, most of it is staff-written or assigned to writers who specialize in food/travel pieces. Rate of payment ranges from about two cents a word to more than five hundred dollars for a 2,500- to 3,000-word article.

3. *General-interest publications.* Many of these magazines, like the *Saturday Evening Post* and *Reader's Digest,* have wide exposure on newsstands. They explore a variety of subjects, and their travel needs vary from an occasional article in *Grit* to several pieces each month in *National Geographic.* Demographically, there are vast differences in readership. *Country Clubber* is aimed at country club members in the metropolitan South. *Town and Country* is published for "upper-income Americans." Articles in those two tend to be sophisticated. On the other hand, *Grit* is "for residents of all ages in small-town and rural America who are interested in people and generally take a positive view of life," according to its editor, Terry L. Ziegler.

As you determine your special markets in this category, you'll do best to avoid the high-profile books and focus your efforts on magazines such as *Easy Living Magazine,* a saver's club publication put out by Webb, and *Goodstay,* a magazine distributed to patients in hospitals. Pay in this category ranges from a few cents per word to thousands of dollars for *National Geographic* articles.

4. *Newspaper travel sections and weekly supplements.* This is the biggest market for travel material in the country, and the easiest way for beginning writers to break into print. The major newspapers are listed in *Writer's Market,* but all over the country, smaller dailies and weeklies are on the lookout for articles on interesting places. Rates of pay vary from less than a

dollar per column inch to up to several hundred dollars for articles sold to publications like the *New York Times.*

As with magazines, newspaper travel writing styles and the kinds of material they're enthusiastic about differ widely. The *Sacramento Union Weekender,* for example, is interested in offbeat, unusual items anywhere in the world, whereas many other publications want pieces on attractions within their geographical area. The *New York Times* travel articles appeal to worldly, experienced travelers; those in *The Islander,* a publication in British Columbia, have a folksy, homespun style.

5. *Men's magazines.* This is one of the least promising markets, since the magazines don't use a lot of travel material. When they do, it emphasizes hunting, fishing or active sports or focuses on exotic, erotic, places. Most of the publications pay about ten cents a word or less, with the exception of the big circulation books like *Oui,* where again it's a case of high pay and stiff competition.

6. *Specialized magazines.* The magazines in this catch-all category appeal to groups of people with highly divergent interests, philosophies, lifestyles, ages, and backgrounds. Travel relates directly to the particular magazine's focus—traveling with baby in *Baby Talk;* good hunting or fishing locales for *Field & Stream;* travel appealing to homosexuals in *GPU News.*

This is not to say that a single travel idea couldn't fit the format of several magazines. Recipients of *The California Highway Patrolman, The Dakota Farmer,* and *Texaco Tempo,* though their occupations differ, might well be interested in the same travel subjects. But almost always each publication demands minor (or major) differences in approach.

Payment rates vary from as little as one-fourth cent per word to figures like six hundred dollars for a 2,000-word article.

7. *Motor club magazines and magazines published by auto manufacturers.* These publications cover all aspects of motor travel, from tuning up the motor to traveling with pets to vacation bargains. Only two, *Friends* (published by Chevrolet)

and *Ford Times,* devote any appreciable share of editorial space to other than auto-related subjects. The magazines concentrate on places their readers might want to visit by car and are looked upon by their sponsors as advertising tools.

Although most of these magazines use material about North American travel exclusively, a few such as *Odyssey, Friends, Minnesota Motorist,* and *Ohio Motorist* buy pieces on foreign travel. *Away* prefers travel with a New England angle. *National Motorist* concentrates on California, Pacific Slope, and western states motoring. *Small World,* the magazine of Volkswagen, emphasizes people, rather than places, in its travel articles.

The motor club magazines will be well worth your analysis. Since they reach only a controlled list of readers, writers aren't overworking the mailmen who deliver their queries. And since many of them are subsidized as an advertising cost, rates of payment to writers are higher than you might expect. Ten to fifteen cents a word is usually the starting rate; twenty cents and more is not uncommon.

8. *Recreational vehicle magazines.* I include in this category recreational vehicles in the broadest sense of the term—motorcycles, boats, airplanes, as well as the four-wheel homes away from home. Of this group, motorhome and trailer publications offer the most opportunities for freelancers, with almost all of them carrying one to four destination pieces each issue. They're among the easiest of all travel categories to analyze. In fact, this is the only group in which one article with very minor changes might fit into any number of magazines. You'll find that these articles always contain a tie-in with camping facilities. Usually, public transportation within the area is covered. Hotels and motels aren't mentioned, but dining out is (the cook occasionally wants a night off, even in a motorhome). Most of the recreational vehicle magazines pay about ten cents a word.

9. *Regional magazines.* Some of these magazines are produced with private capital. Others are put out under the auspices of state or city agencies to promote tourism within their areas. Whatever their sponsorship, these magazines not only want potential visitors to know about their local points of interest, but

also aim to give readers who live within the region positive feelings about attractions in their area.

Perhaps the most public-relations-oriented magazines that use travel material, the regional magazines aren't at all receptive to derogatory comments, but their editors don't like the chamber-of-commerce-brochure approach either. The articles usually focus on one point of interest, putting the subject in its best light. Pay rates vary widely.

10. *House and garden magazines.* These books, devoted to house and garden, in my opinion aren't worth querying, since so much of their travel is staff-written. Rates of pay are excellent—up to two thousand dollars for *Better Homes and Gardens*—but the chances are so slim you'll make more profitable use of your time trying elsewhere.

11. *Travel magazines.* More than two-thirds of these publications have been established since 1960 and the category can be divided into three subsections: those aimed at the general public, monthly newsletters, and magazines published for people in the travel industry. Top publications in the first category pay as much as three thousand dollars for full-length features. The newsletters buy expos items and how-to tips, for which they pay around twenty dollars. I've found when I'm traveling that it's easy to come up with several of these items without doing any extra research.

Writing for the travel industry magazines is an opportunity many freelancers ignore. Although most of them pay somewhat less than ten cents a word, the material they use is easy to write: articles contain a good number of facts and the style is reportorial in most cases. They demand a lot of phone time (checking current room rates, plane fares) but can be done in conjunction with pieces you're writing on the same subjects for other publications. Travel trade magazines, too, are always on the lookout for items about new tourist attractions, so you can often write for them without wandering far from home.

12. *Women's publications.* Most of these magazines are difficult markets to break into. The limited travel material they

use is generally written by staffers or contributing editors. Their needs are varied—honeymoon destinations for *Modern Bride,* family-oriented vacations for *Family Circle* and *Woman's Day,* exotic hideaways for *Playgirl.* If you do manage to get a go-ahead, the pay is great—as much as twenty-five hundred dollars—but your chances are almost as remote as winning a magazine's sweepstakes contest.

Identifying the Best Sellers

The next—but just as important—step is gaining a knowledge of the popular types of articles. There are ten of them and many combinations thereof. Look through a variety of magazines that publish travel material and you're sure to recognize each one.

The *broad brush* piece tells about many of an area's attractions and is the kind you'll see most often. It's a once-over-lightly piece, devoting a phrase, a sentence, or at most, a paragraph, to each of the points of interest.

Titles such as "Seattle—Holiday City on the Sound," "England's Lake Country," and "Bargain Hunting in Hong Kong" alert the reader to expect broad brush treatment of the theme.

The *place/event* piece describes one specific tourist attraction or event in depth, be it an art gallery, posh resort or rock concert. Topics can include everything from restorations such as Pioneer Arizona to the St. Louis Arch to the Shakespearean Festival in Ashland, Oregon. Before deciding to write this kind of article you must be sure that it's interesting enough to justify a piece of the required word length and that there's sufficient information to write about.

Round-ups contain information about several events or places with a common theme—folk festivals, unusual museums, holiday celebrations, and the like. Many round-ups include service information such as dates, hours, and locations. "This Summer's Rodeos," "East Coast Industrial Tours," and "The Caribbean's Ten Top Fishing Spots" are the kinds of titles that identify round-up articles at a glance.

The *service* article, whether broad brush, round-up or place/event, is set apart by its emphasis on costs, street addresses, and sources of further information. It usually begins with from one to a dozen paragraphs of straight prose setting the mood of the places or events, then goes on to deal with dining, hotel accommodations, transportation and sightseeing specifics. You can use the service treatment on a broad topic like Los Angeles or a much narrower one such as a theme park as long as you have enough nuts-and-bolts information (costs, hours open, credit cards accepted, available transportation, and the like).

How-to pieces can cover every aspect of travel from taking good pictures through grimy train windows to traveling with your mother-in-law. Choosing a cruise, finding a hotel that's right for you, packing without pain—whenever you think of a problem associated with travel and have some solutions, you have the beginnings of a travel how-to.

With inflation, articles on stretching travel dollars have become increasingly salable.

Specialty articles are travel pieces that incorporate some specific hobby, activity, or pastime with an area, such as an article on Phoenix highlighting area golf courses, or scuba diving in St. Thomas. A pleasant way to generate ideas for this kind of piece is to pursue your hobby while you travel. Contact hobbyists in the places you visit: they'll tell you where to go in their area. If you collect dollhouse furniture or bottle caps or paper fans, seek out special collections or displays along your route. Tour the yacht clubs or tennis courts or ski slopes. Take copious notes and photos, collect every brochure you can lay your hands on, and your specialty articles will be all but written when you return home.

Travel diary pieces are personal experience accounts of trips. Written in first person, they fit into a limited number of editorial formats, but the editors who prefer diary accounts buy few other types.

The travel diary article usually centers around a humorous incident, an unusual experience, or a reminiscence comparing a well-known tourist spot today and years ago. You'll notice that this kind of article is most often the work of a very well-known writer.

You-are-there articles, heavily laced with anecdotes, quotes, and human interest, are intended to give the armchair traveler the feeling of participation. You'll find excellent examples of this style in every issue of *National Geographic*. In order to write this kind of piece, you must have access to a variety of people who live in the place you're writing about. Most you-are-there articles are written about exciting or exotic locales and events—bullfights in Spain, Samoan village life, San Francisco or Shanghai night-spots.

A variation of the you-are-there is the *mood* piece, usually written by literary figures such as James Michener or Leon Uris. In these articles, the writer becomes an artist, using his typewriter to paint impressions.

Hard news articles, written in reportorial style, are most often found in the travel trade publications. These articles may tell about a new resort that is opening, additional airline routes, or other news of interest to people in the business. "Amtrak Fares Increase," "Largest Casino in the World Opens May 3" and "Hotel Announces Special Weekend Rates" aren't exciting titles, but they denote the kinds of articles making up most of the travel trade publications' copy.

Hard news travel in newspapers is usually staff written.

Photo essays require more skill with a camera than a typewriter. They involve only a short text; the pictures (usually five or six of them) are what sell the piece. Almost any subjects that are photogenic qualify as photo essay material—country roads, city skylines, foreign faces, or footgear. The only hard-and-fast rule is that all the photos in an essay must embrace a single theme.

Going Deeper Into Analysis

Another step in pretrip planning is a thorough analysis of article possibilities along the travel route.

By planning ahead, travel writing offers a unique opportunity to gather information for several pieces at once. Most destinations have potential for more than one article. By keeping prospective markets' requirements in mind (or better yet, written down on paper) and a list of appropriate ideas to pursue, you'll be able to handle on-the-scene research efficiently.

If there's time before departure, I send for brochures. Additional information is often available in guidebooks. I look for attractions that might lend themselves to place pieces, to articles on native crafts, customs, cookery, and recreational facilities. It's important, too, to see if there are any interesting spots nearby that haven't been included in your itinerary, as a two-hour side-trip can provide material for additional articles. Not long ago, I spent a morning in Sacramento gathering information for an assignment. I finished sooner than anticipated and had five hours to spend before my return home. The material I was able to accumulate in that short time because of pretrip planning resulted in sales of three 500-word pieces.

Let's look at some some specific examples. Say you're planning a trip to Mexico and will visit five cities—San Miguel de Allende, Dolores Hidalgo, Guanajuato, Morelia, and Patzcuaro. Your pretravel analysis might go something like this:

First, you study the markets to see what magazines use pieces on Mexican travel, eliminating those that have featured the country in recent issues. Next, guidebooks and brochures at hand, you start listing article possibilities. Perhaps you can arrange your visit to coincide with market days or fiestas. You might be able to attend small-town bullfights or interview well-known artisans. You find that your destinations are rich historically, that they lend themselves to broad brush articles. You'll discover that there are place piece possibilities galore—the old silver mines at Guanajuato, the island of Janitzio in Lake Patzcuaro, the candy market in Morelia. Toys, regional dances, games and sports, deluxe resorts—an hour or two of research will reveal dozens of potential article ideas.

After you've accumulated a number of them, start matching up these ideas with the magazines you've selected as your best bets. Through analysis of what a publication has gone for in the past, you'll be able to calculate what its editor will like in the future.

Not all places promise such a wealth of articles as Mexico, but whatever your destination, your idea-generating mechanism shouldn't be stuck for long. If you approach the problem analytically, coming up with ideas is almost as simple as phoning your travel agent for reservations. It just takes a bit longer.

All you have to do is gather together a good number of back issues of a publication you'd like to write for and start analyzing. One overcast afternoon, I visited the reference section of our local library and asked for five years' back copies of *Travel/*

Travel-Holiday (the two merged in 1977 and retained what basically was the former magazine's personality). After four hours of study, I had a profile of what the editors are looking for.

During that five-year period, *Travel/Holiday* published almost equal numbers of domestic and foreign destination pieces, with a slight edge favoring international travel. About 40 percent of the articles were about cities; another 40 percent focused on whole countries or regions of a country. Approximately 10 percent were about islands; only six articles were about states and one featured cruises.

That information didn't tell me enough. The titles did. Take these, for example: "South America by Ship," "Gypsy Carting in France," "Europe's Scenic Train Rides," "Traveling by Freighter," "Biking in Holland," "Barging Through Britain." Then look at some others: "Copenhagen at Night with the Kids," "Oslo in Winter," "Thanksgiving at Old Sturbridge," "Thurber's Bermuda," "Mark Twain Country."

Upon skimming the articles I found that almost all of them were broad brush or place pieces about popular tourist destinations. With a few exceptions, I had seen a good many articles on the same geographical areas in other magazines. What set the Travel-Holiday pieces apart is that they were angled toward a specific mode of transportation, a certain time of year, a historical or literary figure. I haven't had time yet to query *Travel/ Holiday* on the basis of my survey, but when I do I'll have a roadmap to follow.

Travel/Holiday isn't the only magazine you can use to read its editor's mind like a book. Editors of *Discovery,* Allstate Motor Club's magazine, say, "We like narrative accounts of trips, with incidents and quotes (especially humorous ones) worked in, to keep them light and lively." A quick look through back issues of the magazine confirms this. That quick look will show you also that each issue features four "weekend" articles geared to a theme such as walking, bicycling, gas-saving or budget and that round-up pieces about such subject as zany contests and unusual museums are popular, too.

Each issue of *Travel & Leisure* has a theme, your investigations will show—The Romance of Travel, Strictly American,

The Art of Doing Nothing, The Mediterranean. Not *all* of the articles in an issue follow the theme, but several of them do. For example, the issue on the Mediterranean included ten—everything from "Resorting to the High Life: Italian Style" to "The Glories of Garlic." A good way to anticipate future themes is to analyze past ones. An area that's been highlighted during the previous five to seven years most probably won't be featured again for awhile. Parallel areas or ideas will.

You'll also notice that *Travel & Leisure* uses "series" pieces. These series, on such subjects as Great American Weekends and Airports, as well as shorter articles on hobbies, small hotels and the like, are easy to analyze and offer the best chances for writers new to the publication to make sales.

Many of the magazines that use travel articles have ongoing series or pieces that fit into a theme appearing each issue. *Odyssey,* you'll find, has "Cities and Sights," with pieces of about 500 words tightly packed with information. *Odyssey* also carries "People in Travel," a department featuring people who travel in frequent pursuit of professions or hobbies. *Trailer Life* features "Rolling The Cities." To give yourself the best odds in selling a series piece, analyze back copies to see what places have been written about, then come up with ideas about different spots that have the same sorts of attractions.

When to Pop the Question

Should querying be a pre- or post-trip affair? Read the magazines you want to write for to find out. Most broad brush articles contain information you can be positive of obtaining, so you can send out queries with assurance. Some, though, rely heavily on interviews with local people or insights into daily life that you can't be certain of in advance. If you're positive you'll be able to research the number of cathedrals, markets, or renaissance fairs a publication's articles call for, advance queries for round-up articles won't get you in trouble. But I've found that querying for a place piece before I've seen the place can be disastrous. Guidebooks have a way of putting every attraction in its most appealing light and I've found all too often that places I'd planned to write pieces around were those I wouldn't recommend to any traveler.

Granted, it's great to have assignments before you go, or even go-aheads on speculation, but if you're at all leery about your ability to deliver, save querying until you return home. Assignments or not, I always jot down enough information about publications I'm interested in so that whatever preconceived ideas are discarded en route or new ones are added, my research will allow me a variety of choices when the article writing begins.

Perhaps, for example, I've chosen *Travel/Holiday, Travel & Leisure, Odyssey, Motorhome Life,* the *New York Times, Bon Appetit,* and as a long shot *National Geographic.* My first set of notes, based on analysis of six issues of each, would look something like Table 3.

Divide the number of words in the Preferred Article Length column by 500 (the size samples from which quote and anecdote information is taken). Multiply your result by the number of average anecdotes and quotes each publication uses. For instance, divide 500 into 4,000 for *National Geographic.* Then multiply the answer, eight, by 2.3 and 1.5. You'll see that 18 or 19 quotes and 12 anecdotes are needed for a 4,000-word piece. You'll need one or two quotes and the same number of anecdotes for an *Odyssey* article of 2,500 words. I always try to get a few extras, as it's extremely difficult to fabricate a good anecdote and equally hard (and unethical if it's attributed to someone) to make up a quote.

Pack Your Mind with Techniques

Before you take off, become familiar with the various devices successful travel writers use to give their pieces personality. Keep these devices in mind while you're taking notes on your trip and you'll find much of the work has been done when you arrive home.

Dialogue figures heavily in such articles as *Discovery*'s weekend pieces. Examine any one of these articles and you'll read what the tour guide, the motel owner, other vacationers and the waitress said. These snatches of conversation transmit information to the reader, while giving an air of informality to the work.

Table 3.

Publication	Predominant Article Types	Preferred Article Length	Quotes per 500 Words	Anecdotes per 500 Words
Travel/Holiday	Broad brush, Place	1,500-3,000	0	.17
Travel & Leisure	Service, Broad brush, Place	750-3,000	.2	0
Odyssey	Broad brush, Place	500-2,500	.3	.3
Motorhome Life	Broad brush, Place, Specialty	1,000-2,500	1.0	0
New York Times	Broad brush, Specialty	2,500	0	.17
Bon Appetit	Specialty, Broad brush	850-1,500	.33	.17
National Geographic	You-are-there	4,000-8,000	2.3	1.5

For example, instead of the writer telling the reader, "Not long ago, we spent a walking weekend on Galveston Island, a place known for its history, natural beauty, good shopping and loads of recreational opportunities," a writer wishing to sell to *Discovery* (and this one, Carol Rush, did) would put it this way:

"What's full of history, natural beauty, good shopping and loads of recreational opportunities?" I asked my husband.

"I don't know," he replied from behind his newspaper.

"And where can you find all these attractions on foot with a minimum of driving?" I queried.

The talking newspaper responded, "I don't know."

"And where are we going to spend next weekend enjoying these activities?"

"Galveston Island," he said smugly, putting down his paper. "I overheard you making reservations."

Another device is what I call the *Texture, Smell, Sound* technique. It gives the reader a sense of the place, as Phyllis Funke did in this piece called "Manhattan's Lower East Side," which was published in United Airlines' *Mainliner*.

The music pulsing through the bookstore has a definitely Asian twang. The scent drifting from the restaurant is decidedly Mediterranean-garlicky. And the man pulling a cart down the street shouting to no one in particular, "So what can I do, Mechel? The guy wants it on Thursday," sound exactly like Tevye the milkman, of *Fiddler on the Roof,* communing with his God.

Also helping to give the reader a you-are-there feeling is the use of *visual words*. But there's a trap here. Nothing turns off an editor faster than clichés—palm trees swaying in the breeze, breathtaking sunsets and the like. Unless your visualizations are fresh, this won't be your kind of writing. I particularly like these paragraphs from an article called "New England's Blend of Sea and Season" by Jonathan Evan Maslow, which also appeared in *Mainliner*. It's an anecdote with an abundance of well-chosen visual words.

A sturdy little Cape Cod cottage stood at the tip of a sandy promontory. It faced directly toward the ocean and, as a result, square into the face of New England's fabled northeaster storms as well. I used to spend summers nearby, and each year when I walked past the cottage on my way fishing or swimming or digging for clams, I couldn't help but notice the cliff erosion of the previous winter. One year the house would be six feet from the edge, the next four feet, and then two. Finally, the front porch hung out over the vanishing promontory like buck teeth.

Now this charming summer house, like so many along the New England coast, had been built for a city couple by an elderly Yankee carpenter. His face was weathered as Cape Cod shingles, his hands seemed hewn of human hardwood. When a city "smack" like myself asked him what he did for a living, the craggy Yankee would reply with typical New England under-statement, "I bang boards." I used to see him come by the cottage now and then in his patina-covered pickup truck. With a nail between his teeth he'd stand at the edge of the cliff, his great arms folded across his chest, staring silently at the gulls over the ocean foam—you half-expected he knew the exact moment the cottage would plunge over and down the fifty feet to the beach. But couldn't something be done to save the place, I asked him? He looked me hard in the eye. "Not a heck of a lot," he allowed. "Lest ye think ye can outlaw gales."

Metaphors and *similes,* as you've no doubt noticed, figure in any writing that attempts to let the reader participate vicariously in a travel experience. *Slices of history* interspersed in the travel article give the reader necessary background and help move the pieces along. By reading back issues, you can find out just how much historical information an editor likes, or if he wants any at all. Most of the time, historical information is sprinkled lightly, as in this paragraph from "The Best Dam Tour in Washington" by Herb Williams, which appeared in *Chevron USA:*

> More history can be relived at Republic, one of the West's old gold towns. At the height of the gold boom around the turn of the century, it had 148 mining operations. The boom faded, but the Nob Hill Mine was opened in 1935 and is still one of the country's leading producers. The old mines are visible throughout the area, but the greatest care should be used around them; open shafts and tunnels are extremely dangerous. While exploring, you might run across a few gold mining hobbyists, who work small claims for fun and a few dollars a day.

Another tool in the skilled travel writer's bag is the ability to generate *enthusiasm*. The reader feels good about a piece when it's there. Without it, an article is somehow like unsalted mashed potatoes. The writer's excitement about his subject goes a long way in establishing reader rapport. That rapport is further strengthened by use of the second person—"You won't want to miss," "you'll find that." Likening new sights and experiences to those most readers are already familiar with (about the size of Georgia, twice as high as Niagara Falls) also helps them identify.

Last but not least (in many cases, first) of the article personality elements is *human interest*. We want to know what people in other parts of our country and the world are like. What do they wear? Where do they work? How do they play? But we prefer this information when it's personalized, as in this article from *National Geographic* called "Journey to China's Far West," by Rick Gore.

> Beneath the arbor of an elderly farmer we sit on bright Hotan carpets and admire the ripe grapes overhead. "Our weather is such that we can let them dangle all summer and eat them at will," he says.
>
> His wife brings a plate of bread, cheese, and handsomely curled fried wheat noodles called *sangza*. The bread is hard, so the farmer shows me that it should be dipped in tea. I ask his name. "Aziz," he replies. "Do Uygur people have only one name?" I ask. "We just use first names in everyday life. There is no need to do otherwise."
>
> Aziz and his wife, Imsahan, invite us inside their home. Their bed is a hard earthen slab, about ten feet by twelve, covered with a rough hair blanket and several multicolored quilts An elegant old tapestry covers the wall. Beside it hang a lutelike instrument called a *dutar* and a portait of Chairman Hua. On a table sit an alarm clock and a portable radio. They have another room, which holds their sewing machine and serves as a parlor. When I ask how Communism has affected their lives, they simply say: "Before, we were poverty stricken. We were unable to get things."

Home Again

When you're back home, laden with brochures and your travel notebook, resist the temptation to begin writing until you've done your final analysis—for adjectives, adverbs, sentence and paragraph length and polysyllabic words (see Chapter 7). Analysis of the same magazines used in the pretrip planning illustration produces the results shown in Table 4.

Differences on the chart don't look large, but remember that you will divide the articles' lengths by 100 and then multiply the figures in the adjective, adverb and polysyllabic words columns by your answers to come up with the approximate number of each you'll want in your pieces.

You'll also want to note the form of address an editor prefers, the number of statistics required, and the paragraph in which the lead sentence usually appears (see Table 5).

During this session, also be on the lookout for the kinds of transitions. Fortunately, transitions in travel articles are among

Table 4.

Publication	Adjectives per 100	Adverbs per 100	Sentence Length	Paragraph Length	Polysyllabic Words per 100
Travel/Holiday	12.8	.87	21.8	85.9	13.6
Travel & Leisure	7.2	1.4	18	156	8.4
Odyssey	13.7	.7	21.1	96.2	10.7
Motorhome Life	13.7	.7	22.4	81.8	12.7
New York Times	14.7	.8	23.7	87.1	8.5
Bon Appetit	13.8	.9	22.2	83.3	11.9
National Geographic	14.6	.96	18.5	58.8	9.7

Table 5.

Publication	Statistics per 500 Words	Predominant Form of Address	Paragraph With Lead Sentence
Travel/Holiday	4.5	3rd	1st
Travel & Leisure	10	3rd	1st, 2nd
Odyssey	4.4	1st/3rd	1st
Motorhome Life	7.8	3rd	1st, 2nd, 3rd
New York Times	4.0	3rd, 1st	1st
Bon Appetit	4.3	3rd, 1st	2nd
National Geographic	4.7	1st	1st through 9th

the easiest to make, with time or location often bridging one paragraph to another—around the corner, the next afternoon, two miles down the road, on the first weekend in May.

Be aware, too, of tone. Is it light, chatty, no-nonsense, glamorous, humorous? Some articles sound like advice from a good travel agent; some like a travelogue. Still others have the ring of a good friend sharing memories. Certain editors like names of celebrities who visit the magazines' featured spots scattered through the copy. If they do, that's another detail you can't afford to miss.

Thou Shalt Nots

We've talked about editorial preferences, but not taboos. I've found that publications which use travel articles have more prohibitions than others. Airline inflights aren't pleased when you write more than absolutely necessary about surface transportation, and since many airlines have interests in hotels and resorts, they don't like to give free plugs to their competitors either.

The lengths to which you can go about being candid are also built in. If you think Tokyo is a rip-off these days and say so in your piece, don't try to sell it to *Northwest Passages*. After all, Northwest Airlines wants to encourage passengers to fly to its route cities. Don't knock the rental car agencies, travel credit cards, or luxury hotels, either. Advertisers are offended by negative comments, and magazines are very sensitive to this pressure.

There are non-business-related taboos, too. Some airlines, I've found, will not publish any material related to gambling. Others steer away from anything that's in the least controversial. Donna Dupuy, managing editor of *Sky,* Delta Airline's inflight, says, "We have a foundational prohibition on ever saying anything negative about anything or anybody. The everyday press does a more than adequate job of presenting the negative and unpleasantries of life. Since we see part of our role as making passengers' flights as pleasant as possible, we talk about solutions rather than problems, emphasizing the positive."

Newspaper travel editors (and some magazine editors as well) don't go for mention of specific business concerns, restaurants, or hotels. They feel it smacks too much of advertising. On the other hand, there are some publications that *demand* names be used. Some magazines won't take pieces resulting from free trips the writers have taken. Recreational vehicle magazines generally aren't going to print articles on the large amounts of gas RVs consume, preferring more subtle approaches to the energy problem such as conservation and close-to-home destination pieces.

How do you find out about these editorial no-no's? The answer again is by studying the magazine and using your common sense. Be alert to telltale signs. If a publication never contains material that would offend anyone, don't put negative comments in the articles you submit to it. If statements about accommodations, points of interest and the like are candid, you can be, too. Pore over the ads, absorb the editors' pages, become a Sherlock Holmes in detecting what an editor's policies are from what he has bought in the past. Of course, you'll make a few mistakes—we all do—but by carefully analyzing the magazines you want to write for, you'll keep them to a minimum.

Even though you write a well-crafted piece and have used your knowledge of a magazine's preferences and taboos to the fullest, there are times you just can't win. It is a fact of the travel-writing life that the places of the world featured by magazines are often chosen with regard to advertising. Trade-offs of editorial copy for advertising are common. An illustration of this is the case of a publication (which shall remain nameless) that was offered eight pages of advertising if the editors would devote eight pages of editorial space in the same issue to an article on Reno. They assigned a writer to do the piece and gathered in a good deal of revenue in one fell swoop.

Sometimes, it works the opposite way. The magazine sells advertising on the basis of copy it plans to run. Not long ago I sold a piece on the Caribbean (with accompanying photos) to a small travel publication. Shortly after I'd sent in the material, the editor contacted me, asking what cruise lines' ships were in one of the photos. Then she went to the cruise lines for advertising. The editor of another magazine, who asked to see a travel piece on speculation, told me she would let me know if they could use it after she had talked to advertisers.

One of the most effective ways I know of targeting your

material to fit in with advertising is to read the travel trade publications (you can get copies of recent issues from your travel agent). You'll find out when the Montana Department of Tourism or the West German Travel Commission decides to embark on an advertising campaign. Often the articles mention the publications in which ads will appear. If they don't you can write and ask. Query the editors of magazines slated for advertising about places you want to write articles on and you'll increase your chances dramatically.

Travel writing is vacation with pay. But as with all magazine writing, the pleasure—and profit—increases when you've prepared properly in advance. By paying attention to analysis, you can insure that your byline isn't the result of random chance. You'll know it will keep appearing again and again, that your writing adventures won't be based on luck alone.

Bon voyage!

16

Catching Up with Your Past

God gave us memory that we might have roses in December.

—James M. Barrie

The gap between now and nostalgia is narrowing. With the pace of progress quickening, today's technology makes yesterday's scientific marvels obsolete; 1980s trends and innovations relegate those of the 1970s to old-fashioned status. When times change rapidly, the days when life moved less swiftly seem long ago.

It used to be that it took a generation to generate nostalgia. Not anymore. As Mark Shields quipped on public television's MacNeil/Lehrer Report, "I think Jerry Ford's 4.8 1974 inflation rate has made it into the Guinness Book of Records as the quickest nostalgia."

We don't have to look back very far to find what we remember as those good old uncomplicated days—nostalgia's inspiration. We don't have to *go* far to find nostalgic ideas, either, for they're waiting in the dusty attics of our minds.

Nostalgia is memory transferred to paper. It's a wistful, often bittersweet, examination of items, customs, or incidents from the past. The word *nostalgia,* as a matter of fact, is said to have been coined in 1686 by an Alsatian medical student named Johannes Hofer from Greek roots meaning "return home" and "pain." And whether that home be a ranch in Texas, a mansion in Grosse Pointe, or a flat in San Francisco, it doesn't matter. For you'll soon discover that the best nostalgia pieces have a sort of everyman appeal about them—an element that transcends geographical location, age, sex, economic, and social background. As Walt Wentz, associate editor of *Ruralite,* says, "Nostalgia is the re-creation of personal experience in such a way as to evoke a strong resonance in most readers—an emotional response which approximates the feeling which the writer recalls. Good nostalgia must depend in large part upon shared or universal experiences for its appeal."

The goal of the nostalgia article is to make a tear trickle down the reader's cheek, to elicit a chuckle, a groan, or a sigh. But the piece must also have a purpose—to entertain, inspire, instruct, or perhaps subtly point a moral. The amount of research required for most nostalgia pieces is minimal, making it the ideal kind of article for writers who must spend much of their time at home. All you need to begin writing are ideas, an ability to transmit your feelings for the past, analysis of the magazines you want to sell to, and a good knowledge of the markets.

Market Analysis

Since no professional freelancer contemplates writing an article unless there are potential buyers for it, let's talk about markets first. Though there aren't as many of them as for business, outdoor articles, or travel, there are still more than one hundred fifty listed in *Writer's Market*. Among those that use the most reminiscence are religious publications; general-interest magazines such as *Ford Times, Reader's Digest* and *Capper's Weekly;* automotive magazines; retirement, city, and regional publications. Several of the food and drink, sports, antiques, and music magazines also use nostalgia from time to time.

In order to best analyze your marketing possibilities, first check to see who's buying in *Writer's Market,* then make a notation in the margin opposite each entry (I use a capital *N).* Your next step is to go to the library, armed with a list of possibilities. Check the table of contents of back copies of as many of these magazines as you can find to determine how frequently each one prints nostalgia. You can usually tell by the titles, but in some cases it will be necessary to look at the articles to be sure.

As you study the markets, begin to compile your idea list. Dreaming up ideas for nostalgia articles is one of a writer's pleasures. Refining the idea and structuring the article may be work, but idea generating shouldn't be. You'll do the best job of memory retrieving during a time when you're not pressured by other projects or concerns, for reminiscing is a lazy-day occupation. It's an associative process, too, so you may want some props to help prime your memory.

1. Take out the photo album. Through association you'll be bombarded with memories—your first bike and the struggle to earn the money with which to buy it; your mother's favorite dress and how she made it over for you when you starred in the Christmas program at school; the house down the lane that you were sure was haunted.

2. Sort through mementos from your own childhood or from your children's. As you look at each object, try to put yourself back in time to the days when that object was a prized possession.

3. Look over old letters. Chances are, they'll recall incidents buried deep in memory.

4. List the names of old friends and jot down memories of what you did together. While you're jotting, you will think of people whose names you can't quite remember, and as you do, more memories will be triggered—the boy who lived in your small town's hotel for several months; the girl who came from New York to stay with her aunt and had a *fur coat;* the kid whose dad was the "Holy Rollers" preacher. These in turn will start you thinking about the Salvation Army band on the corner on Saturday nights and the baptisms in the river and the junkman who bought old furs and hides and drove a horse and buggy though everyone else went around in automobiles and how everyone made fun of his kids because they smelled of homemade potato chips. . .and before long you will have written down so many memories that you'll have to get yourself more paper.

5. Think about celebrations, family get-togethers, church suppers, band concerts in the park—the special events of your younger days.

6. As you go about your daily routine, recall how various household or business tasks used to be accomplished.

7. Listen to old phonograph records.

8. Read magazines and newspapers from decades past (and don't forget the ads).

9. Go into a shop that sells different varieties of tea or herbs and spices by the ounce and sniff of each jar. It's amazing what chamomile, anise and peppermint can do for the memory.

10. Visit a museum displaying artifacts from the not-too-distant past.

11. Glance through the nostalgia and collectibles books at your library.

12. Read nostalgia articles, both in the publications you hope to sell to and in others. "Where Have All the Aprons Gone?" which appeared in *Ford Times* might jog your memory mechanism into producing "Whatever Happened to Housedresses?"

You will reject some of the ideas. One-room schoolhouses, first dates, and lemonade stands, you will have seen during analysis, have been overdone. While holidays are the easiest past pleasures for most of us to remember, there's also more competition in the marketplace for pieces about the more popular days of the year. Whatever you decide, don't discard any of your ideas completely. Snippets of nostalgia, like scraps of pie crust, are too good to throw away. Those wisps of remembrance that have floated into your consciousness, while not enough in themselves to build an article around, should be filed away in a folder for possible use as conversational leads in non-nostalgia articles.

Remember It Well

As you test each idea, think of the kind of nostalgia article it would work most effectively in. While analyzing markets, you will have learned that there are seven formats most often used in bringing the past to the present.

The *personal reminiscence* is by far the most popular type of nostalgia piece and relies heavily on fictional techniques for its crafting. As long as its length and subject matter are appropriate, good nostalgia will fit a variety of magazines. Thus, unlike articles of other types, you won't have to redo pieces that are rejected before you submit them to other markets. But your nostalgia shouldn't bounce back with a hateful rejection note if you study the best reminiscence examples you can find and use the same devices their authors have used.

The tone of the personal reminiscence is conversational/story-telling, and success hinges upon the writer's gift for dialogue and description. A story by Truman Capote—actually the reprint of a very small book—that appeared in the December, 1966, issue of *Ladies' Home Journal*, called "A Christmas Memory," could serve as a text on fashioning personal reminiscence nostalgia, I'm convinced (so convinced that I read it over two or three times each year). These opening lines set the stage for an enchanting story:

> Imagine a morning in late November. A coming of winter morning more than twenty years ago. Consider the kitchen of a spreading old house in a country town. A great black stove is its main feature, but there is also a big round table and a fireplace with two rocking chairs placed in front of it. Just today, the fireplace commenced its seasonal roar.
>
> A woman with shorn white hair is standing at the kitchen window. She is wearing tennis shoes and a shapeless gray sweater over a summery calico dress. She is small and sprightly, like a bantam hen, but due to a long youthful illness, her shoulders are pitifully hunched. Her face is remarkable, not unlike Lincoln's, craggy like that, and tinted by sun and wind, but it is delicate, too, finely boned, and her eyes are sherry-colored and timid. "Oh, my," she exclaims, her breath smoking the windowpane, "it's fruitcake weather."

Though the piece is nostalgia, you'll note that it is written in the present tense—a good technique for giving the reader the feeling that he or she is watching the action as it happens.

The piece is much longer than most personal reminiscences and tells about a seven-year old boy and his "sixty-something" best friend cousin's preparations for Christmas. There is dialogue woven throughout, which, along with Capote's talent for empathy-producing description, makes the story memorable. An example is this passage describing the tree-decorating:

> The trunk in the attic upstairs; a shoebox of ermine tails (off the opera cape of a curious lady who once rented a room in

the house), coils of frazzled tinsel gone gold with age, one silver star, a brief rope of dilapidated, undoubtedly dangerous candy-like light bulbs. Excellent decorations, as far as they go, which isn't far enough: my friend wants our tree to blaze "like a Baptist window," droop with weighty snows of ornaments. But we can't afford the made-in-Japan splendors at the five-and-dime. So we do what we've always done: sit for days at the kitchen table with scissors and crayons and stacks of colored paper. I make sketches and my friend cuts them out: lots of cats, fish too (because they're easy to draw), some apples, some watermelons, a few winged angles devised from saved-up sheets of Hershey-bar tin foil. We use safety pins to attach these creations to the tree; as a final touch, we sprinkle the branches with shredded cotton picked in August for this purpose. My friend, surveying the effect, claps her hands together. "Now honest, Buddy. Doesn't it look good enough to eat?"

In "A Christmas Memory" there is no other tie to the present than the words "more than twenty years ago." Many personal reminiscences are like that—simply a look at the past. Others, for editors who like them to be related more firmly to the present, are linked—usually in the first and/or final paragraphs—to some current custom or event.

Recaptured memories in personal reminiscence nostalgia generally center around the writer's childhood, but they can deal with teenage or young adulthood, as does an excellent article called "An Evening at the Waldorf" that appeared in *Gourmet*. The story tells of an Annapolis midshipman on a limited budget who hopes to propose to the object of his summer romance after dinner at the Waldorf-Astoria. It fulfills eloquently the requirements that Alice Rubinstein Gochman, senior editor for *Gourmet*, lists as important to her magazine—a conjuring-up of a mood, of color, an excitement or emotion and the association in some way with food. "Through the recollection," she says, "we come to care about the participants—and we learn something."

Whether you use "A Christmas Memory," "An Evening at the Waldorf," or any of hundreds of other well-crafted personal reminiscences as your text, you'll learn volumes. First of all, there's the matter of plot. Every good reminiscence has one; lack of a plot is the reason for a large measure of rejections. There is tension, some sort of conflict, drama or suspense. Will Buddy and his friend have enough courage to face the Indian who sells the whiskey they need for their fruitcake? Will the girl say yes to the midshipman's proposal?

One editor spells out a salable reminiscence structure in the simple outline: 1) nice stage setting, 2) drama or conflict, 3) resolution, and 4) denouement. The competent analyst could literally read his mind and come up with that same structural outline, by reading the nostalgia he publishes.

You'll see, too, that any details included in nostalgia are necessary to the story. Beginning nostalgia writers often remember too well—and make the mistake of trying to include every detail. An eight-page manuscript telling of day-to-day life in Astoria, Oregon, during the era when canneries lined the riverbanks, which involves complicated explanations of the fishing and canning processes, might well be considered a treasure by the town's historical society. But it won't make the grade with magazine editors unless every bit of detail is relevant. As *Ruralite*'s Walt Wentz says, "Purpose—the imposition of some orderly progression toward a definite end—is essential in *any* story. That's why writing good nostalgia, like writing good humor, is very difficult. One thinks it ought to be easy, just because one is too close to the subject. But, not being a natural telepath, the writer must also be an editor—an editor of his own experiences and thoughts. Nostalgia is *not* easy, simply because, while it must be *honest,* it must also be an artificial construct—each word, each shade of emotion, carefully considered and contrived and placed just so."

Good nostalgia, your analysis will also show, moves smoothly along with no transitional jolts. Passage of time or the description of a subject mentioned in the preceding paragraph—after she had finished peeling all the apples; when the day came to say goodbye; the doll inside the box had a straw sailor hat set atop her golden curls—are two of the devices most often employed.

By analyzing well-written personal reminiscences, you will get a feeling for what editors are buying, and also for what they *aren't*. Reminiscences may be poignant, sentimental, and emotional, but salable ones are never maudlin or schmaltzy. The author must maintain a tranquil detachment from her past and not expect sales from pieces wallowing in personal grief or bitterness. And though fictional techniques are used in creating nostalgia pieces, the stories must be based on true experience. Nothing arouses an editor's ire more than trumped-up emotion, which I've heard one refer to as "gooey, maudlin, mawkish drivel."

Conveying honest emotion is difficult, but it is essential in producing good personal experience pieces. Our tendency is to overstate instead of simply telling the story. When the idea is good—one that will evoke empathy and allow the reader to vicariously share a writer's memories—there's no need for prose calculated to produce buckets of tears. Contrast the paragraphs that follow and you'll see what I mean.

> It was Christmas time in 1937 and my biggest wish was that I would get a bicycle. But my mother said I shouldn't wish for impossible gifts because it was hard enough just seeing that we had food on the table. I wished for it anyway every night before I went to bed, then cried myself to sleep because I knew I would never own that beautiful maroon-and-white bike.

Too tear-jerking? I agree. Let's see what happens when the story is told more subtly:

> Every time I neared the Coast to Coast store that December, I crossed my fingers. Would the girl's bike—shiny maroon-and-white and garlanded with tinsel—still be in the window? But what did it matter if it was, I asked myself with a depression child's wisdom. Christmas, 1937, was not a time for bicycles.

Better, yes. But it could be made even more effective with a few more tries. By telling your story in several different ways (a tape recorder is handy here) you can decide which version sounds right: warm, but not cloying; colorful without purple prose.

Alternate Routes to Memory Lane

Since personal reminiscences are the best-selling nostalgia, you'll probably want to concentrate your backward-looking efforts on them. But if you have trouble in plotting or awakening an empathy of personal emotions—longings, righteous anger, anticipation, sadness, joy—so that the reader can remember, too, there are the half-dozen other nostalgia types that may bring you more success.

Whatever-happened-to and *Do-you-remember-when* articles usually appear in newspaper supplements, but occasionally run in other magazines as well. They are easy to write. The work involved in putting together this kind of article is obtaining information, which can involve a great deal of digging. Whatever-happened-to's center around celebrities who aren't in the news anymore, who've faded from public view. They may be former child stars, diplomats, deposed royalty, or ex-public enemies. Almost always, the subjects of a piece have their former occupations or some other characteristic in common. Events, fashions, crazes and customs of the past are recalled in the do-you-remember-when's.

Celebrity reminiscence roundups, like the preceding category, rarely require anything but straight writing. They do call for a relatively large amount of interview or correspondence time, since they consist of reminiscences on one theme by a selection of well-known people from the political, business and/or entertainment worlds. Perhaps a group of industrialists each tell about that first job; half a dozen famous people describe their first cars and how they got them, their favorite childhood books or their happiest summer vacations. Every December you're sure to find a potpourri of celebrities' most memorable Christmases in magazines and weekly supplements.

Rules for crafting the celebrity reminiscence include—as for every successful article—casting the piece in the magazine's image. If roundups always include memories from six people, that's what the editor prefers. If they begin with one prose paragraph, then continue with the individuals' reminiscences, that's the way you want to do it. When a magazine's articles of this type give equal time to both sexes, you'll increase your chances of acceptance by becoming an equal opportunity writer.

In compiling your list of celebrities, you'll want to come up with more names than you'll need, in case some of them refuse to grant interviews or answer your letters. There will be times, too, when the celebrities' reminiscences may be too much alike to use in the same piece, or inappropriate to the magazine you're writing for.

Most always, the information you need can be obtained via telephone or taped interview. Personal interviews are often difficult to get unless you live in a celebrity haven like Beverly Hills or Gstaad. Your cast of luminaries can include everyone from the mayors of big cities or movie and television stars to corporation presidents and creators of comic strips. As long as a person's name is generally recognized by most of a magazine's readers, that person qualifies. In the case of business VIPs and artists, their names don't have to be known, but their companies or works do. For state and regional publications, the criteria change somewhat: you will not have to gather reminiscences from national figures, but from important people in the area your target publication covers. Oldtimers—even if they aren't well known—are marvelous sources for regional publication reminiscences, too.

Roundups of related items or events come in two basic forms: the non-personal reminiscence that begins with a blurb or paragraph of prose, then goes on to describe a group of items or events from the past, and the semi-personal reminiscence about a group of similar subjects. An example of the first kind is a condensation from "Lost and Found" by Robert Paul Smith which appeared in *Reader's Digest*. The article begins with a longish blurb:

> If you remember the sound of coal running down the chute into the basement, and what Papa said every time he had to crawl under his Model T and open a petcock to check the oil level, then you'll remember the world of Robert Paul Smith. And if you don't remember, look back now, youngster, to the world the way it used to be.

The article itself includes six objects—the carpet beater, the coalbin, the buttonhook, the icebox, the soap scrap saver, and the rumble seat—each of which is described in from about 100 to 200 words. Here's the section on The Soap Scrap Saver:

> It was a little wire cage that held whatever bits of soap were too small to keep hold of. You whipped it around in the kitchen sink to make suds for the dishes. (In those days there were no detergents. You bathed with soap, did dishes with soap, did laundry with soap, and it all came in bars. Except for green soap, which came in bottles and was primarily for shampoo, secondarily for getting in your eyes.)
>
> After you washed the dishes, you had to wipe them dry. My uncle, who taught chemistry, told my mother that laboratory glasses were rinsed in hot water and left to dry on racks. She paid absolutely no attention to this cockeyed notion. She said it was dirty, and we went on wiping our dishes with moderately clean dish towels.

You'll find *historical nostalgia* most often in specialized magazines—an airline inflight will carry a nostalgic history on the early days of flight; a music magazine might feature a remembrance of the big band jazz of the 1930s. Many industrial publication editors are also receptive to well-written pieces that recall the evolution of their companies' products. Like good history, historical nostalgia tells not only *what* happened, but *how* and *why* it did. Writers of the best pieces, you'll discover in your analysis, use many of the personal reminiscence techniques to give their work color—anecdotes, dialogue, metaphor, and other means by which they tell the story so that the reader can have a sense of being there.

The *quiz* generally starts out with a paragraph or two of prose, then continues with a series of questions relating to the more nostalgic aspects of bygone years. The questions usually have to do with personalities, literature, music, sports, or other entertainments of a single decade—the twenties, thirties, forties—with titles like "The Fabulous Fifties Quiz." But, as with all types of articles, there are possibilities for variations on the theme, such as "How Well Do You Know Yourself?. . .A quiz to stir up childhood memories," which appeared in *Glamour.* Included in the thirty-eight questions were "Who tucked me in at night?" "Who was on my first lunchbox?" and "My scariest nightmare was _____." As in how-to's, the secret of nostalgia quizzes is to follow the magazine's format exactly (especially regarding the number and type of questions) and aim your marketing only at magazines that have published quizzes in the past.

With titles like "Were the Good Old Days Really *That* Good?" and "Don't Take *Me* Back to the Good Old Days," the *anti-nostalgia* articles play on the concept that while nostalgia is big business, those times weren't so wonderful after all. For instance, take this excerpt from "Were the Good Old Days Really *That* Good?" from *Retirement Living* (now *50 Plus):*

> Nostalgia hangs heavy upon us—lock, stock and ballyhoo. From old movies on TV to folksy revivals of bygone arts and crafts, the silhouettes and soundtracks of the past seem to be everywhere.
>
> I'm not one to deny the thrill of such backward progression. After all, who doesn't want the chance to be young at least

twice? What I object to are many glaring omissions from the things remembered of those halcyon days.

Nowhere, for example, do I hear lyrical praise or even honorable mention of the old oaken ice box—that cordless delight which could turn 50 pounds of ice into 75 pounds of water in a mere 36 hours by a magic all its own. Doesn't anyone yearn to taste again the sour milk it held, to spoon up the melted butter which curled in a yellow sauce beneath the ice, or to savor a potroast tenderized by semi-putrefaction?

Even while these articles are decrying nostalgia, they're producing it. *Why the nostalgia craze?* is one of the seemingly inexhaustible anti-nostalgia approaches which, while examining the phenomenon, also features memories of the past. Look at the lead of this article, "That Rose-Colored Rearview Mirror," which appeared in *Saturday Review*.

The time, let us suppose, is the late Twenties, the place is the local Rex movie palace, and the man at the Wurlitzer is playing "Charmaine." The music swells and burbles through the darkness, and then the colored lights go on, rainbowing the ochre-and-gold frieze that zigzags across one wall of the theater. Tutti-frutti with hints of King Tut's tomb.

Now, a testing question. Do you enjoy, without too much irony, this sort of retro-reverie? If you do, you are already partly familiar, from the inside, with a larger question, one that will be the subject of this article—an important question oddly neglected by fashionable sociologists and our new psycho-historians. How, in appropriately general terms, should we explain our continuing epidemic, in both America and Europe, of period nostalgia and stylistic revivalism?

Whether we, as writers, can explain this continuing love affair with times gone by, there's one message that should be crystal-ball clear. As long as the "epidemic" continues, for many of us, living in the past may point the way to our freelancing future.

The Final Analysis

If you use analysis, that future will be brighter—whichever type of article you choose to write. Writing on target is not a skill you'll acquire all at once. It will take time and energy to learn how to effectively analyze the articles you read.

But I think you will find the results worth every bit of your effort. There's a definite thrill when an editor tells you, "We like the piece and are planning to use it in our July issue." It's exciting to watch that bank balance grow.

Writing is good times and bad times; pleasure mixed with pain. I wouldn't change my delayed vocation for anything in the world. What I have changed through analysis, however, is the proportion of pleasure, by tipping the acceptance/rejection ratio mightily in my favor. You can do it, too.

Appendix A

Going into Analysis— Two Case Histories

"New Games People Play"

Idea Source: My son, who was at the time a recreation major at the University of Oregon, had in the course of our conversations often mentioned noncompetitive play—a rather new concept as far as American society is concerned. One day while browsing in the bookstore (one of my favorite idea-generating environments) I discovered a book called *New Games* and the idea flashed through my mind.

Marketing: I prefer writing for magazines in which I've previously published since: 1)it's easier to market my ideas and 2)the pay is generally better than first-contribution basis. Therefore, I mentally reviewed the publications I write for regularly with suitability of my article topic in mind. None seemed to mesh. Then I thought of *Sky,* Delta Airline's inflight, to which I had been named a contributing editor but for which I had yet to produce any copy. After analyzing a half-dozen back issues for content, I felt the noncompetitive concept would work, so I sent the idea—along with a batch of five others—to the magazine's editor (who welcomes several ideas in one letter). Shortly after, I was assigned the piece.

Title: Noting that *Sky*'s titles often are interrogative, I started with questions using the words competition and noncompetitive, and came up with two or three mediocre names. Since the editor also likes plays on words, I pursued that possibility and the inevitable "Games People Play" popped into my mind. By prefacing those three words with "New," I had a title well within *Sky*'s length limits and with just the right zing: that was the title that was used.

Research: I bought the *New Games* book and another that one of the bookstore's owners told me about. My reading helped me formulate several questions, which I sent to the authorities mentioned in the books. From my son I got the name of a professor at the University of Oregon's recreation department and phoned her with additional questions. Fortunately, the New Games Foundation, which put out the *New Games* book, is in San Francisco, a four-hour drive from my home. I made an appointment to interview one of its directors and combined that job with other writing business I had in the Bay Area. Other interviews included one with a stress physiologist and another with the director of sports psychology at the U. S. Olympic Training Center, which was then located at Squaw Valley, California.

Writing: After that extensive research and my analysis of previously published articles, writing the 1,700-word piece was a relatively easy matter. I knew that I would need about six quotes, that a statistic or two would suffice and that a short summary lead and a quote closing would work well with the magazine's style. Keeping in mind the ratios of adjectives, adverbs, anecdotes, and words of more than two syllables that I had computed, I began with this lead:

> There's a whole new concept in recreation. Traditional competition, it says, isn't for everyone after all—and games in which there are no losers are winning popularity.

In the following eight paragraphs, I explained the New Games philosophy more completely, describing three of the most popular games in some detail. After that, I told about the equipment needed and the fact that age and size of participants don't matter in most of the games. The evolution of the games in the mid-1960s was the next facet of the subject I explored. This brought me to the final third of the piece, time to get quotes and opinions about competition from a variety of experts into the article. I wound up the piece with a summarizing statement and with my most powerful quote:

> Most recreation professionals see the New Games as an addition to more structured games and sports, an option which will enable greater numbers of people to have fun. As George Leonard (previously identified in the article as author of "The Ultimate Athlete") put it, "By all means let us cherish the traditional sports for their many beauties, their unplumbed potential, and for the certainty they afford. But we have signed no long-term contract to suffer their extremes. The time has come to move on, to create new games with new rules more in tune with the times, games in which there are no spectators and no second-string players, games for a whole family and a whole day, games in which aggression fades into laughter—new games."

"A Potpourri of Political Memorabilia"

Idea source: Upon visiting the printing facilities for *The American Collector,* located just north of Reno, I was given several back copies of the publication. Although I had reported on various antiques sales for the tabloid-style magazine, I hadn't done any features for it, so I began studying the articles. Many of them involved collectors. A few months previously, I had seen a collection of political memorabilia in the local library's display case. I phoned the public relations person at the library to get the collector's name and found that she was a library employee. I contacted her for more information and then queried the magazine's editor and received an assignment to do a 750-word piece.

Title: Analysis showed me that the majority of *The American Collector*'s titles are labels, with alliteration used in many of them. I knew that my key words had to say something about politics and that mementos or memorabilia should probably be used, so I began working with those words. The result was "A Potpourri of Political Memorabilia," which was changed by the editor to an even more alliterative name, "A Potpourri of Politics Past."

Research: The only research involved was an hour-and-a-half interview with the collector at her apartment. Beforehand, I had prepared a list of questions based on those answered in the magazine's previous articles about people with collections. I had also written down other information I would need to follow the editor's preferred format. My requirements list looked like this:

1. Physical description of collector and her surroundings.
2. What is her position at the library?
3. What prompted her to start collecting?
4. How does she describe her collection (get her to talk about the various items, where she obtained them, how much she paid, etc.)?
5. What is her favorite item? The most expensive?
6. How many items are in the collection?
7. Does she specialize in a certain area, period?
8. What is her advice to other collectors?
9. What are her collection goals?
10. Get six or seven good quotes.

    I also brought along my camera, strobe, and two rolls of 35mm color film and took about forty shots after the interview was over.

Writing: Analysis showed me that in pieces about collectors, the magazine's articles almost always began with the story of how the featured person became involved, that the midsections of the pieces described the more interesting items in a collection, and that the last paragraphs contained the collector's comments on any gaps in the collection or items that had been difficult to obtain, goals for future acquisitions, and a wrap-up summarizing statement or direct quote. I needed approximately fifteen adjectives, no adverbs, and one or two statistics for every hundred words. Words of more than two syllables, I calculated, should compose no more than one-seventh of the total, and although an anecdote or two would be acceptable, I really didn't need to have any. With average sentence and paragraph lengths and the other requirements in mind, this is what I wrote:

    Wendy Muchmore has been a collector as long as she can remember. Since she grew up in a family that was active in politics, it was only natural that when she started collecting she would choose political memorabilia.

    The green-eyed blonde describes her collection as a "mish-mash of stuff I like." Unlike most political items collectors who specialize in campaign buttons or memorabilia from a specific period in history, Wendy's collection is an eclectic one—

embracing everything from a silk handkerchief commemorating the 1888 Harrison-Morton campaign to a metal traffic sign from the 1965 inauguration. The handkerchief, which bears the slogan "Tippecanoe and Morton Too," cost $20 at an antique store; the sign was a gift from a friend who Wendy suspects "liberated" it.

"If my collection has any focus," Wendy says, "it's on the offbeat." She adds that although she has about 1,000 buttons, she really prefers paper items. She's especially partial to third party and Democratic presidential candidate posters, and she points to a framed poster of Eugene Debs, perennial Socialist candidate for the nation's highest office, as her favorite. She bought the poster in a San Francisco antique store for $48 in 1969. Most of the paper items she has acquired are flyers, pamphlets, campaign literature, tickets to inaugurations and conventions, invitations, presidential menus and postcards. Most date from the late nineteenth century.

The minute you enter the Reno, Nevada, apartment which Wendy shares with her hamster, Alfred, you know what her hobby is. Richard Nixon, John F. Kennedy, Barry Goldwater and the 1936 Republican team of Landon and Knox look down on her breakfast table. Herbert Hoover, Calvin Coolidge, William McKinley, George McGovern and a dozen other presidential hopefuls share the living room walls with commemorative plates and burlap-mounted campaign buttons.

In fact, almost everywhere you look there's a political memento of some sort—be it an English cookie tin with the American presidents' pictures encircling it or tokens from the Andrew Jackson campaigns waiting to be mounted. There are biographies of political figures and a red candle that spells out "Spiro." It's not technically a political item, Wendy explains, "but I like it—and liking has always been my main reason for acquiring any item since I started collecting as a youngster in the 1950s."

Among the plates that Wendy is especially fond of are a blue William Howard Taft and James Sherman plate, a William Jennings Bryan and a James Garfield for President plate. She bought the Taft-Sherman plate for $40 at the American Political Items Collectors convention in 1974.

Though almost all of the faces on her plates and posters and the names on the printed matter Wendy has collected are of men, she's giving equal time to the ladies now. Since the current women's movement began in the late 1960s, she has been collecting movement buttons at women's forums, seminars and from bookstores.

Although Wendy has bought many of the 5,000 items in her collection at antiques stores, auctions and flea markets, she has found that trading with other collectors has been her most successful method of acquisition. Friends and relatives throughout the country help out, too, by spotting items she might like and telling her about them. Her mother's shop, Muchmore's Postcards in Grass Valley, Calif., is another happy hunting ground.

"A Century of Campaign Buttons, 1789-1889," by the late J. Doyle Dewitt, is Wendy's favorite reference book as far as buttons are concerned. And since she works at the Reno library, reference books on the other varieties of items are only a few feet from her desk. She's a member of the American Political Items Collectors and relies on the club's newsletters for tips on spotting fakes and reproductions.

"I've been taken as far as spending too much for an item—anyone who has collected to any extent has—but I've never been stuck with a fake," Wendy says. She advises collectors that a knowledge of current prices is their best defense against being duped, as a price that's too low is often a red flag which should warn the collector to question an item's authenticity.

What's her ultimate goal in collecting? "Right now," Wendy says, opening the door to her spare bedroom piled high with boxes full of political mementos, "it's to find enough time to get all of my collection organized better. I'm not even letting myself add anything to the collection right now. I'm concentrating on getting it catalogued," she says with determination.

Then, nodding at the television set whose channel is tuned to coverage of the Republican National Convention, her enthusiasm for collecting bubbles up again and she adds, "but when I see all those hats and placards, I can really get excited."

The Writer/Analyst's Checklist

Name of article _____

Publication _____ Month and Year _____

Length _____ Kind of article (how-to, personality, etc.)

Title:

    Number of words _____

    Kind (label, interrogative, etc.) _____

    Any special devices (play on words, alliteration, etc.) _____

Style:

    Adjectives per 100 words _____,

    Adverbs per 100 words _____

    Words of more than two syllables per 100 _____

    Quotes per 500 words _____

    Anecdotes per 500 words _____

    Statistics per 500 words _____

    Picturesque writing devices employed (similes, personifi-
       cation, etc.) _____

    Average sentence length _____

    Average paragraph length _____

    Point of view (1st, 2nd, 3rd person) _____

    Tone (authoritative, conversational, etc.) _____

Structure:
    Lead:
        Number of paragraphs in length_____
        Kind (summary, descriptive, etc.)_____
    Body of article:
        Number of points covered_____
        Kinds of experts interviewed or informational sources
            (government agency reports, professional
            people, etc.)_____
        Kinds of transitions_____
        Any punctuation idiosyncracies_____
    Ending:
        Length_____
        Kind (quote, summary, etc.)_____
    Photos:
        Black-and-white or color_____
        Kinds of photos (action, close-ups, overviews, etc.)_____
        Subjects (landscapes, people, etc.)_____
        Age of people in photos_____
        Any item which must be present (sponsor's product,
            etc.)_____

Bibliography

Bander, R. G. *American English Rhetoric.* 2nd ed. Toronto: Holt, Rinehart & Winston of Canada, Ltd., 1978.

Bergin, David P. *Photo Journalism Manual.* Hastings-on-Hudson, N.Y.: Morgan & Morgan, Inc., 1967. (basic photography)

Bernstein, Theodore M. *The Careful Writer.* New York: Atheneum, 1977.

Bird, George L. *Modern Article Writing.* Dubuque, Iowa: Wm. C. Brown, 1967. (queries)

Borland, Hal. *How to Write and Sell Non Fiction.* New York: Ronald Press Company, 1973.

Cassill, Kay. *The Complete Handbook for Freelance Writers.* Cincinnati: Writer's Digest Books, 1981.

Crawford, Tad. *The Writer's Legal Guide.* New York: E. P. Dutton, 1978.

Duncan, Lois. *How to Write and Sell Your Personal Experiences.* Cincinnati: Writer's Digest Books, 1979.

Eastman Kodak Company. *Encyclopedia of Practical Photography.* Garden City, N.Y.: American Photographic Book Publishing Company, Inc., 1978. (special effects)

Giles, Carl H. *Writing Right—To Sell.* New York: A. S. Barnes and Company, 1970. (queries)

Gunther, Max. *Writing the Modern Magazine Article.* Boston: The Writer, Inc., 1973.

Jacobs, Hayes B. *Writing and Selling Non-Fiction.* Cincinnati: Writer's Digest Books, 1967.

Lutz, Robert D., ed. *1982 Photographer's Market.* Cincinnati: Writer's Digest Books, 1981.

Miller, Wilbur R. *Photography.* Bloomington, Illinois: McKnight, 1978.

Polking, Kirk, ed. *The Beginning Writer's Answer Book.* Cincinnati: Writer's Digest Books, 1977.

Polking, Kirk and Meranus, Leonard S. *Law and the Writer.* Cincinnati: Writer's Digest Books, 1980.

Rockwell, F. A. *How to Write Nonfiction That Sells.* New York: Regnery, 1975.

Samson, Jack. *Successful Outdoor Writing.* Cincinnati: Writer's Digest Books, 1979.

Schemenaur, P. J. and Brady, John, eds. *1982 Writer's Market.* Cincinnati: Writer's Digest Books, 1981.

Strunk, William, Jr., and White, E. B. *The Elements of Style.* 2nd ed. New York: Macmillan Publishing Co., Inc., 1972.

University of Chicago Press. *A Manual of Style.* 12th ed. 1967.

Winkler, G. P., ed. *Associated Press Stylebook.* New York: The Associated Press, 1970.

Woolley, A. E. *Traveling With Your Camera.* New York: A. S. Barnes and Company, Inc., 1965. (travel photo tips)

Index

A